MOVEMENT DIRECTORS IN CONTEMPORARY THEATRE

ALSO AVAILABLE IN THE THEATRE MAKERS SERIES

The Collected Essays of Arthur Miller, Arthur Miller
9781472591739

'Death of a Salesman' in Beijing, Arthur Miller
9781472592040

Edward Bond: The Playwright Speaks, David Tuaillon
9781472570062

Meyerhold on Theatre, Edward Braun
9781474230209

Simon Stephens: A Working Diary, Simon Stephens
9781474251419

Joan's Book, Joan Littlewood
9781474233224

Steppenwolf Theatre Company of Chicago, John Mayer
9781474239455

Granville Barker on Theatre, Harley Granville Barker
9781474294843

The Actor and His Body, Litz Pisk
9781474269742

Julius Caesar and Me, Paterson Joseph
9781350011182

Julie Hesmondhalgh: A Working Diary, Julie Hesmondhalgh
9781350025691

Contemporary Women Stage Directors, Paulette Marty
9781474268530

MOVEMENT DIRECTORS IN CONTEMPORARY THEATRE

Conversations on Craft

Ayse Tashkiran

methuen | drama
LONDON • NEW YORK • OXFORD • NEW DELHI • SYDNEY

METHUEN DRAMA
Bloomsbury Publishing Plc
50 Bedford Square, London, WC1B 3DP, UK
1385 Broadway, New York, NY 10018, USA

BLOOMSBURY, METHUEN DRAMA and the Methuen Drama logo are trademarks of
Bloomsbury Publishing Plc

First published in Great Britain 2020

Copyright © Ayse Tashkiran, 2020

Ayse Tashkiran has asserted her right under the Copyright, Designs and Patents Act, 1988, to be identified as author of this work.

For legal purposes the Acknowledgements on p. xi constitute an extension of this copyright page.

Cover design: Charlotte Daniels
Cover image: Royal Shakespeare Company's production of *The Duchess of Malfi* starring Joan Iyiola as the Duchess of Malfi and Paul Woodson as Antonio (Photo © Helen Maybanks/RSC)

All rights reserved. No part of this publication may be reproduced or transmitted in any form or by any means, electronic or mechanical, including photocopying, recording, or any information storage or retrieval system, without prior permission in writing from the publishers.

Bloomsbury Publishing Plc does not have any control over, or responsibility for, any third-party websites referred to or in this book. All internet addresses given in this book were correct at the time of going to press. The author and publisher regret any inconvenience caused if addresses have changed or sites have ceased to exist, but can accept no responsibility for any such changes.

A catalogue record for this book is available from the British Library.

A catalog record for this book is available from the Library of Congress.

ISBN: HB: 978-1-3500-5446-2
PB: 978-1-3500-5445-5
ePDF: 978-1-3500-5447-9
eBook: 978-1-3500-5448-6

Series: Theatre Makers

Typeset by Deanta Global Publishing Services, Chennai, India

To find out more about our authors and books visit www.bloomsbury.com and sign up for our newsletters.

CONTENTS

Foreword *Maria Aberg and Joan Iyiola* vi
Preface ix
Acknowledgements xi

    Introduction 1
1 Early practitioners and practices 9
2 Themes 27
3 Jane Gibson 41
4 Sue Lefton 53
5 Kate Flatt 65
6 Toby Sedgwick 81
7 Siân Williams 93
8 Struan Leslie 105
9 Ellen Kane 119
10 Peter Darling 129
11 Steven Hoggett 137
12 Ann Yee 149
13 Imogen Knight 159
14 Shelley Maxwell 171
15 Future voices 183
16 Beyond the room: Contexts and structures 197

Glossary 213
References 215
Further reading 219
About the author 227

FOREWORD

I've always had a deep interest in movement. How bodies in space, on stage, tell stories and carry poetry in a way that sometimes text just can't. How the visual narrative of bodies interacting creates a kind of sub-structure to a performance that holds its own visceral, undeniable, ritualistic power.

The spoken word is traditionally well looked after in British theatre. Apart from the playwright, there are literary managers making sure every line is in the right place, verse experts helping actors to decipher and bring life into those lines and voice coaches ensuring they are clearly and beautifully spoken. When I started my career, mainstream theatre sometimes seemed to view the actor's body as just a way of carrying the voice around; a mere vessel for that most important aspect of theatre, the word.

So when I first met Ayse Tashkiran in the scruffy rehearsal rooms of the RSC (Royal Shakespeare Company) ten years ago, I wasn't really sure what a collaboration with a movement director would entail. But a decade's worth of shows later, I can say with absolute certainty that I am the director I am today thanks to our collaboration.

Like any brilliant movement director, Ayse is intimately familiar with the nitty-gritty of the actor's physical body and what it needs. Working on a rake? Ayse knows what adjustments need to be made to protect the knees and spines of everyone on stage. Doing a show in the round? Ayse knows how to help the actors use the '360 body'.[1] Covering the entire stage with an inch of slippery stage blood? Ayse knows how to teach the actors to fall safely so as not to hurt themselves.

But the skill, imagination and knowledge of a movement director does, of course, stretch much further than that. Helping an actor create a physical language for someone who has been a soldier in active combat. Mapping through the physical experience of poisoning. Moving through ten decades of social dancing and interspersing it with war and battle. Creating a detailed physical language for the experience of profound and sudden grief. What dying feels like. What the absence of hope might look like expressed in a movement duet. What it feels like going into labour. What happens to your soul when your body is suddenly liberated from years of oppressive gendered scrutiny. All these are examples of things Ayse and I have explored and worked into our shows. And this doesn't even include her ability to put all movement into a wider social, political and cultural context, evaluating its meaning on stage in relation to text, design and structure.

The collaboration with Ayse is now an integral part of how I make work. It has enriched my process, my shows and my practice in ways that are almost impossible to quantify. Through working with her, I have developed a deep respect for the expertise of the movement director, and I'm delighted that this book will help others to access that expertise too.

Maria Aberg

I first heard about Ayse's work while training at Bristol Old Vic Theatre School. At the same time, my best friend, Polly Bennett, was training under Ayse's teachership on the MA Movement: Directing and Teaching programme at Royal Central School of Speech and Drama, and we would spend hours sharing stories of theatre making across the two cities.

In many ways, this sharing presented a new language, which was at once foreign and yet familiar. Familiar, because within my Nigerian heritage storytellers always begin with the physical life; foreign, because within the British landscape I learnt quickly that the value of the movement director was often misunderstood. As we begin to awaken our understanding of movement directors and discover the variety of shapes that we collaborate in, this brilliant book by Ayse Tashkiran has arrived in our laps. Devour it.

I have had the great fortune of collaborating with Ayse on two Webster plays, *The White Devil* and *The Duchess of Malfi*. The world of Webster is fantastically complex, and his words present what we, as humans, are capable of, plunging us unashamedly into depths of darkness. As an actor this requires existing in a state of vulnerability, and working with Ayse has been where some of the biggest surprises in creation have happened and where the work that I am most proud of has been born.

When you work with Ayse, you begin not with the words on the page but with the people in front of you. Ayse understands humanity in a way that I haven't encountered from any other creative, and the physical language that she offers for adoption illuminates any production that I have seen or been a part of.

True collaboration is understood by just looking at the creative partnership of Ayse Tashkiran and Maria Aberg. When directors understand the value of a movement director, they remove any sense of hierarchy within the room and place movement directors firmly by their sides, for they are, and should be, their co-pilots, navigating and creating the world of the play. The movement director widens possibility for the actor, and I firmly believe that it is within this landscape that the actor can truly thrive.

All of the movement directors in this book contribute to the heartbeat of contemporary theatre.

Thank you, Ayse, for creating visibility for these voices.

Joan Iyiola

Note

1 Maria Aberg is referencing an aspect of movement work where an actor is reconnected to the full use of their body expressively – especially when they are working in three-sided performance spaces or in-the-round configurations. In these instances, audiences may be reading the actor's physical responses through their back and not their face and the front of their body. There is an added need for the use of breath, spine and subtle shifts of weight to be able to communicate with the totality of the body. Several of the practitioners in this volume describe this aspect of movement work (see Williams, Chapter 7 and Leslie, Chapter 8) and may be drawing on Laban's idea of the kinesphere, which is the reach of the body into the space around it.

PREFACE

It was with enormous pleasure and trepidation that I undertook the project of this book. As a movement director, I really love what I do, and each time I walk into a new rehearsal room, I am thankful that I am able to unite my passion and my profession on a daily basis. Movement direction is a way of bringing curiosity to all kinds of movement and marvelling at the way movement expresses, reveals and connects us as human beings to our world. When you relate that to the power of the imagination of actors with their world of intention, narrative and emotion, then there is a potent mix.

Since 2005, I have been collecting interviews with other movement directors, in what started out as a very informal way of hearing what other movement practitioners thought about their work. The original intention was to build a resource, as movement directors' words in the public domain were a rarity. In 2009, I curated a round-table. It was perhaps the first time that this had ever happened: a movement director talking to movement directors about movement direction. On that day, someone suggested that there should be a book; ten years later, here it is. In the interim I have movement directed many productions and taught many students. I have also started to write about movement, but that is a much newer practice.

This is the first book of its kind, and it offers not the full picture but *a* picture of contemporary movement directors and theatre choreographers whose practice is shaping our current understanding of movement in the British theatre scene, with their sense of history, their artistic values and their ways of working. The voices of the group of movement directors who have contributed so generously will leave an indelible trace of the depth and artistry of their movement work on production. I am mindful of my limitations of being unable to include many more movement directors, but you are there in between the lines and in the collective psyche. I am also mindful that my revisionist approach to the twentieth century is situated firmly in British theatre and is limited by my Eurocentric stance. Maybe a theme of this book is one that charts a decade that has seen the emergence of a richer, more complex web of practices and practitioners. As a movement director myself with a set of movement trainings, a set of cultural and artistic influences and an Anglo Cypriot heritage, working in Britain, I can feel how they all jostle together to shape me and inform my movement direction.

Most of all, this book is a celebration of the tireless energy of movement directors and theatre choreographers who are working diligently, creatively and with such care for their contributions. I hope to celebrate their craft and artistry. This book is an invitation into the innermost parts of creative processes, to read of the ephemeral yet pragmatic art of the movement director.

London
December 2019

ACKNOWLEDGEMENTS

My heartfelt thanks go to all the movement directors and theatre choreographers who have contributed their voices to this book. Your passion for your craft and generosity imbue every word, as do your artistry and commitment to our field of movement. Without your collaboration, inspiration and support this project would not have been possible.

My gratitude goes to my artistic collaborators – the directors, actors, designers, composers and sound designers, lighting designers, video makers and writers who have all left traces of joy in our collaborations and deepened my work as a mover. My thanks also to the enablers: the stage management teams, David Edgar and Gabriele Lombardo, the Sabbatical Schemes at Royal Central School of Speech and Drama; the Society for Theatre Research for their award that kick-started this project; Andy Lavender and Martin White for their encouragement in the early days of this idea; Joel Horwood and Matthew Warchus for paving the way and connecting me to their movement collaborators with elegance; and Anna Brewer and the team at Methuen Drama for their patience and their encouragement of a movement person with lots of shows that have ultimately fed into this work but have certainly interrupted the writing process.

I would also like to thank my first readers: Gary Yershon for his amazing generosity, his laser gaze and for saying exactly the right thing; Matthew Saxton for his way with words and his honesty; Hannah Weaver for her inspiring notes; Vanessa Ewan for her unending generosity and wisdom, and for her commitment to the discipline of actor movement, which is a constant source of inspiration; and the four generations of women in my family for their unerring, quiet support – I am truly grateful.

And finally, to all the movement students who have weathered the sabbaticals with good grace. It is through you that I have felt the first two decades of twenty-first-century theatre in movement. This book is for you.

INTRODUCTION

Movement directors work with the physical, living bodies at the heart of a theatre production. They are called upon to create a movement language or physical style or to manifest – through performing bodies – the more enigmatic, elusive or otherwise absent parts of a theatre text. They respond to propositions from the playwright. They interact with the mise en scène generated by the director and designer. They contribute creative movement ideas and invent physical processes, helping to take a production from concept to realization. They collaborate meaningfully with other members of the wider creative team. Movement directors may work closely with a composer, for example, in relation to a complex movement section, a dance or transitions between scenes. Above all, movement directors centralize the actor's body. Through movement, they enable actors to embody the fictional world of the work; and through movement, they help to build an ensemble as a temporary but vividly embodied community. Movement directors have skill and insight into how bodies communicate – not only how performers' bodies communicate amongst the ensemble, but also how the bodies of those on stage communicate with those in the auditorium. They understand how the actors' individual and collective movement on stage has the potential to affect the audience's bodies – thus completing the cycle of the live theatre event.

This book draws upon the voices of movement directors to illuminate a discipline that is *innovative* and *shapeshifting* – but also, sometimes, *invisible*. Their working methods are constantly *innovative*, since each movement director creates a new physical language and a new working process for every production in which they are involved. Each group of actors, each text, each director and each space demands constant (re)invention. In the absence of the opportunity for any formal apprenticeship,[1] they have had to create their practice out of their own skill and imagination in response to the needs of the rehearsal room. Their practice is *shapeshifting*, because each production demands different styles of movement. Each company of actors has unique movement aptitudes, and as such, movement directors work responsively, dexterously and creatively. And it is *invisible* because when movement is well integrated, it arises naturally and spontaneously from the actor – a result that often looks effortless or dazzling but belies the skills or techniques underpinning it. As very little has been written on the work of movement directors, their voice is rarely heard outside the rehearsal room; thus, their practice can seem elusive. And there is a second, unwelcome, type of invisibility. Movement direction sometimes remains unacknowledged, both critically and institutionally. The failure to recognize and attribute work that is absorbed into a production, rather than visibly authored, constitutes a complex issue within theatre and within the history of theatre.

The movement directors in this book all work in British theatre. They are all at different points in their artistic journeys and theatre careers. Some have a sizeable body of work in theatre, and some have worked on the global stages of film, opera and musical theatre, whilst others are at the beginning of their careers. What unites these interviewees is the generous way they share their working processes. Two interviewees identify themselves as 'theatre choreographers'; the rest use either 'movement director' or 'movement director/choreographer'. The issue of how to name their work emerges as a theme. It can be hard to talk about movement. As a working movement director, myself, I am an insider, and well positioned to ask questions. As a teacher of movement directors, I was interested in identifying emerging patterns in our practices. And as a researcher, I wanted to understand the other lineages of movement shaping current movement direction practices.

Significant shifts in our creative industries have prompted long-overdue discussions around the performing body, the ethics of the gaze and touch, and the politics of ownership and attribution. In the context of these debates, the voices of movement practitioners are more vital than ever.

Chapter 1 offers a backdrop to some of the current practices. There is no single, clear-cut lineage of movement direction, but here I identify the work of pioneering practitioners and the circumstances that have informed the growth of this discipline in Britain. The work of movement directors, which originates within theatre, has gone on to permeate other performance genres: opera, film, television, new musicals and mass movement.

Chapter 2 teases out patterns and themes that emerged from my conversations with this group of movement directors. The interviews themselves comprise Chapters 3 to 14. They feature discussions with Jane Gibson, Sue Lefton, Kate Flatt, Toby Sedgwick, Siân Williams, Struan Leslie, Ellen Kane, Peter Darling, Steven Hoggett, Ann Yee, Imogen Knight and Shelley Maxwell. All of these conversations followed their own course, but I had some key questions that I posed to all. Each of these chapters sounds different, because I was keen to maintain the music of each voice and the unique tone of each conversation. A running commentary of endnotes offers some background information on movement trainings and notable teachers. Chapter 15 foregrounds the most recent wave of movement directors and looks forward to how their artistic practices might forge the future of the field.

The voices of an exciting group of practitioners inform this chapter, namely Diane Alison-Mitchell, Polly Bennett, Lucy Cullingford, Ioli Filippakopoulou, Natasha Harrison, Chi-San Howard, Vicki Igbokwe, Jennifer Jackson, Ingrid Mackinnon, Rebecca Meltzer, Coral Messam, Anna Morrissey, Sue Mythen and Sacha Plaige. In Chapter 16, the concluding chapter, I look ahead to the fast-changing landscape of contemporary theatre and suggest how future growth for movement direction might be diversified and supported in a wider context.

Introduction to interviewees

The emergence of the movement director has been complex; no single source of practice prevails. Contemporary movement directors are not united by schools or forms of movement. Nor have their working methods coalesced into a discipline of unified practices. Yet they are united in other ways: they share common perspectives, informed instincts, visual acuity and a capacity for enabling embodiment. These underpin the process of creating movement material. They all have varied yet firmly embedded skills in movement. They share a capacity to draw on a deep yet eclectic movement heritage and an ability to creatively develop movement in the living space between actor, director, playwright and audience.

The interviewees featured in this book are working movement directors and theatre choreographers who come from unique and varied backgrounds. They mainly work in the UK. Several have transatlantic careers. One hails from Jamaica and another from the United States. I have worked in parallel with some and enjoyed the work of others as an audience member.

Jane Gibson (Chapter 3) is a prolific director of movement who has dedicated her whole career to movement tailored for the actor. She worked initially as a movement teacher and later as a movement director. As a voracious theatregoer, I was first aware of her work in the 1980s on numerous productions at the National Theatre and with Cheek by Jowl. Her movement work was characterized by the power of ensemble and a vibrancy in actors' bodies. In terms of her place in the history of movement direction practice, she has been directly taught and influenced by Litz Pisk, Trish Arnold, Belinda Quirey and Jacques Lecoq. Our conversations unearthed the respect she holds for her teachers and the high value she places on movement for actors. Her process is deeply anchored in the narrative and shaped by character. As the first named Head of Movement at the National Theatre, Gibson is one of the leaders of the field. She is amongst a handful of pioneers who have been instrumental in shaping movement direction practice as we know it in theatre and film today.

Sue Lefton (Chapter 4) has worked as a movement teacher, movement director and choreographer across theatre, television, film and opera, in a career that spans fifty years. In terms of her place in the history of movement direction practice, she has been directly taught and influenced by Litz Pisk and Belinda Quirey and, to some extent, by Jacques Lecoq and Trish Arnold. She trained as a child at the Royal Ballet School under Ninette de Valois and later with Marie Rambert. Her ballet training was reshaped by her subsequent actor training. Lefton's movement work is characterized by its seamless integration into the overall production and the way she empowers actors to truly own their movement. She is a long-term creative collaborator of Jane Gibson, with whom she has co-directed several productions. The enormous breadth and scope of her work in theatre and opera position her as a leader in the field of movement. I met Lefton when she was working at the Royal Shakespeare Company (RSC) in the early 1990s. Her productions were my first encounter with a 'movement director' working at the heart of the classical British theatre canon. She planted the seed of what would be my own career as a movement director, although at that time I was training as a performer at the Lecoq school. Our conversations capture her intimate understanding of how dancers translate their skills for the purpose of acting and her relish for language, text and the framing of narrative. She has a quiet wisdom and an appreciation for movement that continues to inspire.

Kate Flatt (Chapter 5) has worked as a movement director and choreographer across theatre and opera. Kate's training as a dancer at the Royal Ballet School, and then at London School of Contemporary Dance, situates her in two contrasting dance traditions. She continued to develop her skills by assisting Léonide Massine and through her own enquiry into popular and folk dance, both of which inform her way of seeing movement and understanding the social roots of community rituals. I became aware of Flatt's work first as a theatregoer watching Phyllida Lloyd's operas and Katie Mitchell's plays at the National. Flatt's input shows how choreographic practices can enhance narratives and shape choruses. Flatt brings her clear-eyed, reflexive capacities to bear on movement work and on the field of movement in general. Our subsequent conversations have been a great inspiration. Her insights into working in opera are invaluable for any movement director beginning to work in that form.

Toby Sedgwick (Chapter 6) works as a director of movement and an actor across theatre and film. He follows in the wake of Claude Chagrin as a Lecoq-trained, visually creative actor devising large physical sections within plays. Significantly, he was, like me, directly trained by Jacques Lecoq himself – we share the experience of having Lecoq's approach transmitted body to body. Sedgwick deploys the best of the Lecoq traditions of making the invisible visible, with a focus on the physical rather than the textual. Levity, comedy and the everyday characterize his movement work. He is one of the movement directors that I have also seen in action, and his ability to galvanize groups of actors is testimony to his deep insider knowledge as an actor himself. I watched Sedgwick's contribution to the Olympic Games opening ceremony with such joy at the involvement of so many non-professional performers. Our conversation revealed the creative enquiry that he brings to bear in the preparatory process and demonstrated his imaginative yet structural thinking. I discovered that his movement style is informed by a cinematic imagination as well as one that has refined a 'poor theatre' movement language of objects, dynamics and images.

Siân Williams (Chapter 7) works as a movement director and choreographer. Her description of her practice resonates with the actor-focused dancing of Geraldine Stephenson (see Chapter 1). At the start of her career, Williams was engaged to create discrete dance sequences, which then led to more extensive contributions to productions. For her work at the Globe, Williams largely draws on her varied dance training and on her love of social dancing. The conversation also revealed how the physical dexterity of vaudeville and classic musical theatre movies has influenced her work; her inventiveness makes sense in light of this background. I have followed Williams' work at the Globe as an audience member, revelling in the liveliness of her style and her skill at using dance to connect actors and audiences. Our conversation was characterized by a spirit of enquiry mixed with pragmatism. Both qualities are, I think, common to the movement directors who, like me, started doing it before they named it. We discussed ideas of authenticity and the particular demands made of actors in plays from the Renaissance in three-sided spaces, which characterize work that Williams has undertaken both at the RSC and at the Globe.

Struan Leslie (Chapter 8) works as a movement director and choreographer, mainly in theatre and opera. Struan's training at the London School of Contemporary Dance and in the United States situates him in two notable dance traditions: that of contemporary dance and Contact Improvisation (CI). Both resonate in his current practice. As the first named official Head of Movement at the RSC (2009–14), Leslie is one of the key players in the field. I became aware of Leslie's work first as a theatregoer, when I noticed the poise and beauty of the choruses within Katie Mitchell's plays and operas. Over the last fifteen years, we have had some frank and creative discussions about the field, and I have had opportunities to see Leslie in action, where his connection to music and rhythm and his ability to see movement have been striking. Our conversations revealed the questions that inform his work on choral movement. I discovered that a quietly political stance, driven by ideas of queerness and the inclusive foundations of CI, informs his thinking about his process.

Ellen Kane (Chapter 9) is a theatre choreographer who comes from a contemporary dance background. She trained as a dancer at Lewisham College and London Studio Centre and was a founder member of the Henri Oguike Dance Company, beginning her career as a dancer before working as a theatre choreographer. She is a long-term collaborator of Peter Darling (Chapter 10), with whom she worked initially as an associate and then as co-choreographer on a range of productions. I was first aware of their working partnership when I did a small amount of movement coaching on *Matilda* several years ago, which gave me an insight into the complex organization required by a production with many incarnations in London and beyond. The level of structural thinking and teamwork at play is dazzling. Kane's interview clearly illuminates how her training as a dancer as an adult has shaped her ability to teach and create with others. The potency of dance skill and the power of long-term collaboration are themes that emerged from our conversation.

Peter Darling (Chapter 10) is a British theatre choreographer, best known for his narrative-driven, actor-centred style of dance. He began his career as an actor before working as a theatre choreographer. In the 1990s, I undertook a formative, extended workshop with DV8 physical theatre company. This led me to follow their creative journey and that, in turn, led me to Darling's work. He has spoken of their influence on him as an actor and then as a theatre choreographer. Darling's movement work is characterized by an inventiveness and a joyful exuberance. He channels an actor's imaginative power and insight into narrative and expresses it through choreography and musical staging. Our conversations, conducted virtually, revealed the collaborative process at play in his practice and the rigorous preparation process that underpins movement dramaturgy in new musical theatre. He is the only practitioner in this book who calls himself a 'choreographer' only, which is the received terminology for creating dances within musicals. He is a long-term collaborator with Ellen Kane (Chapter 9), and they reference each other's work.

Steven Hoggett (Chapter 11) is a movement director and theatre choreographer. He trained by performing with a range of British dance and dance theatre companies in the 1990s, first in other people's work and then as founder and Co-Artistic Director of Frantic Assembly. He acknowledges the influence of a variety of choreographers who worked with Frantic Assembly through their early years. I became aware of Hoggett's work first as a theatregoer watching Frantic's early shows in small studios (such as Battersea Arts Centre) in the 1990s, and more recently I have followed his emergence as an independent movement director and choreographer with interest. Hoggett's movement style is characterized by the powerful connection amongst the ensemble. Having known his work from afar, it was insightful to hear him articulate his process and philosophy, which he did with such generosity. Our conversation revealed his absolute commitment to nurturing a creative relationship with performers and the ease with which he collaborates with directors. His forthright energy and responsibility to the creative process permeated the conversation. Hoggett is currently working across both the UK and the United States, where he is usefully defining the field.

Ann Yee (Chapter 12) is a movement director and choreographer from the United States who works across theatre, opera and musicals. She undertook her training in modern dance in the United States, and her early work in theatre was largely in the UK. She now has a transatlantic career. She is an influential movement director in the United States, where she is defining the field. I was first aware of Yee's work through the voices of the actors I was working with at the RSC. I have since followed her movement direction work with great interest. Yee's movement is characterized by its poetic beauty and the interconnectedness amongst the ensemble. Our wide-ranging conversations took place in the summer of 2018 as she was previewing *Julie* at the National Theatre. They revealed her deep commitment to the lived experience of a company of actors and the artistry involved in collaboration. In the interview, she explored the function of warm-up in depth, and in her words I can hear the movement director in action – connecting, enabling, reacting. Her energy and passion for the medium are an inspiration.

Imogen Knight (Chapter 13) is a choreographer and movement director. The range of her movement work reaches from film and television, to art installations, to opera. Like Ann Yee and me, her practice has emerged and grown throughout the last decade or so, on to the British movement direction scene. Our conversations started informally when we crossed paths as teachers several years ago. The interim period has seen a prolific career develop, and following her work has been a great pleasure. In our conversation, Knight explored how her dance background has adapted to meet the work of actors. She offered real insight on the scope of her movement process from preparation to realization. Her attraction to the rawness and messiness of humanity that is exposed in theatre works was evident. The deep, thoughtful artistry revealed in our conversation made sense of her movement work that is characterized by originality and the unexpected. Her movement work always plays a significant dramaturgical role within overall production. Her energy and responsibility to the creative process permeated the conversation.

Shelley Maxwell (Chapter 14) has emerged more recently than other interviewees on the British movement direction scene. Our conversation started informally when we crossed paths at the RSC several years ago, on what was her first assistant movement direction job. Since then, an exciting and prolific career has developed. In our conversation, Maxwell explored the fundamentals of movement direction and the place of the actor within the creative process. She examined her Jamaican dance lineages and her Cuban training. She offered insight into her method of adapting her performance and dance know-how in her work with actors. Her movement work has bright originality and appears well integrated by the actors. Maxwell's energy and relish for the creative process imbued the conversation, as did her deep commitment to the potential of the moving bodies of actors.

Chapter 15 gathers the voices of Diane Alison-Mitchell, Polly Bennett, Lucy Cullingford, Ioli Filippakopoulou, Natasha Harrison, Chi-San Howard, Vicki Igbokwe, Jennifer Jackson, Ingrid Mackinnon, Rebecca Meltzer, Coral Messam, Anna Morrissey, Sue Mythen and Sacha Plaige. This group of movement directors responded to an open invitation to talk about their work. Unlike the preceding twelve conversations, this chapter emerged from curating diverse voices in short conversations. Some are at an early stage in their career, many are mid-career and many have undertaken the first formal training for movement directors in Britain (see Chapter 1). Their individual biographies are included in the endnotes.

The collection of voices in this book illuminates the complex web of embodied experiences that inform our discipline. Every interview followed its own course, and a different emphasis for each one emerged. In the spirit of feminist revisionist history, I have concentrated mainly on female practitioners and have acknowledged and emphasized the influences of teachers. My hope is that the reader will gain insight into the ephemeral and impactful practice of movement directors through the many voices that follow, and step nearer to the vibrancy of this growing, creative practice.

Note

1 The first formal training for movement directors and movement teachers specializing in movement for actors was established in Britain in 2004. Some of the practitioners in Chapter 15 are amongst the first wave of 'trained' movement directors to undertake a formal, vocational apprenticeship before entering the profession.

1 EARLY PRACTITIONERS AND PRACTICES

Each conversation in this book describes a practitioner's unique personal history of movement trainings and references the teachers and practitioners who inspired them. The interviews illuminate a myriad of influences on these contemporary practitioners, and taken together, they start to map the development of the discipline.

Looking backwards into the twentieth century is a useful way of understanding what constitutes the contemporary in the field of movement direction in the UK. This chapter provides an insight into the work of the earliest movement directors and theatre choreographers, and whilst it does not present an exhaustive history, it discusses a representative range of early practitioners working within the British theatre scene. I begin by discussing the careers of Litz Pisk, Claude Chagrin, Geraldine Stephenson and Jean Newlove. These pioneers were the first to name the practice and developed working processes that are still recognizable today. Some of these early practitioners also directly taught or influenced a generation of movement directors that feature in these interviews.

Whilst the term *director of movement* emerged in the post-war period, instances of actor-centred movement practice, *avant-la-lettre*, are discernible much earlier in the twentieth century in British theatre. Frequently, this kind of work was attributed to a 'choreographer' (sometimes signalled with a reference to 'dances by' in the programme or credits). These terms can be misleading, since they sometimes fail to represent the real contribution of nascent movement directors. I will examine one short phase of Ninette de Valois' work on theatre productions to reveal that she was creating movement material beyond the dances that she was originally engaged to set – a creative contribution that is now more akin to movement direction than choreography. Then I will look at some of the dancers and actors associated with the British Natural Movement and Greek Revival dance who developed their own hybrid techniques, inspired by new, freer forms of dance emerging in Europe at the start of the twentieth century. They too contributed to the emergence of 'movement' practices before they were so named. In this chapter I will discuss the careers of choreographer Margaret Morris, and movement and mime teachers Ruby Ginner and Irene Mawer, all of whom are representative of the practitioners working in this period.

Litz Pisk (1909–97) was a notable actor movement teacher working in Britain from the interwar period onwards.[1] Originally from Austria, her early training combined drawing, scenography and costume design with *Ausdruckstanz*, or new expressive dance, in 1920s Vienna. Her formative training was a dynamic combination of acrobatics/gymnastics, Laban, ballet, historical and folk dance. Like many Jewish artists, Pisk left Vienna ahead of the Anschluss in 1933, settling permanently in England in 1937. She went on to teach movement to generations of actors at the Royal Academy of Dramatic Art (RADA; 1936–42), the Old Vic Theatre School (1947–51) and Royal Central School of Speech and Drama (RCSSD; 1962–70, as Head of Movement from 1964).

Hand in hand with her teaching, Pisk worked on theatre productions, practising as a movement director with greater frequency from the 1950s onwards. She directed movement across theatre, film and, to some extent, television. Her collaboration with theatre director Michael Elliot was an enduring one, based on complementary working methods that sought to harness the actor's emotional and imaginative capacities. Elliot recalls that as collaborators, they could 'always discuss the emotional intention in detail first, where we speak the same language, before finding our different ways to express it' (Elliot in Pisk 2018: xxxiii). Pisk also worked repeatedly with actor Vanessa Redgrave, first on a seminal production of *As You Like It* at the Royal Shakespeare Company (RSC) in 1961, and then on the 1967 film *Isadora*, directed by Karel Reisz. For the latter, she contributed choreography and movement direction, creating the dance and movement language for the role of the modern dancer Isadora Duncan. Redgrave recalls,

> In 1967, we spent weeks together preparing the dances for the film *Isadora*. When Litz drew up her skirt between her legs and began to move, with or without her drum, I saw in her, alive, the amazing spectrum of history, philosophy and rhythms from the ancient Greeks to the Renaissance and to our times. She inherited and transmitted the *katharsis*: the coming together and the mutual release that men and women all seek and can find.
>
> GRACE ET AL. 1997: 14

Pisk's movement practice was, at times, choreographic but almost always ritualistic. Her way of working was frequently described as organic by those who knew her because she started with the innate qualities in each individual actor. Her movement progressions commenced with inner impulses that manifested in external motion. Her capacity to draw out the dramatic potential of movement and her actor-centred approach continues to inspire practitioners today. Jane Gibson (Chapter 3) and Sue Lefton (Chapter 4) trained with Pisk in the 1960s in London and are directly influenced by her teaching, which they embodied as trainee actors. Lefton also went on to assist Pisk on several productions. In particular, Pisk's idea of a 'climate of a time' was intended to help actors access social dances through their imagination. She would draw on references to architecture, art, clothing and music of a historical period to activate the actor's senses as well as their imagination. Pisk focused on the actor's capacity for transformation, explaining that

> The actor does not move for movement's sake and he does not beautify movement for beauty's sake. If he is called upon to dance, he will do so as a certain character in a specific time, place and situation. The actor's body maybe small or big, short or tall and he transforms his body into any body.
>
> PISK 2018: XXXV–XXXVI

In 1975, Pisk published *The Actor and His Body*, a seminal book that starts to chart the terrain of movement direction, and which still influences movement practitioners and actors to this day – especially her identification of an actor's *need* to move. Pisk's legacy to movement direction lies in identifying and realizing the dramatic dynamics within movement in a way that was tailor-made for the actor's inner life and that supported the dramaturgical imperatives of the theatre production.

Post-war movement directors/theatre choreographers were often engaged to fulfil moments of specialized movement. They were hired as specialists to teach specific movement techniques if movement was seen to be beyond the skill of the actors or the director. Their specialism – for example, animal movement, mime or dance – was needed in and of itself and frequently acted as an entry point to a more expansive input. Movement director Claude Chagrin and theatre choreographer Geraldine Stephenson were credited with 'mime' or 'dances by' early in their careers. From the 1950s onwards, the demand for their specialist skills grew. This led them to make greater movement contributions, resulting in a gradual renaming of their work to 'movement by' and 'choreography by' in credits.

Claude Chagrin (born 1935) was a French movement director and performer whose physical training was in mime with Marcel Marceau[2] and physical theatre with Jacques Lecoq.[3] In Britain, she taught mime in a variety of settings, including the City Literary Institute (City Lit.) and Morley College. Throughout the 1960s, she taught actors alongside movement directing on professional productions – with one practice feeding the other. Some suggest that Chagrin was chosen by Laurence Olivier to join the National Theatre. She was, in fact, appointed by William Gaskill to become the in-house movement specialist, but it is unclear in what capacity she worked, beyond contributing to individual productions. We do know that she worked on at least seventeen productions at the National Theatre from 1961 to 1974. In 1964, Chagrin movement directed *Royal Hunt of the Sun*, a new play by Peter Shaffer at the newly formed National Theatre, directed by John Dexter. She was instrumental in creating a stylized physical language that included ensemble movement work and rituals. Her movement vocabulary developed out of her physical theatre training and into a creative dramaturgy that prioritized seeing and feeling over understanding and listening. Critics responded to the dynamics of her work and sometimes acknowledged her work directly in their reviews. When reviewing *A Bond Honoured* (also directed by John Dexter), critic B. A. Young wrote, 'Stage pictures of great beauty are created, with bold, arrogant movements that take the eye' and explicitly acknowledged Chagrin's contribution, writing that 'Claude Chagrin has arranged the movement' (1966: 24).[4] Milton Shulman noted that 'by the use of swirling balletic movements, by the suggestion of violence throughout the skilful manipulation of mime play and by the adroit placing of Sicilian folk songs, this short play has been turned into a stunning parable with a magnificent theatrical impact' (1966: 9). Critics were noticing the physical potency of the movement and were sensitive to the collaboration between movement director, composer, director and, importantly, actor. A third review of *A Bond Honoured* notes that the movement was characterized by 'flamenco fluency' and 'the plasticity of flamenco dancers, using semi-abstract mime for the moments of violence – blows which fell without connecting, red scarves for head-wounds'. He observes that 'above all, there's Robert Stephens carrying further the sculptural technique he mastered for *The Royal Hunt of the Sun*: part-dancer, part-athlete, fixing each posture in bronze' (Bryden 1966: 24). In 1973, Claude Chagrin worked with John Dexter again on the seminal production of Peter Shaffer's play *Equus*. She contributed what we might recognize as the mainstays of a Lecoq-trained movement director – mime, animal movement and chorus work. The central relationship between horse and human necessitated a physically creative approach to express violence, sexual awakening and psychological disintegration. Dexter, in his biography, makes little mention of Chagrin's sizeable contribution, but one has to infer a successful working relationship where physicality was playing a significant part of the whole production language.[5] Chagrin's daughter, Sophie Chagrin Cohen, recollects that Claude's 'movement came from her training with Lecoq and Marceau, and then it was a process of translating her unique vision into a display of ambiance, movement and impeccable timing' (unpublished conversation with Chagrin family, September 2014). Chagrin's work in the UK came to a temporary halt with her relocation to Israel in 1976; she returned to England in 1988/9. While there is no direct inheritance from Chagrin to Sedgwick, there is certainly an indirect one through the shared vocabulary of the Lecoq training (see Sedgwick, Chapter 6). Her legacy is inscribed into the artistic vibrancy of early National Theatre works and the reimagining of corporeal mime for a wider physical theatre vocabulary.

Geraldine Stephenson (1925–2017) was a dance and Laban-trained movement director and choreographer who created mass-movement pieces, and social and historical dances for the actor.[6] She studied physiotherapy and physical education at Bedford College of Physical Education and went on to study at Laban's Art of Movement Studio in Manchester with Rudolph Laban[7] and Lisa Ullman from 1946. Stephenson's formative experience with Ullman and Laban included teaching movement to actors and non-professional performers as well as creating her own solo works for dance recitals. She went on to assist Laban, teaching actors at Esme Church's Northern Theatre School in Bradford.[8]

Stephenson talked of the influence of Laban and Ullman, and how their movement training focused on 'the liberating of one's movement' by putting 'emphasis on centrally generated body movement – so different from ballet' and 'full-body use of the floor, bare feet, wide-ranging spatial directions, and the totally new experience of improvisation, partner and group work' (Goodrich 2003: 29). She had a range of skills at her disposal – skills that would be reformulated in her work with actors.

Stephenson worked on St Mary's Abbey's medieval York Mystery Plays as part of the Festival of Britain, where she was asked to create three movement sequences including Lucifer's fall from heaven. Her credit in 1951 was 'Stylised Movement and Mime'. And with the same project three years later, in 1954, this credit changed to 'Director of Movement'.[9] Stephenson's detailed description of her work on the York Mystery Plays in 1951 shows she was clearly applying choreographic skill to a huge range of movers, both amateurs and professional performers. She integrated movement sequences with speech and text for the choruses in this piece. She paid tribute to the 'mathematical solutions' that Laban imparted; she employed a structural strategy in which smaller subgroups within the larger chorus of 250 performers were led by two of her own students. Actor Edward Petherbridge trained with Stephenson and performed in this production. He recollects that Stephenson was

> a disciple of, and chief assistant to, Rudolf Laban at the time and her classes were both rigorous and freeing – no dancing, rather abstract in their exploration of, it seemed, every fundamental quality of movement. We students played demons, bad and good souls, at the last judgment under her direction at the York Mystery Plays of 1954.
>
> PETHERBRIDGE 2018

Stephenson identified this project as a creative turning point. Working on the Mystery Plays, she discovered her capacity to create movement material for non-specialist movers and found how to generate a movement style that was integral to the narrative demands of the drama. Talking about her approach to movement for actors, she said, 'I think you get the best out of people if you don't impose on them. ... I like to know who I am working with – what my material is' (McGaw 2001: 24). This very individual, bespoke approach is a characteristic of all movement direction today, and one that you will hear repeated amongst the voices that follow (see Flatt, Chapter 5; Maxwell, Chapter 14; Igbokwe, Chapter 15).

Stephenson's long career included choreographing pageants as well as theatre works at the National Theatre, at the Royal Shakespeare Company and in television from the 1960s to the 2000s – often credited as 'choreographer' or for overseeing 'movement' on her many television productions. Stephenson developed what would become a lifelong commitment to

> working with actors and helping them find the movement for their character or teaching them to dance – the process of getting the movement out of them and through them. ... I believe that this is what all dance should have: a sense of drama and a sense of intention. You have to know what people are dancing about. Laban with his *effort* work as much as with his spatial exercises, is responsible for my interest in the content of movement, and for my being able to work with all these different types of people – the York Plays, pageants, actors – professional or amateur, and of course with dancers.[10]
>
> MCGAW 2001: 24

Here, she places emphasis on the actor rather than the director or the production. Two threads emerge from the work of Stephenson: first, dance's dramaturgical potential to communicate drama and second, the centrality of actor-tailored processes. It is notable that several of the interviewees were actors before they became movement directors/theatre choreographers, and that their knowledge as performers remains key to their process (see Lefton, Gibson, Darling, Sedgwick, Hoggett, Knight, Maxwell, this volume).

The influence of Laban in post-war British theatre can also be identified in the work of theatre director Joan Littlewood. Littlewood embraced movement training as part of the development of new work and ensemble theatre practice. She had a horror of 'past tense acting' as well as a reputation for preferring enthusiastic amateurs to conservatoire-trained actors. She did not

> believe in the supremacy of the director, designer, actor or even the writer. It is through collaboration that this knockabout art of theatre survives and kicks .... No one mind or imagination can foresee what a play will become until all the physical and intellectual stimuli which are crystallized in the poetry of the author have been understood by a company, and then tried out in terms of mime, discussion and the precise music of grammar: words and movement allied and integrated.
>
> CLIVE BARKER IN HODGE 2000: 114

Laban's influence on Littlewood dated from her own actor training at RADA, where she was taught movement by Anny Fligg.[11] The influence coalesced when she founded her company, Theatre Workshop, situated within reaching distance of the Art of Movement Studio. Laban's assistant, Jean Newlove (1923–2017), embedded herself full-time in the creative life of the company.[12] This is one of the first company-based movement direction roles to emerge in the post-war period. Newlove had trained in ballet from the age of three, and later in Greek dance. In 1942, she applied to become a dance and movement teacher for 300 women on the Dartington Hall Estate. And whilst she did not obtain that post, the encounter led to an invitation to train with Laban. She initially assisted Laban and F. C. Lawrence on their project for improving efficiency in factories during wartime, and then worked closely with Lisa Ullman in establishing classes in modern educational dance.

The reach of Newlove's contribution with Theatre Workshop ranged from training to creation of performance material. She recalls,

> At Theatre Workshop, apart from the regular Laban training on a daily basis, actors were encouraged to approach their characters through an exploration of their movement habits and relationships. Voice was always considered as an extension of movement, dialogue came later.
>
> NEWLOVE 1993: 8

Newlove recollects the impact of regular movement training on the actors: 'Every day they had at least an hour's movement … we could see how well it was working … and it was very obvious then that people were improving.' Arguably, it was Littlewood who first built the bridge between movement training and acting in her company; bespoke actor movement would not develop until much later in the twentieth century (Newlove 2007). It is clear, however, that the vocabulary provided by Laban offered a shared language for Littlewood and Newlove, and then the ethos and practices of the company shaped the work of Newlove to encompass training, creating, choreographing and performing.

The Littlewood/Newlove collaboration created an environment that prioritized the moving body of the actor. Their daily movement practice would be instrumental in building shared experiences and developing the movement skills of any untrained performers in the company. There is no direct inheritance from Newlove to the contemporary movement directors featured in this book, but there is an indirect one through the vocabulary used by Littlewood/Newlove from Laban training (see Williams, Chapter 7). Their legacy to movement direction lies perhaps in the integrated and embedded nature of movement practice that fed directly into the performance physicality and styles of the company.

Several of the movement directors featured in this book have a long-standing connection with ballet (see Flatt, Yee, Williams, Lefton). This prompted me to investigate both the form and the development of ballet in Britain. The dramaturgical aspects of movement direction find parallels in classical ballet, which is a form structured around storytelling with character development. Ballet's codified dance language is used to express relationship and feeling. Dance repetitions and movement patterns are used to heighten and express emotion. Mime is employed and reintegrated into danced language. Fictional location is, in part, created by the orchestration of bodies in a space. A corps de ballet – a type of chorus – embodies dramatic movement in relation to protagonists.

While ballet training existed in the first quarter of the twentieth century, a coherent progression into a dance profession in Britain was lacking. Ballet as an art form was dominated by visiting companies. This would remain so until the arrival of the great galvanizing forces of Marie Rambert and Ninette de Valois who, in the mid-1930s, established Ballet Rambert (see Lefton, Chapter 4) and Vic-Wells Ballet, respectively.

Ninette de Valois is primarily remembered for her great advocacy and entrepreneurial force in the establishment of British ballet.[13] However, for a short period in her early career, she undertook work that we may retrospectively identify as movement direction.

Irish-born de Valois spent a short period dancing with Léonid Massine (see Flatt, Chapter 5) and Lydia Lopokova, creating and performing ballet dances for music-hall performance, before joining Diaghilev's ballet company in 1923 as a dancer. It was here that she met ballet choreographer Bronislava Nijinska. De Valois drew inspiration from the choreographers of the ground-breaking ballets she appeared in. On her return to London in 1926, she opened her Academy of Choreographic Art. She devised a training programme for professional ballet dancers at the academy while also working on theatre productions. At the Old Vic in 1926, she arranged dances for Shakespeare's *A Midsummer Night's Dream* and *The Tempest*. From 1926 to 1933, she worked on many theatre productions at the Festival Theatre Cambridge, the Abbey Theatre and again at the Old Vic. Her work had three concurrent strands during this period: creating movement for plays; creating ballets that were eventually programmed alongside plays; and training dancers. De Valois helped to cultivate the next generation of theatre choreographers. She supervised a number of her dancers as they directed movement themselves (or 'arranging dances', as it was then called). The scope of de Valois' and her protégées' work extended from Shakespeare to symbolist plays and, according to Kathrine Sorley Walker, included coaching actors and creating a varied range of movement languages – dance sequences, masked chorus work, dream sequences and ritual and symbolic movement. Walker concludes that de Valois 'had raised to a fine art the amplification and illustration of words by movement, using rhythms of music, speech or chanting to give it choreographic form' (Walker 1984: 400). What is being described here is the work of a movement director having a creative impact on actors and the wider production of plays.

Movement direction remained unnamed by de Valois during this period and sat within the framework of 'choreography'. The establishment of the Vic-Wells Ballet[14] in 1931 meant that the focus of de Valois' creativity started to shift wholly towards ballet and away from theatre.

Early twentieth-century Europe saw significant developments in dance as a performance art and the reconceptualization of the body in theatre. A free-moving, natural body connecting to its inner life and to universal rhythms burst on to the artistic scene. Emergent movement training did not rely on codified movement but emphasized expressive movement. A way of working *with* the body started to emerge: movement practice designed for freeing the body and allowing the mover to shape imagination and emotion through his or her own creative impulses. Nascent movement principles proved to be malleable, more so than rigid forms of traditional movement training. This enabled movement to be applied in a wider range of art forms. Rather than learning a systematized technique such as ballet or gymnastics, performers could create movement out of their individual expressive movement and personal aptitudes.

Early in the twentieth century in Britain, the influence of dance pioneer Isadora Duncan developed into what was to become known as Natural Movement and Greek Revival dance (which also percolates through the training of certain movement directors – see Flatt, Chapter 5, and Gibson, Chapter 3).[15] Duncan's influence in Britain spread partly through the efforts of her siblings Elizabeth and Raymond Duncan, whose classes and summer schools were attended by teachers who would go on to become significant Greek Revival dancers and Natural Movement practitioners. Amongst them were Margaret Morris, Ruby Ginner, Irene Mawer[16] and Madge Atkinson,[17] four practitioners who became powerhouses of the Natural Movement and Greek Revival dance in Britain and were instrumental in British dance pedagogy in the first half of the twentieth century.[18] Writing in 1933, Ruby Ginner acknowledged their debt to Duncan, saying that 'the first exponent of this form [was] that great artist of the dance, Isadora Duncan, who regarded movement not only as a means of artistic expression but a power wherewith to reform life' (Ginner 1933: 12).

Margaret Morris (1891–1980) was a British child actress who trained initially in ballet. Over a brief period of training, she also learnt fundamentals of Greek forms from Raymond Duncan, which catalysed a desire to create a new dance language and training. Her early career straddled work as a dance-trained actress, a choreographer and a producer. When she produced work at the Royal Court in the 1910–12 seasons, she was one of the youngest female actor-managers of the time (Trewhitt and Hastie 1997: 3). In this early phase of Morris's work, two elements were developing: choreography for production, and movement as training for performers. Although her work predates any named practice of movement direction, at this point in her career Morris was clearly shaping movement for the stage as a key part of a theatre or an opera event. For example, in 1910 Morris staged ballets for Marie Brema's production of Gluck's opera *Orpheus* at the Savoy. Morris also provides the first example of what will prove to be another emerging model in movement direction: the practitioner who is trained as both dancer and actor (a background shared by interviewees in this volume; see Lefton, Chapter 4 and Darling, Chapter 10). In 1910, Morris opened her first schools and started to develop a movement training that would become known as the Margaret Morris Method.[19] Her physical principles highlighted the use of opposition; the amplification of a movement; and the body as a locus of creativity.[20] Her technique was built on a form of yogic breathing, on swings and arm/leg coordination. Much of her technique was strongly anchored in ballet, yet there was an aesthetic influence from Greek artworks on the angles of hands and arms.[21] Looking at elements of her training now, it is possible to see the imprint of 'positions' from ballet. However, hers was a technique that was to centralize breath and weight, albeit still at the service of shape rather than experience. She emphasized that each class should deploy the techniques to prepare and practice but that classes should always contain some improvisation and composition, too.

Later in her career, Morris moved from theatre towards therapeutic practices. By the outbreak of the Second World War, she had seven schools in total (five in Great Britain and two in France). All but one was forced to close. Then, Morris shifted her work more clearly into the field of dance, and in wartime she created her first full-length ballet in Scotland, where she went on to establish the Celtic Ballet Club, the precursor of the Scottish National Ballet. Her legacy for movement direction is indirect: many of her students would go on to work as teachers or directors or choreographers in theatre. They included Rupert Doone,[22] Joan Lawson[23] (see Flatt in Chapter 5) and Leslie Burrowes, who from 1924 became a performer and assistant teacher for Morris.[24] In 1928, Burrowes became the first dance teacher at the progressive school and artistic community at Dartington Hall in Devon. The method Morris developed would find another iteration in the teaching developed by her student Ruby Ginner.

Ruby Ginner (1886–1978) is an example of a practitioner whose own training as a performer encompassed both dance and acting; she trained in ballet while working as an actress. Arguably, the roots of what would become her own style of movement training grew while she was under the tutelage of Elsie Fogerty, the founder of the Central School of Speech and Drama, who asked Ginner to research the role of the Greek chorus.[25] By the time she had joined forces with mime teacher and performer Irene Mawer (with whom she established the Ginner-Mawer School of Dance and Drama after the First World War), she was undertaking physical explorations of the ritual roots of movement. Of this, Ginner writes that 'in [Greek] drama the dance expressed the action of the play and its spiritual and moral significance; the choric dance was an interpretation by movement of the intellectual qualities of the verse' (Ginner 1933: 38). Her movement approach was wholly practical, emphasizing principles of relaxation and focus on different body parts. She wrote that it was important to work up from the feet to the legs, and on up to the torso and head, then outwards towards gesture. Ginner highlighted her aesthetic of movement in her descriptions of balance and poise. She redefined poise as a moment of stillness between two forces rather than a body conforming to a prescribed alignment. Her translations of sculpture, poetry, the natural world and the seasons into movement are echoed in the preparatory work of many movement directors. However, her engagement with the sung/danced/spoken ritual of Greek drama – the roots of Western theatre – provided the bedrock of her understanding of movement. She sought to understand drama as both a source and a consequence of movement. This formulation is the legacy she left for movement directors. Ginner and Mawer prioritized body and gesture over spoken word in their teaching philosophy. In their writings, they have an expansive and ethnographic frame of reference, seeking movement that would give rise to the primal, the natural, the ritual. In her book, *The Art of Mime: Its History and Technique in Education and Theatre*, Mawer reminds us that the 'two terms, dancer and actor, are in the Indian, as in the Greek, synonymous' (Mawer 1932: 13).

These early movement practitioners diverged from other, more prescriptive, forms of movement (like ballet and gymnastics) and instead placed importance on creation, improvisation and application. They started to shape a holistic practice through which the individual's qualities were harnessed and developed within a group setting. They embraced a new-found, barefooted connection to the earth: their celebration of the natural world led them to hold classes and performances outdoors, in parks and on beaches. They upheld some principles of Duncan's original agenda; however, the insistence on self-expression, which was so present in Isadora Duncan's philosophy, shifted. Her choreographic material had been largely subjective and took the form of solo dance works, whereas these new practitioners created movement for theatre and opera, engaging with the fictional and expressive demands of character, narrative, drama and atmosphere. While I do not want to overestimate the direct impact of these early practitioners, I would like to acknowledge the following patterns: a practice that is connecting drama and dance/movement, allowing the individual creative movement freedom within forms that support and develop movement technique; and a dynamic, new practice that is taking a historically distant Hellenic world, and reinventing it for female bodies at the outset of the twentieth century.[26] A research project in 2009, which encapsulated both archival work and a conference, suggested that the legacy of these pioneers was unfairly eclipsed by later developments in dance.[27]

There are two key parallels between the work of these pioneers and that of today's movement directors: first, the importance of concrete movement training that can be adapted for different levels of ability (from children to amateurs to professionals); and second, fluid careers that move between creating dances and producing for theatre. It may be that the forms of movement have not really lived on in theatre contexts, but the philosophies and practices of these practitioners resonate with the breadth of the work of the movement director. An indirect influence often brushed aside by movement directors themselves was the absorption of Natural Movement and Greek Revival dance methods into the Imperial Society of Teachers of Dance curriculum and the Royal Academy of Dance (ballet) syllabus, which is present in the early training of Flatt, Lefton, Gibson and Williams.

Directors of movement may have only been named as such since the 1950s in Britain. They emerged on the scene to create movement within theatre productions, which meant finding working methods that enabled actors to reach their full potential in movement. They became close collaborators with directors. Often, their creative relationships developed through repeated productions and new creative challenges. A wealth of varied twentieth-century movement lineages – including mime, modern dance, ballet, free dance and gymnastics – forms the background from which these early movement directors emerged. Informed by various types of training and a range of influences, they shared an aptitude for the creation of movement for narrative-led works. This remains true for the practitioners that follow in this book.

Notes

1 Litz Pisk (1909–97) was a movement teacher and early movement director. Born in Vienna, Pisk combined her aptitude for fine art with movement in her early years. Drawing and movement were to underpin her lifelong teaching practice. In Vienna, she studied stage architecture at the State Art and Crafts School as well as training in a variety of movement forms. She attended the Hilde Holger School of Dance (Neue Schule für Bewegungskunst) and became co-owner and teacher there. For further research, refer to the 2018 edition of Pisk's book *The Actor and His Body*, with a contextual introduction by the author for details of Pisk's practice and influence.

2 Marcel Marceau (1923–2007) was a French mime artist who founded a school in Paris in 1978.

3 French movement pedagogue Jacques Lecoq (1921–99). Lecoq's early movement roots lay in sports, which included athletics (running, high jump), gymnastics (parallel and horizontal bars) and swimming. When he embarked on theatre training, he acknowledged that he was filtering creative movement through his sports knowledge. Like all sportspeople, Lecoq would have had an embodied understanding of the connection between breath, rhythm and motion which he then translated into new forms of movement for theatre. In Occupied France he worked as a physiotherapist and acknowledged how useful his understanding of anatomy and rehabilitation was for his later work in movement analysis for performer training. His future pedagogy was to be filled with metaphors of the natural world and of journeys. He created theatre exercises about the elements: climbing mountains; swimming in rivers, lakes and the sea; running in the countryside; being in wind, rain, dusk and so forth. Much of his pedagogy was built on the ability to absorb and

render theatrical the everyday world, such as the rhythm of the village square from dawn to dusk or the motion of a paper bag uncrumpling. Lecoq's theatre training started during the wartime period with *Travail et Culture* where he practised mimed improvisations with teacher Claude Martin (who had trained with Charles Dullin). He also took classes in free dance with Jean Séry (originally a ballet dancer converted to modern dance). After the liberation of France from 1945–7 he joined forces with fellow student Gabriel Cousin to create a first theatre company, *Les Aurochs*. This proved to be short-lived. But they soon joined up with Luigi Cicione (his physical education teacher from Bagatelle) and Jean Séry and founded another company: *Les Compagnons de la Saint-Jean*. They used their collective performance and movement skills to put on large-scale festive events. Dealing with the movement of large groups of untrained performers would influence the formative movement director in his future work on choruses. Several of these company members were asked to join Jean Dasté's newly formed company *Les Comedians de Grenoble*. Donning the movement mantle from Suzanne Bing, Lecoq was asked to train the actors physically as well as perform. In 1947, Lecoq returned to Paris to teach physical expression at the newly formed *Education par le jeu dramatique*, a vocational acting school created by Jean-Louis Barrault with actors including Marie-Hélène Dasté and Jean-Marie Conty. From 1948 to 1956, he worked at the University of Padua in Italy as a teacher and a practitioner. Here he discovered *commedia dell'arte* and was taught the physical parameters of commedia characters by the Italian actor Carlo Ludovici through direct body-to-body transmission. He also mounted some pantomime productions at the Theatre University. During his time in Italy, Lecoq joined Giorgio Strehler and Paolo Grassi in the formation of the school of the Piccolo Theatre in Milan, a company-based school. He also started to movement direct, and in working on Greek tragedies he had to grapple with a movement language for the chorus. Lecoq recalls: 'Par la suite, de nombreuses compagnies me sollicitèrent pour mettre en mouvement les spectacles et faire bouger les acteurs. On me demandait de faire des "chorégraphies dramatique" (ce terme, très difficile à situer, "entre" le plus souvent dans la mise en scène tout court)' [Author's translation: 'After this, a number of companies asked me to set the productions in "motion" and activate movement in the actor's body. I was asked to create "dramatic choreography" (a very difficult term to define, often occupying "in between" place but, most often it resided simply within the mise en scène'] (Lecoq 1987: 111). Here, he identifies the emergence of a new kind of movement work for himself and the company, but he also points towards the liminal space that would be occupied by movement direction. After these formative experiences of both training and production, Lecoq returned to Paris in 1956 to open his own school of mime and theatre. For three years, he combined teaching with work alongside Jean Vilar at the *Theatre National Populaire* as a movement director. Like many of his contemporaries in Britain, Lecoq was combining pedagogic and production practices. It is also significant to note that the role of 'movement director' attained a place in French theatre at the same time that it was being acknowledged in the UK. Lecoq's pedagogic ideas are very well documented in his book, *Le Corps Poétique* or *The Moving Body: Teaching Creative Theatre* (Lecoq 2000). Movement directors Monica Pagneux, Claude Chagrin, Toby Sedgwick, Leah Hausmann, Jane Gibson, Sue Lefton, Joseph Alford, Joyce Henderson and I were all taught by Lecoq, and are working extensively in British theatre. The performer-movement director model also manifests amongst British movement directors, for example Toby Sedgwick and the author.

Born in France in 1935, Claude Chagrin was a teacher and mime and movement director. She attended the Lecoq school from 1959 to 1962 (see also Tashkiran 2016: 135–41).

4 *A Bond Honoured* by John Osborne, directed by John Dexter, 1966 (National Theatre).

5 Dexter (1993).

6 Geraldine Stephenson (1925–2017) was a British movement director and theatre choreographer whose prolific career spanned fifty years working across theatre, opera, television, film, pageants and galas. Also see Petherbridge 2018.

7 Hungarian-born Rudolph Laban (1879–1958) was a significant figure in twentieth-century Western dance and actor training. His lifelong practice in movement, research and training has influenced actor movement training in the UK. Laban was one of the leaders of the wave of innovation in expressive dance, *Ausdruckstanz*, developed in Germany and Austria through the 1920s and 1930s. Well-being through movement practice and connection to nature and to community underpinned this explosion of dance experimentation and analysis. Laban's teachings and theories had been well established in a variety of schools and companies in Germany, and in the UK. His sizeable influence predated his arrival in 1938. Two Laban schools were run by Anny Fligg and Anny Boalth who had been operating in London in the early 1930s. Kurt Jooss and Sigurd Leeder, both Laban-trained teachers and choreographers, had been working together to develop their own training, which became known as the Jooss–Leeder dance training at Dartington. Sigurd Leeder struck out by himself, establishing a second school, the Sigurd Leeder Studio, in London in 1947. Here, full-time diploma courses were programmed and amateur classes offered. Laban was developing two main sets of movement theories, known as Choreutics and Eukinetics. Choreutics 'explained human movement as shaping its own spatial environment: expanding, contracting, elevating and lowering, designing the body as a mass and leaving virtual trace forms in the surrounding space' (Nicholas 2007: 96). Eukinetics was concerned with the actual make-up of motion as expressed through four factors – weight, time, space and flow. Movement training took a creative leap, developing movement practice out of human expressive qualities, rather than movement technique. The emphasis was on movement improvisation, rather than on virtuosity; a practice of expression rather than form. In 1946, Laban and his long-term collaborator, Lisa Ullman, established the Art of Movement Studio in Manchester. It acted as a hub for students who could also go on to train as teachers of this growing movement approach: Jean Newlove and Geraldine Stephenson both emerged from that school. The inheritance of Laban vocabulary for theatre can be summarized as emphasis on movement analysis; collective and individual movement improvisation; non-form-based physical training; use of body weight and swing; character-driven movement exploration and movement choruses.

8 Esme Church (1893–1972) was an actor and theatre director. She became the artistic director of Bradford Civic Playhouse with its allied Northern Theatre School. In 1948, she engaged Laban as Director of Movement, and with Geraldine Stephenson he 'regularly taught the actors movement and directed them in mime plays' (Hodgson 2001: 7).

Actor Barry Clayton recalls:

> In 1948 I managed to go to – what was then the Civic Theatre School – Bradford Northern Theatre School, which was run by Esme Church. And I was of the age where one had to be particularly lucky, because all the people coming out of the forces at the end of the war obviously had priority. So we seventeen year olds – there was Robert Stephens and I – had to be a damn sight better than all these, to us, seemingly older and much more experienced people. And I was two years at the school, and the great thing was that we had for movement Rudolf Laban, who had a centre in Manchester. And he and Stephenson – what was her first name? – Geraldine Stephenson – and he would come. And he was about seventy-five, and he would … 'oh, further back, further back'. and he would come and dig his knuckles in the base of your … [spine]. 'More, more.' And I mean … and he could do all these. We could slash, and we could [w]ring, and we could flick, and all of that you know which … [was basic Laban movement]. (Clayton 2007)

9 Director of Movement was the English translation of the title that Laban used while working in Germany, and that may have influenced Stephenson's choice of terminology (see Hodgson and Preston-Dunlop 1990).

10 'Laban analysed effort and broke it down into four "Motion Factors", which he called Weight, Time, Space, and Flow. All effort contains these four factors. The type of effort depends on how each of these four efforts is being expressed' (Ewan 2019: 27). Laban's efforts were called 'Floating, Dabbing, Wringing, Thrusting, Pressing, Flicking Slashing, and Gliding' (Ewan 2019: 30).

11 Joan Littlewood recalls her time at RADA movement classes: 'On the Saturday morning I walked into Annie [sic] Fligg's class, the legs of my outfit a bit stretched, but I was ready for action. And what action. Fraulein Fligg beat a drum and away we went. … Up! Down! Leap! Stretch! Dyum da deed da. Dyum da dee! Forward and Back. Dyum! It was great. I'd never felt so alive. My stretching-out was putting a bit of strain on those stockings, but what did it matter? Mrs. Bedell's ballet class had given me half past twelve feet, this was action, a first taste of Rudolph Laban's work which was to influence my whole life' (Littlewood 1995: 69).

Anny Fligg was a German dancer who had trained at the Hertha Feist school in Berlin, and who in 1930 taught Central European Dance at Chelsea PT College in the UK. In 1933 she gave a recital of Central European dance in London, and by 1935 she was advertising a Laban training in London.

12 Jean Newlove (1923–2017) was a British movement teacher and choreographer whose prolific career spanned sixty-seven years. While with Theatre Workshop, Newlove married the playwright and songwriter Ewan MacColl, co-founder of the company. Newlove went on to have an international career teaching out of her Laban training and authored two books, *Laban for Actors and Dancers* (1993) and *Laban for All* (2004).

13 Dame Ninette de Valois (1898–2001) was an Irish-born dancer, teacher and choreographer. She was artistic director and founder of the Royal Ballet.

14 The Vic-Wells Ballet was established in 1931 at Sadler's Wells and included the Sadler's Wells Ballet and the Vic-Wells Ballet.

15 Isadora Duncan (1877–1927) was an American-born dancer who is remembered for her radical approach to dance. She used Classical Greek art as a source for movement as well as developing inspirational relationships to music and the natural world. In her 1902 essay 'The Art of Dance', she wrote, 'The dancer of the future will be one whose

body and soul have grown so harmoniously together that the natural language of that soul will have become the movement of the body' (Duncan 2002: 175). In her writing she also challenged ballet as a dance form, suggesting that it was an artistic form in its death throes. She exposed the way it deformed the natural female body through its training, engendering a spirit of conformity in movement and propagating an aesthetic of constriction. By so doing, she opened the door to invention and creation, an impact which has been very well explored in the history of modern dance.

16 Irene Mawer (1893–1962) was a mime artist, and in 1920 she established the Ginner-Mawer School of Dance and Drama with Ruby Ginner. 'The School continued until 1954 when Ginner retired from full-time teaching. Although she always emphasised that Greek Dance was born in the theatre, for the theatre. The Ginner Mawer dancers also appeared on television in 1936' (ISTD 2014).

17 Madge Atkinson (1885–1970) was an actress and dancer who developed 'Natural Dance'. She trained with Annie Spong and Jacques-Dalcroze. She choreographed dances for the Gaiety Theatre, where in 1912 she was 'ballet mistress', and opened her own school in Manchester in 1918. In 1944, she founded the London College of Educational Dance.

18 The three centres of activity inspired by the Greek ideal were the Margaret Morris School; the School of Natural Movement, founded in Manchester by Madge Atkinson; and the Ginner-Mawer School of Dance and Drama in London.

19 In *Margaret Morris Movement* (Scottish Film Council 1973), Margaret Morris expresses her intention to develop 'a natural basic technique from which all kinds of exciting developments can arrive'. She then demonstrates yogi, circular breath, lateral movement of the spine and oppositional movement, that is, the relationship between the left and the right. Her method starts with limbering up by running and swings/walking. To strengthen the feet, she uses slow controlled walking with contractions of the foot. Breathing is central to her work and is coordinated with arm and spine positions. She goes on to oppositions with arm positions coordinated with stepping in opposition, balance, tension and relaxation. She has a sequence to exercise the eyes/head and the neck. She devised exercise for pelvis/thoracic mobility through isolations. She used stretches, swing relaxation and scissor bounces.

The first two of these principles can be observed in two British Pathé extracts from 1938. Available online: http://www.britishpathe.com/video/margaret-morris-movement; http://www.britishpathe.com/video/margaret-morris-movement-1/query/Margaret+Morris+Movement.

20 Opposition in physical terms can mean moving the torso in one direction and the pelvis in the other, like a twist. Or it could mean creating diagonals by pulling the right hand and the left foot, or left hand and the right foot away from each other – using oppositional forces creates interesting tension and movement dynamics.

21 Additionally, she explored balance postures where an arched back creates backward balance as well as more familiar vertical and horizontal balances. Her technique has forms that twist at the waist, which in turn send the torso and pelvis in opposite rotations.

22 Rupert Doone (1903–66) was an actor and choreographer. After working briefly with the Ballet Russe, he formed the Group Theatre, an avant-garde theatre group experimenting with an expressionist physical style and political content. Michel St Denis was a guest director. From 1939 he was director of Morley College Theatre School.

23 Joan Lawson authored many books on folk dance and classical ballet. She set up the National Dance Branch for the Imperial Society to form a syllabus that offered the study of a wide selection of dances from Europe (see Chapter 5).

24 Leslie Burrowes (1908–85) also went on to train with Mary Wigman in Germany and, in 1932, opened a studio in London.

25 Royal Central School of Speech and Drama, University of London, is a conservatoire of acting and teaching. Founded by Elsie Fogerty in 1906 at the Royal Albert Hall, it moved to its current home at the Embassy Theatre, Swiss Cottage, in 1957. It has a long heritage of actor movement training that includes Litz Pisk in the 1960s and continues to this day through the MA MFA Movement: Directing and Teaching programme that teaches teachers of movement and movement directors.

26 Alexandra Carter suggests,
> Their forms have lived on, of course, albeit in the more limited context of the private sector. Dance in public education came to be dominated by Laban's Modern Educational Dance, which, although systematized on a conceptual basis, still relied in practice on notions of the natural in its assumptions that the child will dance spontaneously. … What these, N[atural] M[ovement] and Classical Greek Dance have in common is the privileging of the physiological/organic functions of the body and their structural relationships as the foundation for dance. (Carter and Fensham 2011: 28)

27 Pioneer Women: Early British Modern Dancers was a project that ran from June 2008 to May 2010, organized by University of Surrey in collaboration with National Resource Centre for Dance.

2 THEMES

Les acteurs écrivent avec leurs corps… C'est une des lois du théâtre.
HÉLÈNE CIXOUS (IN PERRET 1987: 127)

Themes

This chapter presents a thematic grouping of key ideas articulated by the interviewees. These are inevitably filtered through my experience as a working movement director. Variously, the interviewees from Chapters 3 to 15 illuminate the following themes in relation to movement for production: ***movement backgrounds, preparation, collaboration with directors and performers, working methods and movement dramaturgy*** and ***audiences' bodies***.

Movement backgrounds

The group of practitioners in this volume come from a range of movement backgrounds. Their skills are wide ranging and originate in the fields of dance, physical theatre, actor movement and holistic practices. Each interviewee shared details of their unique lineage and training history, which comprises their physical history and determines the resources upon which they can draw. My endnotes expand on the variety of movement techniques and forms mentioned by each individual. The work of these practitioners is enriched by a wide range of embodied knowledge that they re-form, reimagine and streamline to serve the needs of rehearsal. Their movement knowledges are a basis from which they translate and communicate movement to actors, a process which is richly imaginative and constantly inventive.

Movement directors come with movement skills. These skills are developed over years of training and practice. The process of learning a type of movement endows the movement director with embodied knowledge of that form and a deep connection to the power of movement. A facility with one form of movement enables them to access other types of movement quite readily, as the one form acts as a lens through which they understand other forms. Movement practitioners tend to undertake lifelong learning and may accrue embodied knowledges from a variety of physical disciplines. Forms of movement are a vital resource, as movement directors draw on a range of methods that they translate and synthesize into movement principles which can be activated in different ways to suit the artistic journey of a production.

Lecoq-trained movement directors such as Sedgwick, Gibson and Lefton have an embodied understanding of sport-inspired forms, mime, acrobatics and Feldenkrais. The movement directors featured in this book who have trained in contemporary dance, including Flatt, Kane, Leslie, Maxwell, Yee and Knight, have an embodied understanding of isolations, repetition, experiential anatomy and skills in musicality and choreographic strategies. Ballet is evident in the background in several interviews in this book, as is yoga and Contact Improvisation. Several of the movement directors I interviewed draw on their experiences as actors, including participation in company-led movement practices. If one were to remove the specific movement vocabulary from a particular discipline, a set of principles remains which can be translated into a language for movement in the theatre. Movement directors work by extrapolating such principles from the movement disciplines they are acquainted with and communicating these to actors in creative, production-specific ways.

Deeply undertaken movement training also imprints methods of kinaesthetic learning, observation skills and movement analysis; creating the warm-up or training for a company, for example, requires these systematic skills and body knowledges. Movement analysis is frequently an amalgamation of different vocabularies and ways of seeing. For some, the method follows anatomical lines. Others conduct movement analysis reminiscent of Laban[1] vocabulary, that is, time, weight and space. Others approach it through the levels of tension and push/pull – terms drawn from Lecoq training.[2] Whatever vocabularies are used, movement analysis is a useful part of embodied learning, as it provides the means to discuss movement with actors and directors.

Preparation

The movement directors in this book see themselves as collaborators with specialist skills. As creative collaborators, they engage with the totality of a project. Sometimes pre-rehearsal preparation is undertaken independently by the movement director, at other times alongside the director and with other members of the creative team over time. Extended periods of preparation suggest a way of letting ideas and images percolate through the text, score or source materials for the production. This phase may take many forms – physical, visual, aural and intellectual. It is an opportunity to dwell with ideas and to reflect upon them intellectually, imaginatively and emotionally. This period anchors and nourishes the movement director to meet the challenges of the pressured rehearsal timeline and the unknown nature of the company of actors. Before rehearsal commences, the movement director undertakes another phase of preparation, in which they investigate myriad possibilities and make careful choices in readiness for the actual rehearsal.

Almost all of the interviewees discuss the integration of movement into a production. By this, they mean that movement should sit well within the overall production language and its emerging aesthetic, but also that it should be fully and authentically *embodied* by the actors in the company. The framework for a movement director's involvement is shaped by the director's conception of the play as well as the text or score. Movement directors respond to that conception, and they feed into it by contributing informed selections of movement matter and physical ideas. This collaborative mode in the preparation phase serves to reveal the tone of the production, and it helps to identify the working methods of the director. In this phase, these practitioners negotiate how they might work together on the floor, who will lead at which moments and whether there should be simultaneous rehearsals. All of these negotiations have an impact on the rehearsal culture and the creative progression of the movement work.

Collaboration

Contemporary theatre directors are leading larger and larger creative teams. Each member of these teams contributes to the final work. These creative teams frequently collaborate over many productions and cultivate a shared language. Productive, repeated collaborations can positively shape how movement develops throughout a project and can influence the final work dramaturgically.

As movement directors share time, space and actors with directors, the two have, inevitably, close and complex collaborations. In a rehearsal room, an intricate process of communication often takes place between collaborators as they develop and influence the movement material. Different movement directors express this part of the work differently. It might involve the director leading the rehearsal and the movement director following their lead and feeding in en route. Or it might be that the movement director leads on a section of movement, creating and drafting movement material in the moment, and then involves the director en route (back and forth); or their contributions may be more intertwined, with director and movement director shaping a section in tandem – one pressing the narrative forward, the other developing the movement material simultaneously. They may work separately and then subsequently bring new material back to the shared rehearsal space. These separate moments necessitate extensive preparation, either ahead of rehearsal or ahead of a shared rehearsal day.

Movement directors and directors may work together repeatedly over many productions. When they do, they create shared movement languages and rehearsal strategies in the face of new creative challenges with new actors. The interviewees articulate how they contribute ideas and dramaturgical input through the movement. The degree to which they contribute dramaturgically changes from project to project, and most of them identify how each director and each unique project requires distinct modes of input. Movement directors translate ideas into actuality. There is a recognizable commitment to integration of movement in the aesthetic and performance language.

The movement directors featured in this book work with a range of directors, and they talk about adjusting their approach not only to the unique demands of a particular project, but also to the ever-evolving working methods of the director. Directors who collaborate with movement directors are, on the whole, movement savvy and ambitious for a certain vibrancy that movement work can bring to a production. A common thread amongst these movement directors is the way that movement can flourish in a productive rehearsal culture – a rehearsal culture that is well supported by the director. And at its best, their working relationship with the director can be highly stimulating, mutually supportive and built on reciprocity.

The movement practitioners in this book articulate the other central collaboration as being with the performers – actors, singers and dancers. The interviewees see their approach as relational and dialogic.

The creative, imaginative and emotional matter of the actor's journey necessitates movement proposals that feed the development of character. Movement supports engagement with the text and has to work in harmony with the way a performer uses their voice. It contributes to the actor's expressive remit to represent the breadth of human experience. For singers and dancers, movement requires other strategies that are built on their particular aptitudes and strengths. Their expressive terrain of song and/or dance means that rhythm and musicality are at the core of their embodied skills. Actors often become expert in one sliver of a specific movement technique that is filtered through character perspective. Singers' and dancers' movement is shaped by borrowing from the actor's world of intention and emotion. The movement director's tailor-made working methods produce integrated, embodied results – often like well-crafted bespoke suits, built around *these* bodies and *these* qualities and *this* process. These methods result from careful negotiation, an expert eye and the pursuit of authenticity and fit. The interviewees who define their work as theatre choreography sometimes engage an extended team of dancers and assistants so they can test out ideas and draw on their expertise in many dance forms ahead of the actual rehearsal (see Yee, Darling, Kane). In these cases, material is prepared or storyboarded in advance of rehearsal by a team of movement people then adapted to fit around the specific aptitudes of the performers once rehearsal starts. Frequently, the material is significantly reshaped and reimagined with the direct involvement of performers. It could be said that prepared material is *recreated* with performers.

Dancers, actors and singers all use different physical techniques. The interviewees who work with mixed casts identify the particular strengths of the range of embodied techniques at play and seek to extend their expressive potential. Actor movement methods are transferred to dancers and singers. Dancers participate in character-led processes such as moving with intention and motivation. Singers are supported to work expressively, physically and vocally. Eventually, shared movement vocabularies will soften differences between the movement aptitudes of the different types of performers. And to the audience's eye, all performers will enter into the overall movement style of a production.

The creative relationship between actors and movement directors entails a delicate negotiation. Contemporary actors are increasingly trained in movement and recognize that their acting practice is a process of embodiment. So, actors and movement directors already occupy shared terrain. The movement practitioners in this book are sensitive to an actor's journey and frequently reference creative negotiation that has to leave much space for reciprocal moulding. Some movement directors describe practices that aim to release actors into character work and facilitate emotional connection through intensely physical means. Others describe play, improvisation and warm-up as a way of addressing nerves, reticence or anxiety. All of these movement directors discuss how ensembles are effectively built through movement work, but also how individual actors benefit from the discovery of feeling and experiencing that movement offers.

The movement practitioner's understanding of an actor's craft is shaped by the background of the movement practitioner. Text is sometimes seen as an actor's primary language, and movement as more remote. Some see an actor's primary strengths as connection to language and psychological investigation; others see an actor's core skill as embodying and manifesting stories. Movement practitioners nearly always work with actors who are negotiating spoken and/or sung communication. Movement is sometimes shaped by the text – but not always. An actor is likely to be filtering the 'what' and the 'how' of movement experiences. They will be checking that movement choices can authentically enter into the truth of their evolving character choices and their narrative logic. Once actors identify a character's *need* within the narrative, they start to connect impulse, feeling and action. All movement directors negotiate with each actor's personal construction process of character creation or performance building.

Amongst these practitioners there is also an acknowledgement that whilst movement is a significant element in the actor's experience, it is one aspect of a rich creative journey. The actor's body is at the centre of a matrix of creation that involves their own instinct and creative process, scene partners, audience communication, text, the dramaturgies of the production and choices made with the director. As there is sometimes a danger of actors feeling that movement directors are interfering with or invading their process, these movement directors talk of an attentiveness to the developmental aspect of embodiment which grows over the course of a production.

Within one production, the work of movement directors may manifest in many diverse ways. They may, for example, create bespoke sessions for particular character movement or work with a group of performers to create large-scale organizational and compositional movement. Regardless of the form the movement work takes, most of the interviewees articulate the centrality of movement that ignites and maintains the imagination and imaginative choices of the actor. Actors come from a wide range of creative backgrounds, and may have undergone a variety of types of training. They may utilize one of many kinds of acting processes. In light of these wide-ranging differences, the movement directors featured in this book seek to access the imagination in ways that are sympathetic to a variety of acting processes. Some of these movement directors approach facets of human experience through quite elliptical or abstract means to instigate unexpected or heightened responses. Regardless of the point of departure, they use movement work to generate usable material that can be readily and inclusively embodied.

Whatever the production set-up, movement directors encounter actors whose movement experience is varied and is likely to be discontinuous and fragmented. The building of continuity underpins several movement directors' ambitions (see Gibson, Hoggett, Leslie). In response to unknowns and rehearsal timelines, movement directors create space for regular practice for the duration of a rehearsal period (see Knight): they all use warm-up to reconnect actors to their movement potential. By carving out this space and time, actors can pay attention their bodies. These movement practitioners also anticipate the movement vocabulary for a production by endeavouring to provide physical infrastructure for the demands a show might make on actors' bodies.

A current swell of explicitly physical theatre work takes its reference points from continental Europe – from dance theatre, live art and experimental performance. Here, the actual replaces representation: 'I run until I am out of breath' rather than 'I act that I am out of breath'. Characterization is replaced by actors undertaking tasks. The interpretative aspects of fiction are replaced by slippages between actor and character. Classical texts are radically reshaped by replacing language with physical scenes.[3] Several movement directors featured in this book work in this hyper-physical way. The sustainability of movement work in a hyper-physical production must be questioned and planned. In these instances, it is actually more important to establish infrastructures to ensure the actor's body is well supported and safe during the demands of a production.

Many other forms of movement feed into the body language of productions like undercurrents. There is a cyclical nature to forms that become popular for a while and are then replaced by different, 'newer' ones. Examples include acrobatic practices such as aerial work and parkour, or martial/dance forms such as capoeira and hip-hop. All of these have been integrated into movement languages. Actors are, by necessity, at the centre of these developments, and movement practitioners are alert to harnessing extant movement potential. Shelley Maxwell (Chapter 14) clearly articulates the way she uses transferable principles that might already exist within the actor's body knowledge. She goes on to articulate acute observation of what resides innately within the actors, which can provide a basis for developing creative movement. Other practitioners work along the same lines. Actors rarely have time within one rehearsal process to learn a whole movement technique, especially since they are likely to be using one element of it. A movement director will make some decisions ahead of rehearsal about what might be of use and what will not. Then they create bespoke methods for each production and tailor them to the particular set of actors in a company.

Movement directors and theatre choreographers collaborate intimately with actors/performers and directors, and their work plays out through this dynamic, triangular relationship. They have also established themselves as part of creative teams influencing and enriching dialogue with composers, designers, video artists, writers and musical directors, some of whom you will see referenced in the interviews. Constant, multifaceted collaboration is an essential part of the movement director's and theatre choreographer's craft.

Working methods and movement dramaturgy[4]

Out of their own responses to the text and the framework set out by the director, movement directors start to translate the textual into a visual, dynamic movement language. They become adept at imagining movement in relation to the ideas of the director and the emerging aesthetic of the creative team. Movement sections are often located in the liminal spaces in the text or in response to sparse stage directions, such as 'They dance' or 'They scale the Andes'. Or they may even be created *outside* the written text – for example, by adding a wordless movement prologue that introduces the world of the play.

Different patterns of working emerge amongst these practitioners that are often used in combination or in part for any one project:

- Preparing new movement material ahead of rehearsal, either alone or with others such as assistants or associates. Teaching that material in rehearsal, and adjusting it according to the particular strengths of the performers and the dramaturgical demands of the production, for example, in relation to the style of the design and music.

- Preparing a movement framework with production-focused parameters to generate specific qualities of movement or movement material. Selecting and developing material created from tasks and improvisation.

- Preparing environments that generate a shared experience of movement and then activating the resulting movement vocabularies with the performers in the room. Rather than creating material, this type of shared experience may imbue actor choices and/or stimulate the director's eye.
- Undertaking one-on-one work with an actor in a wholly responsive mode. These embodied experiences facilitate the actor to shape their work with no obvious dramaturgical outcomes. This might be more usefully thought of as movement coaching within a movement directing framework.

The movement directors in this book reveal how some movement processes are completely absorbed into the actor's craft. The physical history of the character – the psychophysical events they have experienced – leaves traces in the body. Everyday intimacy such as characters embracing, kissing or having sex are equally in need of navigation, because these are very recognizable and ordinary in life but are subtler in relation to the actor's personal body and the character's actions. In the same way that staged violence is underpinned by stage combat technique to avoid physical harm, staged intimacy has to have its own technique, too.[5] Movement directors are almost always mediating this terrain. Imogen Knight (Chapter 13) talks clearly of the importance of managing intimate or violent movement languages in a transparent and ethical way in the rehearsal room and usefully extends that detailed consideration to the audience's body.

Creation of an ensemble, chorus work and group movement constitute a significant part of the movement director's work. Movement directors start building the ensemble through the warm-up (see Yee, Leslie, Hoggett, Knight, Gibson). This is often based on fundamentals of awareness – through engagement with proprioception, mobilizing joints, readying muscles and connection to breath. During warm-up, movement practitioners discover the capacities and tendencies amongst the cast. By developing this group activity, they lay down the physical infrastructure that they later draw upon to create movement. After the warm-up, movement directors might tip the ensemble movement towards improvisation that generates shared experiences, language, worlds and tasks that are likely be used in the production.

Chorus work, group movement and mass movement are deployed by these movement directors and theatre choreographers to create material that operates in a range of ways:

- Creation of worlds through shared energy qualities and social codes to represent a society with complete internal coherence. This will fulfil a dramaturgical function that will be buried deeply in character work and an audience's reading of a society that is represented.

- Chorus movement that creates physical images and/or expresses a protagonist's inner world. These choruses use heightened physical language to facilitate a protagonist's emotional journey. They can also be used for journeys, glimpses of the past and time lapses.
- Musical chorus work – the most recognizable form of chorus movement work. Singing, dancing and moving are interrelated within the structuring force of a song, with its style of music and with designated numbers of singers and performers. Here, the whole framework is mobilized to fulfil the dramaturgical imperative of the song, but it also offers the movement director or theatre choreographer creative licence to invent a physical narrative.
- Types of narrative moments that involve group movement, such as parties, celebrations, rituals, ceremonies, dances, battles, epic journeys, time-travel back or forward. Movement directors will sometimes approach movement-driven scenes like these via an indirect route, creating abstract movement language. Methods by which they arrive at these languages are diverse, but they are mainly disruptions to time and space and/or extension of the movement vocabulary strongly in a new direction and away from realism or quotidian movement.
- Scene changes – these can be a dramaturgical linchpin for movement direction, as they provide opportunities for speed, contemplation, breath, transformation and motion. Movement practitioners use their skills in timing and use of space. Scene changes often draw the creative team and stage management team into a close collaboration.
- Mass movement, whether that is an opera chorus, a group of actors or a community chorus. Movement directors use a combination of structural strategies and internal mechanisms for organizing large groups. Having micro-choruses with a leader within the mass is one such structuring method; numbering and phasing are another. Both Flatt (opera) and Sedgwick (Olympics) discuss how organizational choreography can be deployed as a means of unification, to bring a contrapuntal chorus into unison or to instigate a new pattern.

All of the interviewed movement directors and theatre choreographers have been involved in shaping group work. This starts with the content of a warm-up and threads all the way through the production. They invent creative and practical strategies to activate and organize performers. The resulting movement informs the overall dynamic and language of a theatre work.

The interviewees articulate how they contribute new ideas and dramaturgical input through movement. The degree to which they contribute dramaturgically changes from project to project, and most will identity distinctive modes of input with different directors on each unique project.

All creative collaborators contribute to the dramaturgy of a production in some way. Sound design, lighting and movement act on the sensorial and perceptual capacities of the audience member's body; as such, we may say they operate in a *liminal* place. Music and song and set and costume design may be said to occupy more *tangible* places in the audience's reading of their experience. But regardless of the experience or the reading of the production, all those mediums are dramaturgical.

Movement dramaturgy is shaped by the following elements:

- Responses to the source material
- Interpretation of a brief
- Research and preparation
- Embodied skills of the movement director/theatre choreographer
- Actor's movement skills, aptitudes and responses
- Choices of movement material and how that material is organized in space – that is, use of space that is real (designed performance spaces) and imaginary (implied or fictional spaces) – and in time (duration, dynamics, timing and repetitions)
- Qualities of movement used by the ensemble or an actor (organic, organized and patterned).

Unlike most design elements, or costume or music, movement is living and changeable. Movement also exists subtly in the energy qualities of characters' ways of moving, or the psychogeography of a fictional world. All of those are intricately woven into the actor's lived experience of the performance. Therefore, movement is likely to be constantly shifting and developing. It might be thought of as occupying an unstable dramaturgical role.

Imaginative and emotional truth in the ways actors' bodies move is a goal for movement directors. To that end, they are often involved in creating a poetic movement language to communicate unreal and, sometimes, unimaginable physical experiences undertaken in narratives – such as dying, flying, killing and being killed, being violated and violating, injuring and being injured, being poisoned, growing old, going backwards in time. All of these will rely on the development of a metaphoric physical language for acts beyond the scope of realism. Plays often offer physical conundrums, such as humans who turn into rhinoceroses (in *Rhinoceros* by Ionesco, an example given by Lefton, p. 61) or a character ageing to 400 years old (Hoggett's example, p. 142). Movement directors respond to these creative challenges and initiate a working method. Then the actor, movement director and director work together to create a language of movement that solves these challenges. An author offers a phenomenological challenge to work outside lived experience, and the movement director is instrumental in responding to the challenge and ensuring that embodied movement experiences are reinscribed into the performance score.

The compositional aspect of movement with regard to large groups of actors requires inventive, structuring skills to manage and mould movement material effectively and to facilitate physical vocabularies for all concerned. Movement material, such as the selection of social dances or extant dance forms, is clear in its dramaturgical drive and impact. In the case of 'diegetic dance' (to deploy Kate Flatt's formulation), the writer inserts a dance into the narrative, the characters dance and they know that they are dancing (see Chapter 5). When a dance is indicated by a text, the movement practitioner will either draw on recognizable social dance forms or invent a dance language to respond to the writer's offer. Many (Williams, Lefton, Flatt, Gibson, Leslie) talk about using social dance forms. They prepare movement material such as motifs, patterns or steps which are taught to actors. For an actor, dancing starts with an impulse to move. The embodied history of a character, their relationship to their community and the world in which they are dancing are all significant. Actors may require or request responses to a range of character-led questions and will ask the same questions of a dramaturgically offered social dance as they will of the text.[6] Contextual information feeds the narrative logic of their character's world view. Movement directors often create a holistic approach to such danced moments, considering contextual, relational, sensorial and kinaesthetic dimensions as they prepare and create.

Several of these practitioners extend actor-led approaches to singers and dancers. For Yee, Kane and Darling, the form leads. When working on musical theatre, they prepare choreographed material and establish their relationship to the music ahead of time. Darling highlights the narrative drive of choreographic material and character objectives that feed into the dynamics of a dance or musical staging. When preparing for dancing within a play, the same practitioners identify an actor-centred approach that pays attention to intention, character perspective and relationships. The actor necessarily approaches choreography differently to the trained dancer; movement directors work with the actor's own, unique movement tendencies frequently moulding material around them with precision.

Some of the movement directors interviewed do not have dance backgrounds and do not create dance material. It is notable that several of the movement directors (Hoggett, Yee, Knight) deploy task-based methods and improvisation to create choreographed movement languages. This can develop movement built through the use of extension, repetition, heightened gesture and relationship to music – but, ultimately, it becomes movement material rather than dance, as such. In these instances, movement language is generated from the actor's movement capacity and their response to tasks, and the dramaturgical work of the movement director lies in the creation of the tasks and in selecting, organizing, editing and structuring the subsequent material. These generative tasks are largely invented by the practitioner in response to each production, but they may be inspired by existing practices such as contemporary dance and somatic practices (see Yee, Leslie and Knight).

Particular British physical theatre and dance theatre companies have influenced some of the practitioners in this book. For example, DV8 played a significant role in the work of Darling; early Leah Anderson, Nigel Charnock and Volcano were influential on Hoggett; Complicité and Moving Picture Mime Show were inspirations for Sedgwick; The Kosh influenced Williams. The physical styles of these companies are characterized by their accessible and explicit movement ideas, particular body politics (Charnock/DV8's queer themes) and movement languages that depend on athleticism, endurance and high energy.

Audiences' bodies

Being a body is the primary means by which we experience and encounter the world. Bodies in movement – those of the audience and of the actor – are involved in conscious and unconscious exchanges for the duration of a live stage event. Changes to the bodies of an audience act as a hinterland for theatre acts. A gradual synchronization of heartbeats quietly generates waves of shared rhythm through respiration. The internal senses of perception and feeling are carved out through the physical presence of an actor's body and an actor's emotional navigations through a narrative.

The movement practitioner affects the audience's physical experience by means of the movement on stage. Movement might be thought of as a route to the non-literal selves of the audience as well as the influencer of their actual lived selves. Movement offers a common, shared terrain between performer and theatre audience. Movement directors and theatre choreographers navigate and focus on that shared terrain. In the moment of performance, all bodies are imbricated in imagination – both *vicariously* and *actually*.[7] Actors are often engaged in active and heightened states of motion, whereas audiences are often in more resting and observational states.

A movement director is always in dialogue with the audience – initially in an imagined way (during rehearsal, thinking carefully about how movement will affect an audience) and then when they join the audience during preview performances, seeking to feel and sense how movement work affects the audience. Audiences react to movement all the time. The discovery of mirror neurones proves that the action of the actor within a fictional experience ignites real physical responses in the audience.[8] Each individual audience member will have a personalized experience that is informed by their own physical histories. Our mirror neurones do not distinguish the real from the fictional: my leap of joy might be as a result of fictional actions, but the reception of that leap in you is real.

All of the interviewed movement directors and theatre choreographers are in some way considering the physical experience of the audience throughout the whole production process. This grows incrementally through rehearsal and takes a leap forward once the audience is actually present in previews. This is when they start to feel and see the work through the presence of the audience's body. Then their job is to mediate between the movement of the actor, its overall place in the production and how that communicates to the audience.

The movement directors in this book respond in various ways to managing the movement work in relation to the audience's presence. These include how to reboot energy through tempo; how to reimagine work as it moves from rehearsal to stage; and how to collaborate with the creatives and cast to mould the movement work into repeatable, living aspects of the whole.

The craft of the contemporary movement director or theatre choreographer is built out of deep movement knowledge and a relish for all types of moving, performing bodies, for the full range of human behaviours and for the creative stimulus of narratives. They prepare with their embodied imaginations; they work with flexibility, responsiveness and unending invention to solve problems within the rehearsal room. They mobilize all of these skills to speak articulately to the bodies of the audience. In the conversations that follow, the movement practitioners will speak of their own unique perspectives on their creative journeys and their artistry.

Notes

1 See Chapter 1.
2 See Chapter 1.
3 A seam of mainstream British theatre is in conversation with the post-dramatic. Theatre academic Peter Boenisch identifies a distinctive strain within European theatre of reconceiving classic texts in relation to 'actualite' rather than a closed contemporary setting. The work of Ivo van Hove and Thomas Ostermeier might typify this approach, and in the UK, directors such as Katie Mitchell, Maria Aberg, Joe Hill-Gibbins and Ellen McDougall belong to a family of directors who treat their work as a physical score and take a very active dramaturgical approach to the text as a stage event.

   Thomas Ostermeier (born 1968) is a German theatre director and artistic director of the Schaubühne Berlin since 1999/2000. His work is characterized by a radical approach to classical texts. For an in-depth interview, see Ostermeier and Boenisch (2014).

   Also see the work of Ivo van Hove (born 1958), an award-winning Belgian theatre director known for his experimental approaches to classics. He is artistic director of Internationaal Theater Amsterdam. In one example, amongst many, a metaphoric physical language is used in which a car crash in *Obsession* (Barbican Theatre, 2017) is replaced with a three-way Contact-Improvisation wrestle slicked in car oil. (Also see Chapter 11.)

4   Dramaturgy is the practice and theory of dramatic composition. As a movement director, this is the scrutiny of my own decision-making process, the principles by which composition will occur and the drawing out of possible readings of movement material – whether that be dynamic, visual or contextual.

5   For an insight into developing movement techniques that navigate intimacy for/with the actor, please refer to Ewan and Green's (2015: Chapter 9) influential teaching approach.

6   Movement practitioners might encounter actor questions such as, 'Why am I dancing like this?' 'Who am I dancing with?' 'Why am I dancing with them?' 'What is my history/experience with this way of moving?' 'What is my objective with this move/step/activity?' 'When did I learn this?' 'What is the relationship to the music?' 'What is my character's attitude to this dance event?' 'What space am I in?' 'What is the norm, and do I deviate from that norm?' 'What is my way of doing this?' 'What is my relationship to the other people dancing?'.

7   Theatre academic Rhonda Blair finds it 'provocative to know that my brain is lighting up in a way similar to another person's and that my muscles are automatically mimicking hers. I find it powerful to believe, based on some evidence, that we could be "wired for empathy" insofar as our bodies and brains mirror each other in terms of perception, and thereby prepare us for action. I find it powerful that imagination, which fundamentally is about the organism having pictures of itself in different situations and contexts in order to know how to negotiate its environment as well as possible, happens not only consciously, but also extensively and richly below the level of consciousness, so that it might be possible to view what we are doing when we're making theatre as helping the viewers' bodies imagine themselves inside the stories we tell' (Blair 2009: 102).

8   Mirror neurons are a type of visuospatial neuron which respond to actions we see in others and that fire in the same way as when we do the action ourselves. 'Mirror Neurons in the pre-motor cortex and in Broca's area of the human brain are activated both when I engage in specific instrumental actions, and when I observe someone else engage in those actions. They are activated under the following conditions: (1) when I engage in an intentional action: (2) when I observe some other person engage in that action; (3) when I imagine myself or another person engage in that action; and (4) when I prepare to imitate another person's action' (Gallagher and Zahavi 2008: 177).

Theatre academic Stanton B. Garner Jr discusses these neurons in relation to movement: 'Neural mechanisms that respond to the movements of others by vicariously enacting their execution operate automatically; in this sense we are cognitively wired for movement responsiveness' (Garner 2019: 2).

3 JANE GIBSON

Movement is everything, isn't it? It's the beginning of everything [2018][1]

How do you describe what you do?
I work in theatre, television, film and opera, and the common denominator is that I'm coming from a movement perspective.

How is movement affected by those different mediums?
They are all very different; although the foundation is exactly the same. My foundation is totally based in movement, and everything springs from there; dance springs from there. I worked on a play at the Royal Court that was in traverse:[2] the director required help with how to keep people moving. I did quite a lot of work to render the space dynamic through the actors' intentions in relation to their status. There were dances in it: there was an actor who had to do a Madonna-style dance in a hijab, wearing six-inch red stilettos, and a burka. This is quite demanding for a young actor to do. Sometimes there is movement that directors perhaps expect the actors to be able to do without any help, so your job is to work with that actor, encourage them and enable them to do it. That's something that I might do in the theatre.

In films, I do a lot in relation to historical dance, or period dance (dance from a particular time in history). That's a different requirement. You get paid a lot more, but you have fewer days, so you have to work extremely hard and very fast. Joe Wright, the director of *Pride and Prejudice*, was very interested in the dances and wanted to explore them.[3] He watched rehearsal, videoed the dances, responded to them. By watching, he was able to think about his shots. It was the same with Ang Lee, who directed *Sense and Sensibility*.[4] I was there to do all the etiquette and work on movement and self-image of that time. He was very interested in the movements of courtesy. He is from a Taiwanese background and bowing is still in his culture, so he understood where the bow came from.

My work is very dependent on the director, on how much they open the door to you and let you in. The more they understand movement, the more likely you will be given time to do it, and then you are able to do good work. The irony of it is that the directors who least need movement input (that is, those who are very open to movement and believe in how much it can bring) are the people who *need* you the least.

I am aware that we bring movement skills with us but that we also invent our approaches; I'm interested in both your skills and your approach.
My skills have been built up over a tremendously long period of time. When I was a child I was dancing like crazy. I did a lot of ballet and Greek dancing. When I was seventeen, I went to Central, where I came across Litz Pisk.[5] That was the part of the training at Central that I really responded to. We used to do masses of 'pure movement' with Litz where every movement had a meaning, or a purpose, and was a piece of theatre. It was very intense in such a good way. She talked a lot about movement coming from the centre of the body. She was also teaching historical dance. Afterwards, I went to Lecoq – in 1968/9.[6] He was still teaching every day, so I had him for all those hours, and that was just an incredible piece of luck for me. Having said that, it's never by chance, there had been a show on at the Arts Theatre, where I worked as a dresser – across the road from Central starring Julian and Claude Chagrin.[7] I thought they were rather amazing. They had been to Lecoq, and that's where I made that connection. There's this osmosis from these rather fantastic people that you have the good fortune to come across. You learn from them, you assimilate and you bring things together. I mean Litz, in a way, was very far away from Lecoq. Litz was Central European, very intense. Lecoq had this very playful side. You amalgamate them in your work.

Slightly later, I became a student teacher with Trish Arnold, so that's where I learned a tremendous amount; she was training me to be a movement teacher.[8] Trish's great strength was her phenomenal ability to correct movement: she was very specific. That has served me well because it's a quiet approach. Another big influence on me was Belinda Quirey, who I came across with Sue Lefton.[9] Belinda was an incredible influence on us in terms of our historical dance. And we spent many years working with her. She cast me in a TV show she was doing called *May I Have the Pleasure*, a history of dance, because she said I didn't 'look like a dancer'. The whole point of social dance is that ordinary people, real people, really dancing, at that moment in time, danced them – not professional dancers. I learned a tremendous amount from her. You had to spend a great deal of time, because it was a question of a respect, an understanding that these dances would take a long time to learn. Even though they appear very simple, they are actually not very simple. For example, the Pavanne, which Belinda described as a 'dance of baffling simplicity', has to be understood in terms of the society and the beliefs that were in place at the time. And that's what I bring if I'm asked to do a historical dance. You cannot just take the surface of those dances – the movements are profound. For example, why did people start to waltz? Why did they suddenly go into each other's arms and face each other? Something they'd never done before. These significant historical shifts are worth communicating to the actor. Sue Lefton has been very important to me, as a colleague and a friend, and a truly wonderful movement director. She has been someone to talk with deeply about what we do; to be a movement person can be very lonely.

I've acquired my skills really through working with those people and building those relationships. It's a *soul* relationship really. It's not just through the work, it's something else, there's some sort of spirit that connects you with those people, because movement is everything, isn't it? It's the beginning of everything, and although it is said 'In the beginning was the word', actually there was a lot of movement before the word.

How do you set about preparing to work with a director?
I make sure to ask a lot of questions, so I get an idea of the play that *they* want to do, why they want to do it and what's required. You try to make a very good professional relationship. You're definitely on the production side; you belong to the production team, you don't actually belong to the actors. Because of the nature of the work, you have to be very careful that you belong to the centre of the production, so when that becomes clear to the director then, you have a more relaxed relationship with him or – very rarely – her. Obviously, I read the play. And then, having read the play, I meet him again. Or her. Then I would usually, at that point, say what I think the themes of the play are from my point of view. My response is going to be much more intuitive, whereas they would have worked very hard on that play before they started rehearsing and they've really analysed it, whereas I don't work in that kind of detail. I read the play and I get a sense of a theme. For example, [when] we did *Othello*,[10] I was very interested in how to explore envy and jealousy, so I started by reading *Envy, Spite and Jealousy*, a book about how the Greeks saw those emotions.[11] Then I would, if the director gives you that freedom, begin to explore the play without having to work on the scenes. How does envy actually manifest itself? And where is that in the body? What's the difference between envy and jealousy? You're feeding the actors, and you create the kind of environment where the play can take place.

What happens when you get into the process of movement directing?
I try to keep my focus on the work and not on my relationship with the actors, not even on my relationship with the director, but my relationship with the director and the actors through the work. You're there to discover something with the actors. I am very passionate about what I do, and I try to really 'insist' – Lecoq

used to use that word – to 'insist' on something that you want to do. If I was to take a specific play, then I do quite a lot of thinking before I go to work. I have an intuition about what kind of space it is, what kind of landscape it is, what kind of light it is, and that informs my first session with the actors. I really have to have a minimum of three sessions in order to get to 'see' people and so they can 'see' me. If I get to know them, I can go somewhere, so that's the minimum, but you can be working much more.

Your job as a movement director is to put the dream of the director into the space. To visualize it for them, to make it happen, because many directors are, for want of a better word, intellectual – quite academic in some ways. They have incredible ideas, they have imagination, but some cannot put the thing in the space. They can visualize, but they can't always actualize, and that is your job to do that, to put it out in front of them – to realize their dream.

Declan [Donnellan], who is tremendously powerful in terms of his ability to stage, is someone who really knows what movement can bring to the theatre and still uses a movement director.[12] One of our projects was *Troilus and Cressida*, and that is the most difficult play you could possibly do.[13] One of the key themes as far as he was concerned was of 'heroes'. So, in response, I asked myself, 'How do I get these, perhaps self-conscious, English actors to be great warriors and great heroes, and come out to the crowd?' How do you do that? How do I dig that out? We also worked on *Andromaque*, a Racine play, with French actors.[14] Declan's focus was the problems faced by children of famous people. So, you think, 'It's all about a kind of disaster in the family.' I'm thinking about the landscape of the piece, I'm thinking about the weight of the piece.

Then you're bringing things to the rehearsal, and the directors can sit back and look and watch and just think. And, even if they're not on the front foot when you're working, if they are seeing what's going on, they validate your work. You do sometimes have to impose an atmosphere in which people can work. If you're working with twenty-five actors and then, at a long table behind you, there are people chatting, not giving focus, it's hopeless. A lot of it's quite practical. We are trying to make a working environment, but you're not the director, so you have to be careful as they might be a director who likes chaos in the room, and they don't mind mess. But I might say, 'Let's just clear the space.' It is very much a question of having to respond in the moment to everything: it isn't a set of rules.

Having thought a lot before you go in to work, you've got access to things instantaneously in the space, and you work spontaneously. I don't really make a shape: I have a starting point, and I see what is going on between the actors, and me, and I build from that. And it's all based on movement. I have to have the bodies that are actually 'available' to me, so if they're not at the beginning, I would have to do quite a lot of pure movement with them.[15] You can't just leap into expressive movement; you have to have a body that's actually working as a whole. You know your blood's running, you feel movement through your body, you've got an appetite to move, you've got to encourage that in the actors. Then you can start to go into other areas. So, it's very much a conversation between you and the actors; if they're 'available' to you and if they respond, there's nothing better, but if they don't, there's nothing worse.

You access actors through their imaginations, and that's how you get the movement work out of them, because they have this incredible imagination. And when they engage their imagination, they can do these amazing things physically. Whereas if you were to say, 'Now we're going to do a pirouette, we're going to jump,' they would say, 'No, no, I can't do that.' But if you say, 'You're Eros, and you're balancing, standing on one leg, and shooting arrows and getting people to fall in love with each other,' they'll probably do it through their imaginations.

Now that I've had a long career, I put much more onus on the actors to warm themselves up first, because I'm very tired of being on the nursery slopes with actors; I've been on the nursery slopes for so long. For example, Declan's very good, and the actors will warm themselves up from 9.30 to 10.00, so that I am then ready to really go somewhere of interest at 10.00 am. All the work depends on the actors being warmed up, because I do make demands, and you've got to be very careful that people don't get injured. A proper warm-up takes time, time out of my session; so, ideally, they warm themselves up first, and then when I come in, I can actually start to do movement that is quite demanding.

When I was at the National as Head of Movement for ten years, I was available to the actors in one-to-one sessions.[16] You had time to lay them on the floor and open up their shoulders, for example, and that was rewarding.

There's a whole negative side to being a movement director. You're dealing with many more complexities with the body; people can be very vulnerable about their bodies, or nervous, not really wanting to move, just wanting to sit and look at their script. At least in voice you've got a text, whereas with movement – well, Shakespeare doesn't really say what everybody should be doing. You have to do that with them. They have to find it. A lot of it's to do with enabling the actor. I really put my focus on them and particularly on the ones that are very positive, and they usually are in the majority. It can be quite demanding and quite alarming, because you're standing up there with your body, just one of you, and there could be twenty-five actors standing in front of you, with all their hang-ups. You want to do some pure movement with them, and then you see that they can't release anything, they're completely tense, they're very uncomfortable, and you're thinking, 'I've got to find a way round and make a connection' so they can make a connection to the work. So, I work very spontaneously in terms of what's presented to me. I was teaching in drama schools for twenty years; that's a very different thing where trainee actors could get really stuck in and hope to transform a little bit over the three years. But working with professionals, that's completely different: you need to respect what they can bring and work around where they're 'at'. Often, you're working with people from a whole spectrum of ages, from very,

very old to very young, and you've got to be very careful in terms of 'health and safety'. I always do say, 'Don't feel you have to do anything I'm doing; you can always stop at any point. You know your bodies much better than me, you know if you've got an injury.' If they have an injury, they never tell you and you have to say, 'If you've got something wrong, just make sure you look after it and stop.' That is a practical thing.

How do you approach a dance?
Sometimes you're asked in specifically to do a dance, and you try to get as many rehearsals as you can. You find that actors can be quite insecure about dancing. You need to always do a dance which is well within what they can do, so that they're really who they are 'in' that play when they do that dance. Not suddenly having to be someone else, struggling. The way I approach working on a dance with actors is through their imagination and creativity, and through the narrative and who they are actually playing in that piece of theatre. So, they are not thinking about dance, as such, by explaining why the dance is there and how it is moving the narrative forward, because that is what they are usually doing with in a play. By approaching it from an actor's point of view, by considering their character carefully, you plant in their mind the idea that for everyone at that time, dancing was absolutely current. Actors are often frightened of dances because they don't regard themselves as dancers, so you have to circumnavigate that by talking about the context of the piece and the characters they are playing, and by choosing movements that are simple, that they can *really* inhabit, they will be able to play their actions and objectives through the dance. So, you learn to simplify a lot as you get more experienced, you simplify and simplify, so that that actor is totally on top of doing what they're doing.

Are you aware of having a style? Either in the actual movement work that ends up in the piece, or a style of process?
I would hope I don't have a style because I would hope that every job that I do, you wouldn't really perhaps recognize it. It would be difficult to say that I had a style, because you're a movement director, you're a chameleon. I don't think I have particular stylistic things that I do, I think it's more open than that. I've worked with many directors, and every one of them is different. Everyone has a different approach, and you're feeding into that, and you're collaborating with them, and you're sharing with them and you're enabling them. I would hope that the style is something to do with the play: what the playwright has written and how you can make that work. I find a lot of theatre is disappointing because of the lack of vibrancy in the bodies, and when I say vibrancy, I don't mean they should be leaping around and jumping, I just mean to be alive to each other and to respond as we do in life without even knowing. I'm always a bit disappointed that movement directors are actually only ever called in when there is some massive, recognizable

'movement thing' to do – why shouldn't they be there for two chairs and a sofa and hardly any movement? We just communicate so much with our bodies without even knowing we're doing it, but someone else from outside sees that. I think it's left to the actors to do it all really, I think directors think, 'Oh, we've hired that actor, and he's good, she's good, they'll just do it.' They're not given a chance to keep on learning really interesting things to do with what neuroscientists are exploring, this total link between the brain and the body.[17] What does this discovery mean for movement? For example, information is not always moving from the inside out. It's often from the outside in. These are the things that are really wonderful to explore in terms of theatre, but you want to work with experienced people, who've got something to offer and who can bring something.

I don't know whether I've got a recognizable style, I don't think I really have a set vocabulary of movement. Every play has a different vocabulary that you actually have to discover. And that's a creative thing; often the actors are creating that. You're getting the body ready so that it can respond very quickly to impulses and respond to the imagination. It's not a vocabulary that you're teaching, and therefore you're not bringing a vocabulary to every play. You're trying to create one with the actors.

Can you talk about the different phases of a production? Do you see yourself operating differently through the phases?
Very often, the director throws you into play straight away. Early days are quite dynamic and full of energy. As you assess the whole situation, you realize that all the actors have a different relationship to movement. You have to be sensitive. If there's a dance in it, you would start to do that as soon as possible. I always work with a live musician. The rehearsal process follows along at the rate that the director is setting; this is in an ideal world, where you are part of the production organically all the way through and you haven't been called in at the last minute. At the run-throughs, you take your movement notes. Note giving can be a slightly difficult area so you've got to be sensitive. You need to take them, because you want to improve the work, but at the same time, you don't want to be taking the floor in the wrong way. You have to be attuned to what the director's doing, because you can undo something without even realizing. Everybody needs to know that you are in your place and you're happy with it and you're not jockeying for position. It depends on how much the director wants you to give notes alongside them, or whether they are happy for you to run and give notes one-to-one afterwards; you have to discover how it works. In the tech, you usually do quite a lot of work because the work has transferred from the rehearsal space to the stage space, and everything goes completely haywire. Mostly, the actors don't fill the space as they're still in the rehearsal space in their minds. With Declan, for example, I usually have a big session in the new space, where we can actually feel the difference. If you've got proper time, actors adapt to the new space. In a tech, the director is

often sitting, negotiating, like the captain of the ship, and you're running up and down, because you're actually adapting the material. Unless, of course, you get the sensation from the director that you're really irritating them, in which case you just sit and watch. In previews, you follow through as you may be required to make changes. At the National, the previews were just endless with masses of changes every day right through until the last moment. Something that can happen with companies in preview is they all start to work on the same rhythm, so you break up this tendency. That's something that you could virtually think about in every play.

If you're called in to a production at the last minute, you have to work like a surgeon, you have to work fast. It's a bit more like working on a film. Whereas on a film the actors expect to work fast, for theatre actors, it can be disruptive when you come in late and start fiddling around or teaching something at the last minute. They've been on a long process and they think, 'Well, who are you?' In fact, you are somebody who knows something, but you can understand that response.

You have such a sizeable body of work and across different media and across genres – how is your work affected by that?
I don't think my work is affected. I think the strength, and what's indisputable, is that I have a really solid base in movement, and people know that, they can feel it. I'm not just pretending I know things. I have got a foundation. It's a bit like when you take your car to be done, I'm not just doing a spray paint, I'm working on the engine, and if required, I can do an hour of pure movement with nothing airy-fairy at all. I can go through the whole body in a logical way. I think that is something that people ought to think about when they want to work in the theatre, they need to have a proper base skill and to keep learning. I think that an actor would always know whether there's anything genuine in front of him or not. I think you do have to have knowledge.

When were you aware that you were a movement director? And what did you start calling yourself when you started doing it?
I was a movement teacher at LAMDA [London Academy of Music and Dramatic Art] and at various drama schools, and when we founded Common Stock Theatre Company, Trish and I were both doing the movement side of the company, so I think already the credit was probably there. Then Peter Hall asked Di Trevis to form a company at the National to do three plays, and she asked me to be her movement person, so that was a chance for me develop a body of work – a chance to become freelance.[18] I had learned so much from teaching for twenty years. I wasn't suddenly working with very famous people or very marvellous actors. I had a long time with all these different students, some of them very difficult, and it was part of my experience that I could bring into the profession. So that's when I think I probably became a proper movement director.

Movement direction has been given lots of slightly different role titles such as movement, movement director, director of movement etc. Why do you think this has been the case?

What on earth do you call yourself, it's just a terribly ridiculous title, 'movement' – no one knows what it is. 'Movement director' – you could be directing traffic into the car park, moving the furniture. 'Movement consultant' sounds like you're in a hospital. At one point my agent said to me, 'I think you should call yourself "director of movement".' Sometimes I ended up doing masses and masses and masses, and then she said, 'I think you should be called "director",' and I sort of said, 'okay, now I want to be called director of movement,' so the first thing was 'director' rather than 'movement'. They didn't really like that very much because they want to be 'director', but if you're serious and they want you enough, they agree it.

I think that theatre companies do use the term 'choreographer', and most of them understand that and it is easy even for me to sometimes call myself that, because if I say movement director then people say, 'What?' But choreographer they do understand, but it's often not choreography. Choreography does imply dancing really, it implies a sort of set number, of steps in space, the figure and patterns; movement directing is something else – it's movement. All dance is movement, but not all movement is dance.

And then it's a question of how high up the list of credits you get. I don't like being under 'the florist', in terms of the theatre. I like, if I have done an enormous amount, to be close to the director. I don't want to be down under the sound engineer. So that's another thing. I did fight for every single credit at the National, I had to fight for my credits and fight for some sort of profile.

If I am asked to do quite a lot on the play, I sometimes ask to be called the 'associate director'. I have done that with Declan sometimes, because I have to explain to the management, if you like, that it's not really about status, it's about how the actors relate to me. So the credit, it's not just about the public understanding what you do, it's often about the actors as well.

What do you think the future of the work of the movement director is?

There is something about the profession which is quite unrewarding. You can just park your ego at the door because there's no room for it at all. You really have to serve other people, and your work really may not get noticed, which is actually the point.

I think that contemporary dancers have entered the field. While I was at the National it was beginning to happen, I was getting a lot of letters from contemporary dancers who wanted work. I found that they wrote to me with very long CVs of all the things they had choreographed, and all the things they'd danced in, and how they wanted to come and work with actors – there was never any 'I understand it must be quite different working with actors, because I understand actually that they have to speak, and they have to deliver large pieces of text, so that must be very different to what I do, and I would like to know, is there a way that I could find out about [it]?' They have to adapt what they're doing, because actors can no more do a Graham contraction and speak at the same time than fly to the moon.[19] So presumably they're adapting everything, but where is the knowledge of dealing with people who have to deliver text and where the word is coming out of the body, and what is that body like, and what sort of quality has that body got to have? In classic British theatre, it's about the word. They have to be able to speak. At the forefront of all the movement work that I've done is the fact that you have to deliver a text. You have to be able to speak. How can you really separate movement from text, actually? You can't separate that off in the play, really. That is the whole thing with Shakespeare, isn't it – that it's incredibly amazing text, the muscularity and the power. How can you have a body that doesn't have any sort of dynamic in it, or any sort of real energy in it, delivering that text? I think the body, you know, has to be in a particular place for that text to come out of it.

The amount of television and film that's done by actors is quite a curse, because they have completely lost the idea of how to exist in the space. They're used to the camera coming right up to their face, the director making all the decisions, and suddenly in theatre they're in the space – 'Where is your body? You're not really there' – and you're thinking, 'How am I going to get them on to a level where I can actually "see" the person?' There is an energy that the stage requires. They have to have a body that reverberates in a stage space – imagine an actor on the vast Olivier stage.[20]

The future of movement directing work lies in the hands of the director because directors have to invite you in; they have to be happy that you are there. They have to be unthreatened by you: they have to accept that you do know things that they don't; they have to be happy that you can achieve things that they can't; and they have to have a generosity of spirit towards you. And from time to time, it would be helpful if they acknowledged your work.

I have recently worked with two young directors, which was very enjoyable. For example with Oliver Dawe, who has given me lots of space; he isn't threatened by the work that I do, he supports it and he supports me, and he is very kind. We worked on one man/woman show at the Hackney Showroom with a wonderful actor who was 'available' to movement through his imagination.[21]

It would be good if directors could recognize that you can prepare the bodies in a particular way to function in a particular way for that particular production. We are happy to provide things in order for something else to happen: we are putting the ingredients out there and giving them to the director and saying, 'Here, what will you do now? You make the whole meal.' Young directors need to see that you are bringing special skills in how the body can be prepared and used in the service of the theatre.

There are many roles that are completely accepted as integral to a theatre show, but a movement director is still not part and parcel of a production – you will look for it and often not see it, and sometimes you look for it, don't see it and there actually was someone there and they never got a credit – that drives me even more mad.

Notes

1. Jane Gibson trained as an actress at Central School of Speech and Drama with Litz Pisk, with Jacques Lecoq in Paris and with historical dance teacher Belinda Quirey. She apprenticed as a movement teacher with Trish Arnold at LAMDA and went on to teach there for many years. She is a founder member of Common Stock Theatre Company. Jane initially joined the National Theatre as part of Di Trevis' company and was then appointed as Head of Movement. For a decade, she worked on a prodigious range of productions at the National Theatre. She is associate artist with Cheek by Jowl, where her productions include *Lady Betty* (1989), *Hamlet* (1990), *Andromache* (2007), *Macbeth* (2009), *Tis Pity She's a Whore* (2011) and *Winter's Tale* (2016). For the Royal Shakespeare Company, her productions include *Revenger's Tragedy* (1987), *Much Ado About Nothing* (1988), *The Plain Dealer* (1989) and *Don Juan* (1991). Her movement and choreographic work in film and television is extensive – the following is a selection: *Emma* (1996), directed by Douglas McGrath; *Cousin Bette* (1998), directed by Des McAnuff; *Tom Jones* (TV series, 1997); *Far from the Madding Crowd* (1998), directed by Nicholas Renton; *Pride and Prejudice* (2005), directed by Joe Wright (Emmy nominated); *Atonement* with Joe Wright (2007); *Sense and Sensibility* with Ang Lee (1995); *My Week with Marilyn* with Simon Curtis (2011).
2. Alia Bano, *Shades* (2009), directed by Nina Raine at the Jerwood Theatre Upstairs, Royal Court.
3. Joe Wright (born 1972) is a British film director. Jane Gibson worked on his filmed version of the Austen novel *Pride and Prejudice* (2005).
4. Ang Lee (born 1954) is a Taiwanese film director. Jane Gibson worked on his filmed version of the Austen novel *Sense and Sensibility* (1995).
5. Central School of Speech and Drama is an acting conservatoire in Swiss Cottage, London, now called Royal Central School of Speech and Drama, University of London. For Litz Pisk see Chapter 1.
6. See Chapter 1.
7. See Chapter 1.
8. Trish (Patricia) Arnold (1918–2017) was an influential movement teacher. Born in Scotland, her formative career was as a ballet dancer. Her own movement teaching was variously influenced by Lecoq, Pisk and Sigurd Leeder. She taught actor movement at LAMDA as Head of Movement from 1963–74, and she was to influence a generation of movement teachers and directors, notably Sue Lefton, Jackie Snow and Jane Gibson.
9. Belinda Quirey MBE (1912–96) was a notable dance teacher and dance historian and the author of *May I Have the Pleasure* (1987). She was a student of Melusine Wood and a dance teacher and dance historian in her own right. She taught at many schools, including London Contemporary Dance School.
10. The 2004 production of William Shakespeare's *Othello* by Cheek by Jowl.
11. See Konstan and Rutter (2003).
12. Declan Donnellan is artistic director of Cheek by Jowl, a company known for its strong, actor-centred, ensemble approaches to classic texts. Jane Gibson is an associate artist of the company and often movement directs on its productions.

13   Cheek by Jowl's production of *Troilus and Cressida* by William Shakespeare (2008).
14   Cheek by Jowl's production of *Andromaque* (2007–9).
15   'Available' is almost a direct translation of Lecoq's usage of the French expression of actors being 'disponible', which means physical readiness and psychophysical openness.
16   Royal National Theatre is a national English theatre on the South Bank in London.
17   Developments in neuroscience have had a significant impact on how we might understand the relational aspect of thinking and doing. The discovery of mirror neurons is a movement milestone, as is the investigation of the relational dimensions of kinetic and sensorial aspects of movement and the psychophysical nature of emotion. The mind/body divide has been dismantled; the mind is the body. For further research, see publications that have influenced theatre practitioners, such as Antonio Damasio's *The Feeling of What Happens: Body, Emotion and the Making of Consciousness* (2000).
18   Peter Hall (1930–2017) was a British theatre director who was artistic director of the Royal Shakespeare Company from 1958/60 to 1968 and the National Theatre from 1973 to 1988.
  Di Trevis (born 1947) is a British theatre director and actor who has worked at many leading theatres. From 1986 to 1993 she was the first woman to run a company at the National Theatre. In 1986, she was involved with *The Mother* in the Cottesloe and in 1987, with *School for Wives* in the Lyttleton and *Yerma* in the Cottesloe.
19   Martha Graham (1894–1991) was one of the pioneers of twentieth-century dance, and her legacy is the creation of a viable alternative to ballet as a technique as well as her prodigious choreographic output. Here, Gibson refers to one aspect of Graham's contraction and release technique. This can be described as movement that relies on a strong contraction of the pelvis and then the flow of motion that emanates from its release. This has become one of the fundamental techniques underlying many contemporary dance trainings.
20   The Olivier stage at the National Theatre is a large open auditorium and poses challenges for actors and creatives alike to create focus, connection and intimacy between the stage and the audience.
21   *Frau Welt*, written and directed by Oliver Dawe, starring Peter Clements at the Hackney Showroom, London, 2017.

4 SUE LEFTON

You start with the two, body and mind together, joined by the breath [2018]¹

Sue, can you talk about your background – you trained both as a dancer and then as an actor.
Yes. When I first went to Central, I was a fully trained dancer.² I had been due to go into the Rambert Company but had always suffered from back trouble. Marie Rambert sent me to have back X-rays, and it was found that I had a condition which meant that my back was too weak to dance professionally.³ I had a bit of a gift for acting and so went to train at Central. Of course, when I learned we were to have movement classes every day with someone called Litz Pisk, I immediately assumed that I would be the best in these classes, especially considering that most of the other students had never even put on a pair of tights. But to my consternation, Litz literally walked right past me for a whole year and never commented. At first, I was fully confident that my work was better than anyone else and could only think she was reluctant to praise me in front of the other students, since the discrepancy between my training and their lack of training was too great; but gradually, as the situation continued, I began to think there must be something going on in my work that Litz was trying to tell me by saying nothing. Slowly, I came to recognize that as a dancer, I had been trained to be aware of how I looked as I performed each step. I had to always observe each position in the mirror, to 'shape' every movement and where 'technique' was everything; after all, it had taken me many years to achieve a ballet technique. Litz taught intentionally without mirrors. And slowly, although I couldn't have defined it, I began to get a real sense of why she appeared to ignore me. Gradually I came to understand her very subtle notion of letting something happen to one's body from the inside out, and allowing the imagination to lead, with no knowledge of how it looked. Suddenly, I realized that all my dance

training technique had to be jettisoned, let go of – it wasn't the point! It was terribly frightening and difficult to do. The dance training technique was inside me, part of me; since I had started at the age of four and had only recently stopped, at the age of seventeen, it was almost impossible to know how to set about it. A good year later, I quite suddenly got it. I surprised myself. Suddenly, in one of Litz's classes, I found myself deep inside the movement with no awareness of what it looked like, just as the actor has to be deep inside their character with no awareness of it, and of course at that moment Litz acknowledged my 'breakthrough'; she stopped by me and said, 'Very good, Susan.'

Once I had the breakthrough, I still went backwards and forwards, it was hard to remain in the 'acting state of movement' all the time. But why should it happen quickly? Important things do take time. A great thing awaited me, which I hadn't imagined would happen, although Litz alluded to it from time to time, and that was the ability after some years to begin to utilize that dance technique, to welcome it back so to speak, to serve me rather than me serving it. The balance, extensions, strength, ability to sustain a movement, to turn, to leap, etc. enabled me to help students and actors to enlarge their movements to a greater dynamic theatrical level than I would have been able to do without the dance technique, and also I found it easy to turn my hand to choreography and dance history, which needs a grasp of steps and a basic understanding of musical structure.

But I am very aware, I suppose, of the funny division between the dance world and theatre world, and how impressive a trained dancer can appear to directors, actors, critics, etc., and how these people can somehow get the dancer's body so utterly confused with the actor's body. A dancer's technique is impressive, but it's a different art form entirely. It's painful to watch actors trying to perform like a trained dancer, and this does occur when an uninitiated dancer is trying to work as a movement director. The actor doesn't have a dance technique, so they look like a parody of a dancer. An actor's body speaks words from a play and lives in a different world. An actor's body speaks words from a play and has the human foibles of character; for instance, a character dances to celebrate life after having been released from a prison camp. On the other hand, dance training is by nature abstract and does not have space for spoken language. It requires a heightened form of technical training – years at the barre – so the foot, knee, pelvis, stomach, thigh is being sent in many different directions at the same time in order to 'shape' a perfect position. Of course, a very great dancer can transcend the technique, s/he does not need to 'think' about it, s/he can forget it and live dramatically within a piece of narrative ballet or abstract dance piece. To achieve this level, the dancer's training starts as a child. Of course there is a place for an actor to train in dance, ballroom, flamenco, tap, etc. – but so that they can play a character in a play, who happens to dance.

And I do say to people who want to work as movement directors but have a body trained in dance, 'Don't despair, because, finally, you'll be able to welcome back your technique.' But you have to have the courage to suffer the undoing of it first. You have to recognize that the trauma of letting go of something that you've worked so hard to obtain is part of a recognition that you don't yet know enough about an actor to have any right to work with them in your role as a movement director.

When did you realize that you were a movement person? And then when did you realize that you were a movement director? Has it been important, labelling yourself as a movement director, professionally?
In my very early days, just after I gave up acting, actor friends would say, 'Call Sue in to do that dance because she's been an actress, and she will understand, and she won't give us anything too difficult to do.' So that was how I started out, and this was at a time when you could count the number of movement directors on the fingers of one hand. Choreographers were – as a rule – called in to a rehearsal in order to choreograph 'the dance', and that was the extent of their contribution. Gradually, people started to ask me not only to choreograph but to teach bows and curtsies, in the period of the play, and then directors started to ask me to help with staging, and the movement direction work grew from there; and I suppose I didn't really notice how things were developing, because for me it all felt so natural to be in a rehearsal room and to help develop the physicality of a piece of theatre and put it on to the stage.

When we were very young, my colleague Jane Gibson [see Chapter 3] and I started to direct shows together, and as I became more experienced in the world of movement in a play, I began to realize that I, as a movement person, actually ended up directing sections of the play – often the apotheosis of the play. In order to do this, one had to study the plays more thoroughly, their themes and the text. I would read the script a lot and develop ideas that could be fed into the play physically. Even though you are not directing the play, you are working at heightening the play's energy, defining the period the play is written in, working on mass scenes and small two-hander scenes where one would work on more personal physicality between two characters etc., and in order to do this you have to know the play almost as well as the director, while always viewing the play through the prism of the director's lens. Jane and I often discussed, in those early years, our sense that there were areas of a play we virtually had to direct, and it was Jane who first coined the title Movement Director, when she discussed with me her proposal of asking for the unprecedented title of Movement Director for her credits in the programme and on posters at the National Theatre, where she had just been given the position of Head of Movement. To Jane's credit, she succeeded in achieving the title of Movement Director. I very quickly assumed this title too, and this is how the term itself came into being. However, I do think there is still a place for 'movement by' or 'choreography by', if it fits the description of what I have worked on in a particular production.

Looking broadly over your career, how do you describe what you do as a movement director, theatre choreographer and film choreographer?
In films, you're very much left alone. You are handed the job, which is looked on as a specialized area. The choreographer casts the dancers, teaches the dances and oversees and advises on the music, with only the briefest input from the director. When the music starts on set, it's over to the choreographer. At one time, I used to be on the film set quite a lot, seeing to things apart from the dances, but financially these days this is not so possible. If you are around the set, you are incorporated – when you're not there, you're not. It is rather paradoxical; the more you are there, the more you are wanted. So that's how it works in films. Basically, you come up with your own dances and then show them to the director and make sure they're the right dynamic, and then they will film them. And often they'll ask you for help in filming them. Which is very interesting for a movement person because being visual, one knows where the dance should be filmed from. You can make friends with the camera person, because they are also visual, and often the camera man might say to you, 'Where do you want this dance filmed from?' A lot of the people on film sets are very technical, and they don't consider themselves as *arty* at all. You have to really make a practical relationship with them if they are going to let you 'in'.

Then you have this other area, where you're asked in to do the choreography in a play. And you might be offered three sessions, where you go in and literally do the choreography for the dance at the end of the play, for example. That always feels, to me, very odd. The actors look at me out of the corner of their eyes and think, 'What is she going to make us do?' But with experience you learn that one of the major things is to try to make people feel comfortable and to set them a dance which is really simple to do. This doesn't mean that the dance is easy to choreograph; on the contrary, it can be much harder to choreograph something simple that looks good, than something complex.

Then you get into the kind of murky waters of the movement director proper; no longer The Choreographer, no longer the person with a clearly defined creative input. I see my work as being responsible for the 'movement' in the play, and I understand what that means to me, but each director I work with will understand the term 'movement' in a totally different way, so I never really know beforehand what will be required of me. When you come to do your third or fourth show with the same director that implies your relationship has worked. You begin to maybe feel more at liberty to put your ideas to the director, who has now become more of a colleague. But that's an individual relationship which has to be worked on. And gradually, if that director gets a lot of work, the movement director may work alongside them, maybe for many years as I did very happily with Adrian Noble.[4] My one piece of advice to young movement directors would be – start out quietly and don't push your ideas on the director, and be as flexible in your work as possible. And, if you find that you have been asked to do a job involving ballroom dancing and only just managed to muddle through because you had so very little knowledge of what ballroom dancing entailed, know that you just about 'got away with it' and may not the next time. Go to ballroom dancing classes till you really get to understand the rudiments of it. Improving your knowledge may cost you time and financial investment. I spent at least the first twenty years of my life learning, in various ways, alongside my working life.

When you sit back and watch work that you've been part of, can you identify a movement style or an aesthetic that you recognize as particular to you?
Yes. I think I do have a style in the *way* I work. I would hope that style is revealed through an outcome that felt organic and that movement 'grew' out of the play. I would like to think I had helped the actors to commit physically to 'the world of the play'. I would hope the movement would be something that looked like it grew out of the production; it didn't 'stand out' in the wrong way. A dance by its very nature would 'stand out', but I would hope that it felt integrated and that the actors remained within their characters as they danced. And more broadly, that the actors seemed alive and daring in their physical world on stage.

Can you expand on building a relationship with actors?
What does help actors is the fact that having trained as an actor and having worked as an actor myself, my vocabulary is the vocabulary of a theatre person, rather than a dancer or movement director. I try to encourage good work and to appear to ignore, rather than remark upon, bad work. And one must remember that the rehearsal room can be a very sensitive and vulnerable space for an actor, especially in the area of movement and dance, which is often way out of an actor's comfort zone. Using strange, unfamiliar movement language in a rehearsal room can work initially, but the result will tend to be that you set up a 'separation' in the mind of the actors so that they imagine that they must move into a different art form when they come to the movement sections.

Voice and movement are absolutely integral to human nature; when you see someone grieving, or you see a baby laughing, it's always the two things together, sound and movement, so always I encourage actors to make sound as they move, and that tends to make them feel better since using their voices is familiar to them.

What is the relationship between an actor who is dealing with comprehension and dealing with text? How does that relate to movement, in your experience?
Well, I think the more you focus on the text in a rehearsal and you really think about the words and the meaning of a text without engaging the body in the process, then there is a kind of pulling away from the body, and the body feels left out and therefore *is* left out. Now the actor's mind and body are split, and the mind cannot allow the body to participate in case the text is forgotten, disturbed, lost.

If you start with the two, body and mind together, joined by the breath, then this split is avoided and both text and body can enliven each other.

The more the actor works without their body fully engaged with the text, the more wooden their body becomes, and the text will be lack lustre because the body from which the voice emanates has been defunct.

How do you see that happening in a rehearsal process? Is there a point at which it's integrated?

It depends on the director; it's always the director, it always comes from the top. If the director wants it, then they'll give the space to the movement work. That is, they'll give the space to the movement director and also to the potential of movement in the performance. The director must encourage the movement director to work and also give permission to the actors to investigate the movement that lies in the text. This work can open up very interesting things to do with space, rhythm, character, emotion. I think that it greatly improves the acting, but then I'm biased.

Do you see that as early investigation in a rehearsal process? Or is that something that should be a constant?

I think it should, in a perfect world, be a constant. However, following on from your question, let's say we have been working on Lorca's *Blood Wedding*. Towards the end of rehearsals, the 'movement' exercises will cease to be explorations of earth, work and heat, where there is a great deal of moving around in the space, but instead it's time for this work to reside now within the actor's body, the person/character s/he is playing. So, yes, the explicit movement work is no longer really in evidence towards the end of rehearsal. In order, however, for this depth of movement work to be done, the director has to be willing to give the movement director a good deal of time out of the precious rehearsal period. However, too often the director will only allow time for specific movement moments to be rehearsed. In this case, the movement director is pushed to accomplish something tangible at most rehearsals, and the actors will come to feel manipulated.

In what way?

Well, rather than the actor 'owning' their character's 'physical life' by working on movement consistently through the rehearsal period with the movement director, learning how to layer the movement work deeply into their characterization and then into the collective 'world of the play', the actor will find her/himself being 'instructed' as to how to move in this bit or that bit, without ownership of that moment of their performance, and this is what can make an actor feel 'manipulated'. I should add that I am not here referring to set pieces of group movement, which tend to be more movement director-led.

What skills or approaches do you bring to your work, and can you see the origins of those skills?
You mean where were the origins of those skills, and at what point did they become mine? As I said, I was trained by Litz Pisk.[5] I was also trained by Jacques Lecoq, and I was trained by Belinda Quirey.[6] Is that what you mean by an origin?

We are part of a lineage, I suppose.
Yes, we are part of a lineage, but each of us is unique, and I think the proof of a good training is where each individual, each training teacher, can absorb that teacher's work into their being and then make it their own. If we're going to get movement directors, real ones, they've got to work day after day, week after week, month after month and year after year. You can't just do it as an occasional job, because you don't get the chance to develop. And so, it's a two-way thing, isn't it? The more the young movement director gets the opportunity to be in the rehearsal room, the better they get. The more accepted they become in the rehearsal room, the more necessary they become in that rehearsal room. A person can only become a fully fledged movement director if they spend enough time in a rehearsal room, because it's only then that you learn how to solve the challenges that are thrown at you left, right and centre, and you discover how to solve them in the heat of the moment. And also, of course, there has to be a forum where new movement people can be initiated, so there needs to be some kind of an apprenticeship plan. But that no doubt costs money. At Central, therefore, what you're doing by running your course, you're starting to make a culture whereby the work becomes more and more accepted and essential, but as always the final analysis comes down to money.[7] If the Arts Council and theatres in the UK begin to understand that they always need to budget for a movement person – not just when there is obvious movement in a play – as they would do for a designer, lighting, sound etc., then we'd be beginning to get somewhere.

Having observed your work with movement directors in training, you bring in understandings from music and rhythm; of culture and status; from paintings – how did you come across these as a source for your movement directing?
Well, of course, pure movement is the basis of everything. But then one tries to bring in all sorts of aspects from other art forms to inspire the actors' imagination to become physical. Music was natural to me because of my dance training, but then it's interesting to use music as a physical exploration, and this can be done in many ways. For example, you could use music in the most obvious way, which is to do a dance to a piece of music – maybe a Restoration dance, which has a very simple musical shape to it, and the dances, too, are very much social dances so that everyone in that historical period knew how to dance them. The Restoration dances illuminate how people enjoyed themselves in that period, and they very

much liked dancing and spent a lot of time doing it, and the nature of those dances, of course, determined the architecture of those public dancing spaces. As I became more familiar with dance history and the use of period dance in an actor's training, I came to see more and more how much the dances reflect the time that people are living in, and of course paintings of the period are a gift to actors, as they can look at these paintings and imagine the people in them coming to life. But then, of course, leaping to the opposite extreme, a movement person could work with different pieces of music which have very definite 'textures' to help actors to find physical variation and bodily quality. Taken further, we could ask an actor to find a character in a play that moves and speaks with this quality. A piece of punk rock, for example, has a very different texture from a Christmas carol. It's one of the very many different ways to help student actors discover different and varied physical 'textures'.

With art, with paintings, I think it's all there, in the fantastic legacy we've got in art, the most marvellous creative minds at work, and we are at liberty to look at it and use it to create exercises for the student; to take on a work of art and become the person in the sculpture, for example, you must first be accurate. A head tipped too far will convey cynicism rather than wonder. This accuracy will help the student understand *why* they need to spend so long – three years – working towards a neutral body, that is, a blank piece of paper on to which a new character can be drawn, with no eccentricities or tensions to blur the picture.

And I think, finally, this brings me to something which is so interesting, when you see a stage performance – whether it's a play, opera or musical –and the bodies of the performers express no more than a person who has put on a 'costume' and been given a 'prop' and told to go and stand on the stage. The bodies on stage are not alive to the physicality the play or opera demands, and we – the audience – are getting very strange messages, because we are hearing the language, and the music, and understand from this that the people on stage are in a terrifying situation. As we look at the stage, however, there is no sign of danger in the bodies of the performers; we as an audience pick this up instinctively. We have, however, paid for a seat at the top theatre or opera house, so they must be doing it right, mustn't they? We, then, as an audience – semi-consciously, I think – have to imagine for ourselves that instead of seeing these placid bodies in front of us, they are in fact in a state of terror. We do this in order to prevent them from dampening our experience of the performance and to keep us from finding the experience disappointing.

How do you think that arises?
Lack of good movement training and lack of movement directors. I don't think the director always has to be able to work on movement, they have so many other things to take care of in the production of a play, but a movement director working in collaboration with the director is what we need.

Looking at other interviews, I was very struck by the research that you and the company of **Rhinoceros** *did together by going on a field trip.*[8] *Could you talk a little bit about that process?*

The play was called *Rhinoceros*, and in it people are at first scared by a rhinoceros in their midst and then, bit by bit, they transform and become rhinoceroses themselves.

In order for the company to transform into the rhinos, it seemed essential to me that they go to London Zoo and spend time looking at the rhinos. As we watched we learnt more about how to become one. We sensed their weight, rhythm and breath, and the actors would point things out to each other so the observation became shared. Gradually, we also came to think about why Ionesco used the metaphor of the rhinoceros in his play and came up with ideas about why this might be. The animal's thick skin, the horn in the centre of the head for fighting, and which seemed to lead the animal forwards carried by its weight and to pre-empt any sensitive view of the world, the blind anger when the animal becomes enraged. This was intended as a day spent in physical study, but being near those animals took us more deeply into the play and its meaning, in a way we wouldn't been able to by simply watching a rhinoceros on YouTube. The cast were left with a visceral connection to the title and the play.

If you look into the future of movement direction, how do you see it developing, changing?

In my sadder moments, I feel that we've had a kind of ebb and flow, and what's tended to happen in theatre is that you get something called 'physical theatre'. Physical theatre is a thing in its own right, and it's not necessarily a play; it's theatre where the physicality is very much to the fore. All theatre is physical to me, it's a funny word, you know. I wish it wasn't called 'physical theatre', because it makes out that there is either physical theatre or non-physical theatre. Theatre cannot exist without the physical. Otherwise, you'd be much better off hearing a wonderful recording of *Hamlet*, sitting at home with your eyes closed, imagining. Once you're sitting in a theatre, you've got the play in front of you; if the actors don't *realize* the play for you physically, your own imagination is undercut.

It's essential to keep pushing for the 'movement director' to be present full-time within the rehearsal period of a play. I do feel that theatre seems to be wanting more movement and dance and that therefore the presence of a movement director in rehearsal is increasing.

There is a fundamental thing that the actor has a body and the audience member has a body, and so theatre is a terrain that we both share in time and space, unlike TV or film, where, essentially, the live experience isn't there.

Yes, the technology takes over: however, it's wonderful to watch a good movie; but if you want to keep live theatre going, you need to keep developing exciting and innovative work, and if we start to finance movement directors to work alongside the director who is often overwhelmed with work and isn't necessarily naturally gifted in movement, I think this could help that to happen. But most of all the budgeting in theatres has to reflect this need, and sometimes I worry that the cost of live theatre might cause it to shrink and gradually die out.

It doesn't seem to be dying out.
No, it seems to be very alive and kicking.

Notes

1. Sue Lefton trained initially as a dancer at the Royal Ballet and at Rambert and went on to train as an actress at Central School of Speech and Drama with George Hall and Litz Pisk, under whose auspices she later taught movement at Central. She went on to become Head of Movement at Guildhall. Lefton has worked across theatre, opera, television and film as a movement director and choreographer. She has also directed a range of plays and co-directed with her colleague Jane Gibson. Movement direction in the early days at the National Theatre included *Grand Manoeuvres* (1974) directed by Michael Blakemore; *The Hypochondriac* (1981), directed by Michael Bogdanov; and *Equus* (1973), directed by John Dexter. Her fifteen-year collaboration with Adrian Noble at the Royal Shakespeare Company included movement on *Henry IV Parts 1 and 2* (1991); *The Thebans* (1991); *Romeo and Juliet* (1995); *King Lear* (1993); *A Winter's Tale* (1992); *A Midsummer Night's Dream* (1995); *Travesties* (1993); *The Cherry Orchard* (1995); *Twelfth Night* (1997); *The Lion, The Witch and the Wardrobe* (1998); and *Brand* (2003). In opera, Lefton has worked on the Mozart Trilogy of the *Da Ponte* libretti – *Cosi Fan Tutti*, *The Marriage of Figaro* and *Don Giovanni* – for the Opera National de Lyon (2011), Verdi's *Macbeth* for the Met in New York (2007), Bizet's *Carmen* at the Opera Comique in Paris (2009) and Handel's *Alcina* at the Vienna State Opera (2011). Choreography in film includes *Casanova* by Lasse Hallström (2005); *The Libertine* (2004), directed by Laurence Dunmore, starring John Malkovich and Johnny Depp; and *Elizabeth* (1998), directed by Shekhar Kapur, starring Cate Blanchett.
2. Central School of Speech and Drama where Lefton trained on the three-year acting course, graduating in 1966.
3. Dame Marie Rambert (1888–1982) was a Polish-born ballet teacher and a pioneer in establishing British ballet in the twentieth century. She trained with Dalcroze in Eurythmics, which she taught when she joined Les Ballets Russe in 1912–13 to work with Nijinsky. With the outbreak of the First World War, she moved to Britain. Rambert established Ballet Rambert in the mid-1930s, based at the Mercury Theatre. Fredric Ashton was one of her students. The company eventually shifted away from ballet to contemporary dance and continues creating new works to this day.
4. Adrian Noble is a British theatre director and was Artistic Director of the Royal Shakespeare Company from 1990 to 2003.
5. Litz Pisk – see Chapter 1 for details. She taught actor movement to Sue Lefton and Jane Gibson.

6   See Chapter 1 for Jacques Lecoq and Chapters 3, 5 and 8 for Belinda Quirey, historical dance teacher at London Contemporary Dance School.

7   The advent of the MA MFA Movement: Directing and Teaching at Royal Central School of Speech and Drama in 2004 was the first course of its kind to specialize in developing actor movement for movement teachers and movement directors. This was soon followed by the Guildhall School of Music and Drama offering a MA in Training Actors (Movement), an apprenticeship in movement teaching rather than movement directing.

8   Production of Ionesco's *Rhinoceros* at the Royal Court, directed by Dominic Cooke, 2007.

5 KATE FLATT

It's a constant reconfiguring and renegotiating in order to capitalize on the creativity that's emerging [2018][1]

How you would describe what you do in relation to opera and theatre?
What I do is led by the piece, whether that be movement work or choreography. Whatever I am working on will require research, planning, preparation and discussion. That really underpins how I take the work forward. Not to be asked to work on a project early enough to have that thinking and research time can be annoying. If something is sprung on you, it is almost impossible to work well. I probably work best when I know that I've got some uninterrupted time to get to know the director's process, so I take care to discuss how they want me to work with them.

Can you identify the origins of your skills and approaches?
My skills are multifaceted as I had a very wide training. My initial training was in ballet, and one of the things you learn with ballet is *character dance*, which is actually Central European dances that were incorporated into nineteenth-century ballet. I also studied with Joan Lawson, who herself had studied European folk dances and taught me at the Royal Ballet School.[2] She had studied dances from different European countries and had travelled a great deal. They were the loveliest things to tackle during my dance training. During my early training I also studied Greek dance and Natural Movement, the precursors of modern dance. And of course, ballet itself, which I worked at rigorously, with pointe work and all that

entails in strength and refinement of the classical form. At ballet school, I studied choreography with Léonide Massine,[3] who had a very particular movement approach that probably had some relationship to biomechanics.[4] He used a notation system and an anatomical approach for movement analysis. He'd really look at the body not as a trained body, but as a natural body. The notation focused on what was rotating, extending, flexing and what was used in the torso. I assisted him over a period of two and a half years, so I had a lot of exposure to it. That training in analysis was crucial to what I later developed in my career. He was applying it to ballet, but actually its application for actors is relevant as well, as there is a lot of heightened use of the body. It is an exterior approach but with value. I then went on to study Martha Graham technique and Cunningham technique; both offered important information about how the body works.[5] The expressionism of Graham and the linear clarity of Cunningham couldn't have been more opposed to each other and both were deeply informative. I studied T'ai Chi with Gerda Geddes and still practise it now; and I studied Alexander technique for back pain during my training.[6] I also studied choreography with Nina Fonaroff, who made us think about the building blocks of choreographic timing, that is, time and phrasing, and taught me to develop an eye to *see* what is in front of you.[7] I also learnt a little Baroque technique, and social and ballroom dance, with Belinda Quirey.[8]

I travelled to Eastern Europe to study social dance in its traditional setting, watching people with all kind of bodies dance in rural villages. Suddenly, I could understand a dance and its characteristics in a context where the meaning or reason behind the dance was still all intact. And I did the same at rituals and festivals in Spain and in Mexico, looking at dance in its traditional context. I was doing field research before I knew what it was. When I had to deal with waltzing again – when I taught Sean Connery to dance – I went back to ballroom dancing lessons.[9] There's a lot of knowledge in here [*gestures to her body*] that I may have to revisit to keep my collection ready to use. Going back to a class enables me to approach sessions with the actor with deeper knowledge, newly refreshed. What I haven't had is actor training. My intuitive responses were in relation to what I was seeing. More often than not, I had to address something I didn't yet know I knew. This might mean whether I could believe something or not, whether it was 'true' in that person's body or heightened in that person's body. The work is a lot about perception and looking, and observing, and understanding, and drawing on planning and research. They say actors watch people; I think it's really important for movement directors and choreographers to watch people, too.

Can you expand on different ways of watching?
You so often don't get chances to sit back and watch, and when you can it can be very informative. In one instance when I was working on *Dr Faustus* with David Lan, Richard McCabe, the actor playing Mephistophilis, turned up with this rather interesting, twisty walk.[10] After discussing this choice with the director, I was

able to encourage the actor to use his choice of a 'sepulchral walk' more liberally through the production. And then I suddenly realized that in my position, asking questions got you further than telling – training as a dancer or as a dance teacher is to inform, tell, instruct. If you take the word 'director' out of 'movement director', sometimes, not always, you are informing but via a questioning process. Rather than being the person who knows and informs, you are the person who is trying to 'find out' with the actor.

When it comes to movement, there's this idea of something being imposed upon an actor, and that can induce fear. You need the actor to understand physical detail, but you can put that in a framework for him or her and say, 'We're going to work on this only technically for now'. You have to come in with a definition of what it is you're going to do for an actor, because they offer themselves as an open vessel, and you are in a collaborative relationship with them. Your job is to get the actors to go down that path with you. In contrast to how a dancer works, an actor is a creative being in the workplace. It is changing in the dance world, with greater use of improvisation and task making. But I do I think actors feel they have a very big stake in what goes on, and actually their relationship is primarily with the director. There are psychological complexities to movement direction that mean you need to be sensitive to the world that the actor is in. I'm naturally cautious and feel that there are areas that need to be addressed very firmly with the backup of the director about what is emerging with the actor.

Katie Mitchell as an auteur always does back up the area of discovery by describing the world of the play and then eliminates everything that doesn't belong in it.[11] Phyllida Lloyd, who I have also worked very closely with, has a broad palette of inclusion of discovery within the room.[12]

How do you introduce movement into the rehearsal room?

It really does depend on the piece. You might have to find strength in the body, be releasing tension, working on alignment and opening awareness, so that people are in a receptive state – because ultimately that is what needs to happen.

I use approaches like visualization, which works well for dancers, who are working their bodies full-time but which, I think, does work for actors too – I will use some imagery within the warm-up. For example, getting them to shut their eyes and imagine looking into a black velvet curtain (which actually is, I think, a Bates eye exercise), which softens the muscles at the back of the eyes.[13] It allows for a focusing in and it connects to that Alexander technique idea of not fixing the eyes to hold yourself. I might do some T'ai Chi pliés, connecting to the ground, connecting the legs to the back, to the centre – and that is related again to my contemporary dance background. I'm always preparing the body with a repertoire of forms to draw upon. Some actors might resist simple walking exercises – they think they're being sent back to drama school – so actors do need to be informed about the purpose of an exercise, and I will re-explain it for a particular company or character.

There are two things: one is that I always have the actor warm up by doing material that I might use in the work; and then there are the centring exercises, ways of finding your legs, freeing the lower back and activating the major joint combinations in the body. Some of this might be about connecting to breathing or might be sensations to do with what happens if you move your shoulder this much [*indicates an inch between her fingers*]. It's actually quite anatomical, which is a way for actors to understand more about their bodies, their skeletons and their muscle groups. Preparing the body is an important aspect of the movement director's job, because you have to deal with safety and know that there may be 'damage' already in anyone in the group, and that is always worth finding out. But the questions that I feel are crucial when working with actors are, Where is your weight when you're standing? How balanced and poised is the head on the spine? Where are the tension patterns? What have you brought into the rehearsal room with you that you don't need in this place? So that the body is in a prepared state. I've devised various warm-ups that are specific to pieces. For example, on *Dream Play*, the play was in rep with several days off.[14] I wrote out the warm-up and I handed it to the actors, saying, 'You've got to do this even on your day off as well' – otherwise the work would deteriorate. And the actors did it. But there was one thing missing from it, so I had to add in a really tough set of core strength exercises, because the women were really racing around the theatre in high heels, changing costume all the time and moving furniture, and the physical problems only came to light at the tech. I had to add those exercises into the warm-up to avoid injury. The safety of the body, keeping an eye on all of those issues, I do feel is increasingly an important job. Preparing the body is important, and saying to the director, 'Having a twenty-minute warm-up is safer than a ten-minute one.' There might be a variety of approaches with some simple core stability one day or freeing and loosening another day, or it might be some straightforward walking exercises. Or it might be some aerobic material if it's a show that needs stamina. You try to cover the basics of what's needed, and you equip the actors with tools to take responsibility for their work.

Sometimes it might be a more advanced area of skill training, for example, I've done ballet with actors, or waltzing with actors, which can be a technical skill that has to be acquired by all in order to have a common language in a piece.

I remember watching* Three Sisters, *in the archives at the National;* [15] *I can see some vestiges of ballet that feels like it had been shared as a language.
Oh, it's beautiful … The work involved both ballet in Act Two and waltzing. The company had regular ballet and waltz sessions, and we worked also on slow motion as one key theme of the play is time. The actors needed to have movement languages they would need to use confidently in their work with Katie [Mitchell].

And in terms of the movement language, there's a plasticity to the body.
I achieved that through different means but a lot with time exercises. This may be an innovation of mine. Katie had wanted to do lots of slow motion, which led me to asking, 'How slow is slow?' I then brought a metronome to rehearsal. We set pulse speeds, and we would set an action to that pulse. I think it's written up a little bit in my article, and that certainly gave a common understanding to the movement language.[16] And the notion of moving slowly is something where you feel an internal pulse; it unites the group moving at one speed in slow motion. We took that work forward with *Dream Play* and did lots of fast-forwarding and rewinding, which was another way to escape naturalism.[17] But time work is actually related to the tempo-rhythms of Stanislavsky and in this case the theme of the play.

Did it become a route to stylization?
It produces it. It's an abstraction, and it's a technical skill. Changing 'time' or the feel of time abstracts movement away from naturalism and turns it into something else. Time work, I'd say, is a creative innovation, because when I was talking with Katie, in one of our research periods, I said to her what the choreographer has to bring, essentially, apart from the technical insights of the body, is how we deal with time in its purest form. Merce Cunningham said that dancing is the action of the body in space and time. And that's the prerequisite. He also said that dancing is not about representing anything. If you're not trying to represent something through dance, you can be dealing with it like playing music – as a technical skill. But that's a refined set of thoughts, and you have to make them very clear to actors, and I don't think I've always done that, and it's come unstuck if I haven't. When I work with actors and singers now, I say, 'We're now going to work with ..., and this is in order to ...' When you explain, they trust that they're in safe hands. Otherwise you're in a slight danger, offering unclear thinking, and that's the rigour of the work.

So how did you work on **Three Sisters** *for example?*
The 'Swan Lake' duet that was in Act Two of *Three Sisters* was such fun to do. First of all, there was the gift of Dominic Rowan and Anna Maxwell Martin.[18] I brought in a DVD of the *Swan Lake* danced by the Bolshoi, which is the most exaggerated style of ballet, and it was because I'd imagined that Andrey and his sister had been to a performance in Moscow of the ballet, one of the first productions they'd gone off to see, and they'd come home and done it in their living room, when she was about ten, and they went on to do it at parties and they had a wonderful time doing it. I had filtered a possible backstory for their connection to ballet. When I questioned Katie about the quality she was looking for, she said that the 'Swan Lake' needed to look a bit badly danced. I purposely sent the two actors off to watch the DVD and when they came back, they were able to talk about what they remembered and offer examples in their bodies. Only then did I teach them some fish dives, and the lifts, and the beginning of the actual *pas de deux*, and then Anna said, 'Oh, and she

does this', and she flapped around the room, and Dominic said, 'And he does this.' I taught him to run like Nureyev. We had these fragments of taught material and the things they had discovered whilst playing, and we made the piece out of that – letting the process build out of observation, memory and actual teaching. I would say I movement directed that rather than choreographed it.

It's that meeting point, isn't it, of narrative and character through lines, plus movement in space and time, all coming together in a room?
It was a response to the director's very accurate sense of period. And in this instance, giving the actors the scope to respond to something particular. All of those things coming together is what I would call movement direction. Another instance was teaching a fragment of a Hungarian military recruiting dance to Solyony (played by Tim Macmullan); the brief was to impress Irina. Once I taught it to him, he then did it completely unannounced during a rehearsal; it was a sensational moment of surprise.

Watching their work, I thought that the character traits were danced, and feelings were danced and moved.
They really were, I mean, Katie gave me a lot of scope, and although they were little fragments all the way through, they accumulated to quite a lot. And we did do waltzing regularly and the 'time' work, as well, so that when we came to the slow motion, everybody knew what we were going to drop into. Katie gives a very clear brief, which makes it much easier to work; a clear brief but without telling you what you should do.

How does it work with other directors?
Some other directors are more relaxed about that intervention and the flow, inviting a shared ebb and flow of discussion, and are quite delighted to have someone else to chat to. Some directors regard you as an expert in your field, and therefore you are hired to make an offer about a section that they have no idea how to do and give you carte blanche to deal with that particular element. You might work directly with a composer to shape a section.

How do you prepare for working with a director? How do you elicit a brief?
That first meeting with the director is very important. And I'll describe one first meeting with Trevor Nunn, who I have worked with several times, but it was only ten minutes long, and I just plied him with questions.[19] For *Three Sisters* and *Dream Play* we had two or three longer meetings with Katie, and Phyllida [Lloyd] similarly, testing-the-water meetings, discussion meetings, sharing-a-particular-moment meetings, 'What are the dances of this era that you're talking about?' 'Have you got an example?' If I couldn't describe it, I would bring a video or a DVD in and ask them to look at it.

You have to approach the project as if you are working on the whole of the play, even though you might only be doing a particular section. Therefore, understanding the whole and how far the director's got with their other collaborators is really important. But you have to come with ideas to offer or suggest some diegetic dances that might work.[20] Waltzing was from that particular era, for *Three Sisters*, for example. You're bringing something that's a very particular knowledge, or research that you've done, and sharing that. Decisions made before the rehearsal in the planning are vital. The clarity of the brief is the thing that gives the possibility of flashes of insight, which you can share. If the brief is clear, then the flashes of insight will come in the right measure.

All rehearsal is done under time pressures. How do you work swiftly and effectively?
Work swiftly – you just know you're never going to have much time. If you've got twenty minutes of warm-up time, you sneak things into that warm-up. Negotiating time is key to realizing the work. In an opera rehearsal I've actually said, 'Okay everybody, this is going to take me forty-five minutes to sort out, everybody else relax.' And that's what you do, you go and sort it all out. Or if something comes up, I have said, 'I think that's an area of more important exploration, can we give this more time?' Sometimes the director will do that too; they spot something and say, 'Can we come back to that place on Thursday when you're here again?' I think it's a constant reconfiguring and renegotiating in order to capitalize on the creativity that's emerging.

The early days of rehearsal are very fruitful.
It is a very important time. Well, it's like digging a flowerbed, you've got to do the digging and muck spreading before you can go anywhere else. Phyllida and Katie both considered that a very important time. Thinking back to a couple of big shows I've done with Trevor also, he doesn't really stage anything at all before he has explored the territory of the piece for quite a long while. I think that that is crucial. It is a potentially very creative time, but it's also laying out the possibilities – those things that might get discarded might get used elsewhere, or somebody will suddenly remember, 'Oh, you know it's like that thing we did on day two' and we go, 'Oh yeah.' That early part is very good. Then later in a rehearsal period, the negotiation gets quite hard to get movement calls, but you need the actors to maintain the quality that you need. An astute director will always give you the time; but with a less experienced director you may find yourself having to fight for it. And that is really hard.

And then as you move through to production week, tech, how do you use that?
Constantly looking, really; looking and noting. Working on the original *Les Mis[érables]*, I remember noticing character detail at the moment where Roger

Allam as Javert came up over the barricades. His movement was feral, with an unstable centre line to the body as he descended, in his obsessive pursuit of Valjean. It gave me all the clues I needed about his character at that moment, and I was able to ask Trevor if that was what he wanted. And he thought it would be really helpful that the actor knew about that too. And of course, in tech you are also listening to a director's notes and trying to keep in contact.

With some directors you need to hand everything over, and they encompass the whole thing – your work becomes subsumed into the director's envelope. And then your job is sort of over, except that I try to stay on board by giving warm-ups in a familiar way. By then, when you are planning the end of your input, you are normally working with someone who's going to take over the warm-ups, usually a member of the company. That handover through previews to first night is incredibly important, and that might be where you talk to the actors and say what's going to happen and how it will happen. And you just gradually pass that on in discussion with everybody, so that nobody feels something's sprung on them. It is the performers who have got to carry the work and get up there and do it. The continuing care of them, as the stress increases, is quite important. And it's familiarity, it's support, it's feedback that is needed, and giving actors incredibly judicious notes is the biggest help you can be. For example, 'Are your knees very tense when you're doing that, can you find a way to make this easier?' or question, 'What are you doing here, at this moment? Physically I feel it could be clearer.' Some directors will never give time to the movement director – time in the big notes sessions with the company – so you are having to do feedback in the corridors and dressing rooms.

Do you ever hand your notes to the director?
Yes, sometimes, and often I will email them, so that she or he can process them.

And then how do you keep in contact with a production after first night?
That depends on what else I'm doing. If it's gone well, it's very easy to come back. If it's gone badly, it's harder. With longer runs there's usually somebody in place who takes care of it, but I like to do spot visits now and then. With operas, I might go in four or five times because things can slip or get reinterpreted. Maintenance on a long-running show is incredibly important. You're reliant on a good dance captain, who is doing his or her job properly in relation to your work. It is important to take the person who you think will maintain the work, and I would see it as my responsibility to choose that person and agree it with the management.

How does working across theatre or opera change what you do?
I do work differently with an opera chorus, because an opera chorus is an entity that's either hired for a season or longer, on a full-time contract, where everybody knows each other. There's no point in doing warm-up games with them, they've

done them all before. So, ENO [English National Opera] chorus, for example, will issue chorus guidelines for new practitioners coming in, because they feel they have a stake in what goes on and want their professionalism respected.[21]

Nothing prepares you for sixty-five people in the room with a big chorus call. I took voice lessons to improve my vocal delivery. I found I got tense, and when you're moving around demonstrating, your voice gets lost. If you've got to get your message across to sixty-five people, it changes everything about how you work with a group. You demonstrate clearly, you treat it like a performance. It's so different. There's no intimacy. You have to be incredibly clear with instruction. Often, there is not a lot of room to improvise. If you are improvising, you have to make it clear by saying in 'what manner' you want people to improvise, and you have to say 'why'. Phyllida Lloyd is a director who is intent on breaking down the barrier and hierarchy between professional stars and professional chorus, so that you'd have one world. The way in which she and I have worked most successfully with the chorus was with Verdi's *Requiem*, *Peter Grimes* and *Gloriana*.[22] For *Grimes* and *Requiem*, we broke the chorus down into a core group with different specializations. First, we would work with the core group of a dozen, and then we'd have the whole chorus. This core group would then help to inform the relationship with the rest of the staging. It was the only way to keep in contact with the material and them, and through these means we discovered a way – we really sorted out that scheme, if you like.

And presumably, that also gives a different relationship to ownership?
It does. British choruses are very good and committed to the results. With the ENO for example, with *Carmelites*, we had eleven chorus nuns, and the rest of the chorus were revolutionaries, and sometimes they had very formal things to do and sometimes more wild ones, which they did very well. The briefing of them was totally clear and with an underlying idea of trust. You have to work closely with their singing coach as well, and the chorus master. It's a special world ruled by the music.

How do you actually work, logistically, practically with a chorus?
Verdi's *Requiem* was interesting. On stage there were ninety-six people, which conveniently divides as eight times twelve. We had done some planning with a core group of twelve chorus and core group of twelve actor movers. With the opening, we wanted everybody on stage, so we divided their chairs up into eight blocks of twelve and numbered them. We wanted the performers all sitting there staring at the audience as if at a funeral, and then, as the action started to break up the group, as people's fear started to make them move, we got to the *Dies Ire*, people's terror started to emerge, and people started to move backwards or climb over chairs or push things over. We did it by teaching twelve chorus members and gave a model as to how one of the groups of twelve could do it, which we'd worked on, and then we

got twelve of the rest of the chorus to do their version. And then once we got this staging set up, I set a choreographic swathe through it, with the actors jumping and rushing through scattering the chairs. It was actually very, very logistical.

In one production, I managed to get the chorus swaying very slowly, all slightly in contact with each other, and that was with eighty people. They were a festival chorus who were very keen to get involved and knew the music perfectly, because they all know the music by the start of rehearsal. Essentially, it's important to be logistically clear, and having prescriptive planning for everyone works when you have so little time.

I have taught dance to choruses, for example, by giving them little figures of dance, and they choose which ones to do when, so you get a cacophony on stage, for example, across sixteen bars, and the stage erupts with the life of their choices of this material. These logistical strategies are key, really, when you've got that many people.

It's the same thing with smaller choruses, too. You have to know the score inside out. Reading and knowing the music is essential for the job. You could follow the words and score, but it's not the same as knowing what musical terms mean, like *stretto*. 'Can we go from the *stretto*?' The figure numbers, what the function of those are, and knowing how to get the right cue for action, 'I need to know eight bars before, actually, otherwise we'll not hit that moment'. Being clear is really important, as is knowing the score. Opera is a very different animal from text-based theatre. First of all, the music rules. You have to understand what the conductor's asking for, what the chorus master expects, the language it's being sung in. The verbal cue is needed on which they will move, so not the 'and' and the 'one' but the verbal cue. It took me so long to get that sorted out.

And when you're thinking compositionally with large numbers of performers, do you feel yourself working differently?
I tend to think in big, stage pictures. I enjoy that. I'm less interested now, than I was when I was younger, in the choreographic detail of the steps. So often with the chorus the steps might be very simple, or what they actually physically do might have simplicity to it. Maybe it's just a way of breathing, or their heads going in one way. If there are steps, you have to be absolutely sure that they can do them well, consistently, so I make simple choices. Or, if they're going to be complex, that you choose people who are going to be able to do them effectively. To me, the integrity of how they do the material, perhaps, is more important than anything else. I have to believe that they know those dances really well. I think a hallmark of my work is that it's so integrated that you feel that it is naturally the next thing they would do.

And do you, as you're constructing, consider which voices are singing what?
Absolutely! You have to know what the sopranos and the mezzos-sopranos are singing. Sometimes they might be singing the same words, different parts. I

remember doing an accompanying section where I had people circling, in small groups of six, in a chorus in *Boris Godunov* in Paris.[23] It was in Russian – a language I don't speak – and they had to have me knowing exactly on what syllable and beat to move. It took a while to get it right as in opera, you can find yourself in a very stylized world, or a very historic world, and with complicated things such as headdresses, fans, trains, wigs. It pays to be simple, because the world of what they have to do musically is very difficult, and it can fall apart if you haven't got it right, and you won't have any time to go back to it. I think opera's probably the hardest work I ever do, because of time constraints. You don't have a full tech like you do in the theatre. There are piano and orchestra stage calls – three hours of madness that nothing prepares you for.

That's very helpful.
Well, it can be stress all the way with opera.

Looking more broadly at the field of movement, and the actor, when did you start calling yourself a movement director and a theatre choreographer?
I had this little bit of a war with myself about the terminology. In 1991, I did big chorus movement staging on Berlioz's *Damnation of Faust* in Paris, and I suddenly realized I was doing a different job.[24] I think it was then that I started to use the words interchangeably, depending on the production, and I always say to the director, 'Do you think it will be better if we put "movement director", we don't want to give the message that this has got dancing in'. Whereas for the *Three Sisters*, Katie definitely wanted it to feel that there was dancing in it, and all the photographs, the publicity were dance photos, and the play is a tragedy – that was deliberate on her part.

I think it depends on what the production is, and that shapes how I think of my title. Primarily I would say, if there is music involved, or I've been devising things to do with music, it's 'choreography' and I'm called 'choreographer'. If it's not to do with music, or there is no dancing, then it's 'movement direction'. *The Carmelites*, which was movement direction, well there was no dancing in it, but there was music. I guess it's not about the end result, it's actually more about what I'm inputting. And that discussion and debate goes round and round.

My last question – what do you think the future work of a movement director might be?
I couldn't predict that. But I know what I'd like to see, which is more respect for the skills of movement directors. And the problem is, because you're in the director's pocket, you can become a sort of 'secret weapon' – the risk of which is that you might not be acknowledged. But actually, I would like to see directors recognize more actively the specialist work that movement directors do, and can do, for their production. But that takes an enlightened lead from somewhere like the National

Theatre. The RSC [Royal Shakespeare Company], for example, back in the 1980s, my feeling was that the powers that be had a limited idea of how to qualify, accept and respect what movement direction work was doing.

I do think there needs to be some teasing out of respect for what those skills are and, perhaps, choreographers from dance not just thinking they can move into it without understanding more about the field. Movement directors are now equal members in creative teams. They still need appropriate crediting, recognition of authorship. The industry needs to recognize and remunerate that in a commensurate way with other creative collaborators. Movement practitioners deserve greater industry support from Equity in a comparable way with choreographers.

Notes

1 Kate Flatt OBE has worked as a movement director and as a choreographer across theatre, dance, film and opera. After training as a dancer at the Royal Ballet School, Kate attended the London School of Contemporary Dance. In her early career, she assisted Léonide Massine. On opera, her work includes dance choreography, chorus movement and staging; selected productions include *Peter Grimes* (Opera North 2006), *Gloriana* (Opera North 1992); *Turandot* (Royal Opera, 1984), *The Carmelites* (1999); and Verdi's *Requiem* (2000) for English National Opera with Phyllida Lloyd. Work for the Royal Opera includes *William Tell* (1990), *Viaggio a Rheims* (1992), *Aida* (1994) and *Turandot* (1984). She created the dances and chorus staging for *Betrothal in a Monastery*, Glyndebourne (2006) and at the Arts and Sciences complex, Valencia in 2008. She was part of the choreographic team collaborating with filmmaker Sally Potter on *Carmen* at English National Opera (2007). Choreography for film includes *The Dancing Room* (1995), a full-length dance work made for BBC2 with Sally Jacobs, directed by Simon Broughton; feature films include choreography for *Chaplin* (1992), directed by Richard Attenborough; *Restoration* (1995), directed by Michael Hoffman; and *The Avengers* (2012), directed by Joss Whedon.

   Theatre work includes research on *The Waves* (2006) with Katie Mitchell. At the Royal National Theatre, productions include *Ends of the Earth* (1996); *Albert Speer* (2000); *Power, Three Sisters* (2003); *Dream Play* (2005); *'Tis Pity She's a Whore* (1999); *Dr Faustus* (2002); *The Skin of Our Teeth* (2004); *Skellig* (2004) with David Lan at the Young Vic; and *Hamlet* (2004) with Trevor Nunn at the Old Vic London. She was the movement director for the original musical staging for the Royal Shakespeare's Company's *Les Misérables* (1985). At the invitation of Dame Ninette de Valois, Kate taught choreography at the Royal Ballet School. Kate has also authored a range of articles on dance and choreographic practices and in 2019 published a book entitled *Choreography: Creating and Developing Dance for Performance*.

2 Joan Lawson (1907–2002) was a British dance teacher and the author of many books on folk dance and classical ballet. She set up the National Dance Branch for the Imperial Society to form a syllabus of a wide selection of dances from Europe.

Royal Ballet School is a British dance school offering a residential classical ballet training and education to young dancers. It is currently housed at White Lodge in Richmond and Floral Street in Covent Garden. The school was born out of Ninette de Valois' early ballet schools and companies. The school is affiliated with the Royal Ballet Company and the Birmingham Royal Ballet and has many notable dancers and choreographers amongst its alumni.

3   Léonid Massine (1895–1979) was a Russian-born actor, dancer and choreographer who worked at Les Ballets Russes. He appears in the film *The Red Shoes* (1948), which he also choreographed. It is said of his process that 'Massine drew inspiration from a diversity of sources, among them: painting and sculpture, architecture, film, literature, commedia dell'arte and puppetry. … His works are infused with vivid characterizations articulated through expressive movement'. Available online: http://massine-ballet.com/html/about_massine.php (accessed 16 August 2019). He taught dance composition at the Royal Ballet School from 1968–71.

4   Biomechanics are part of an actor training system developed by Meyerhold, a Russian theatre director, producer and actor trainer born in 1874 and executed 1940. It aimed to develop rhythm in relation to both space and motion. His physical 'etudes' emphasized extreme extension, precarious balance, quasi-acrobatic lifts and jumps: 'The exercises combined the gymnastic, the plastic and the acrobatic; they developed in the students an exact "eye" … they helped them to move more freely and with greater expressiveness in the stage space' (Iygor Ilyinsky quoted by Robert Leach in Hodge 2000: 43). Very significantly, movement was understood as 'scenic movement' with its non-naturalistic routes to expressive and highly visible movement language or character bodies.

5   Graham technique originated out of the work and theories of American choreographer and dancer Martha Graham (1894–1991). She developed a codified system that uses contraction and release in seated, standing and travelling positions. Breathing and the torso are central to the technique, as are interior curves, extensions and spirals. Yielding and resisting gravity underpin the strong, dynamic, angular forms that characterise her technique. The encounter between Robin Howard and Martha Graham's company in London in 1954 was to set off a chain of events. Despite the critical bewilderment of the British press towards her dance works, Robin Howard started a relationship with the Graham Company, which would nurture the idea of Graham technique being integrated into a new training for professional dancers in Britain. This eventually led to the opening of the London Contemporary Dance School (LCDS) at the Place in 1969 and, shortly after, the creation of a dance company comprising of graduates in London Contemporary Dance Theatre and led by Robert Cohan. The Graham-trained teaching faculty was further enhanced by the appointment of Jane Dudley as Head of Graham Studies and, in 1972, of Nina Fonaroff, who joined as Head of Choreography at the LCDS. Kate Flatt, Struan Leslie and Imogen Knight all trained here.

Cunningham technique was formulated by dancer and choreographer Merce Cunningham (1919–2009), with its emphasis on the flexibility of the spine and the potential for the body to move dimensionally and quickly using changes of direction.

6   Gerda Geddes (1917–2006) was a dancer, a teacher and one of the first Western women to learn T'ai Chi in China. In post-war Britain, she was to kick-start the

teaching of T'ai Chi in a variety of settings but notably at the LCDS, where she taught for almost thirty years.

Alexander technique is a system of addressing physical tension through an inhibitory route and by redirecting the body towards efficiency and relaxation. The technique was developed by F. M. Alexander (1869–1955) as a response to his vocal problems as an actor. It is widely taught at British theatre trainings, though it is arguably a technique more attuned to vocal technique than a movement experience.

7   Nina Fonaroff (1914–2003), born in the United States, was a Martha Graham Company dancer (1936–46), a choreographer and a teacher. Through Martha Graham she met Louis Horst, who was to become a major influence in her life. She taught at Sarah Lawrence College, Bennington College and Teachers College at Columbia University, as well as teaching movement for actors at the Neighborhood Playhouse. In 1972, she moved to London to teach choreography at the LCDS, where she remained through to 1990 and where her students included the filmmaker Sally Potter, who Kate Flatt has worked with.

8   Belinda Quirey. See Chapter 3.

9   Sir Sean Connery is a British actor (born 1930).

10 *Dr Faustus*, directed by David Lan at the Young Vic in 2002, with Richard McCabe playing Mephistophilis and Jude Law as Dr Faustus.

11 Katie Mitchell (born 1964) is a British theatre and opera director. See Chapter 8.

12 Phyllida Lloyd CBE (born 1957) is a British theatre director working in theatre, opera and, recently, film.

13 Bates eye exercise is based on a therapeutic method for eye health created by William Horatio Bates (1860–1931).

14 *Dream Play* by August Strindberg in a version by Caryl Churchill, directed by Katie Mitchell, Royal National Theatre, in 2005.

15 *Three Sisters* at the Royal National Theatre (2003) by Anton Chekhov, in a version by Nicholas Wright, was directed by Katie Mitchell. Andrey was played by Dominic Rowan and Irina by Anna Maxwell Martin. In the *Observer* (17 August 2003), Liz Hoggard wrote, 'Although the play is located in an upper-middle-class milieu – all ticking clocks, Christmas fairy lights and expensive china – there is an extraordinary other-worldly quality. Scenes are punctuated by dreamy slo mo sequences, reminding the audience that, although this is nineteenth-century theatre, we are fully cognizant of modern cinema techniques.'

16 See Flatt and Melrose (2006: 41–6).

17 *A Dream Play* after Strindberg, directed by Katie Mitchell, National Theatre (2005).

18 Actors in this National Theatre production were Angus Wright, Anastasia Hille, Dominic Rowan, Susie Trayling and Charlotte Roach, amongst others.

19 Sir Trevor Nunn CBE (born 1940) is a British theatre director who has been artistic director of the RSC and the National Theatre. He and Flatt worked on *Les Misérables*. Their production came to a close in 2019.

20 Diegetic dances relates to narrative and is commonly used within film criticism (especially in relation to sound). A diegetic dance is one that is inscribed within the

narrative of the work and where the character is dancing and knows that they are in the action of dancing. By implication, this suggests that non-diegetic dances are outside the narrative as might be seen in fantasy sequences (that is, not necessarily part of the character's reality) or dances that are not moving the narrative forwards but occupying an abstracted or expressive realm.

21 English National Opera Chorus. Available online: https://www.eno.org/about/whos-who/chorus/ (accessed 16 August 2019).
22 *Peter Grimes* by Benjamin Britten with libretto by Montagu Slater (2006) and *Gloriana* by Benjamin Britten with libretto by William Plomer (1992), directed by Phyllida Lloyd for Opera North; Verdi's *Requiem* for ENO.
23 *Boris Godunov,* directed by Yannis Kokkos (1991), Opera National Paris, Bastille.
24 *Damnation of Faust*, directed by Yannis Kokkos (1991), Theatre de Chatelet, Paris.

6 TOBY SEDGWICK

Everything moves … it all comes back to that – 'tout bouge' [2019][1]

How would you describe what you do?
What do I do? As a director of movement, every job is different. When I started out, directors would ask me in if they had a problem to solve – it was more specific in those days. I never intended to be a director of movement, but people started asking me to create movement pieces. I think it was because of the way we told stories with Moving Picture Mime Show.[2] We had an inventive way of looking at something physically, as opposed to through the text or by other means. Most of our images were cinematic and extensions of reality. We'd throw ideas out into the audiences' imagination so they could see something evolving in a physical way, and their imagination embellished the image.

How was the transition from making your own work, as part of a company, to working as a director of movement?
It evolved, because we were all fresh from Lecoq training, and the pedagogy of Jacques Lecoq enables you to come up with illustrative but dramatic images of stories. Theatre is always, whatever happens, a story that unfolds.

Why did you go to Lecoq? Did you want to be a performer?
Yes, primarily because I wanted to do my own work. When I was fourteen, I saw a piece by Julian Chagrin. His wife Claude Chagrin was a successful movement director – I think she did *Equus* the first time.[3] They had been to Lecoq in the early 1950s. I went backstage to see Julian afterwards to tell him I thought his show was great; way before its time. I remember him saying that if you wanted to do your own work then Jacques Lecoq was *the* school. So I thought 'I'll go to Lecoq' – it

was as simple as that. I have always loved making people laugh. As an actor, most of what I've done is comedy, rather than as a director of movement, where the material is more diverse.

Can you describe what you might do as a director of movement?
It's very difficult to describe what I do because as a director of movement, every job is so specific. It's probably better to take an example such as *Frankenstein*.[4] There were two aspects: one was that we wanted to create the Creature, and the other was to show how his movement evolved from 'birth' to standing. That became a whole progression that I worked out by researching how the brain might work in its simplest form. Breaking it down into stages – from moving the hands to moving the spine, all the way up to standing. So that the Creature's brain informs him about his own physicality. I created a sequence of ten stages of a movement progression with Benedict Cumberbatch and Jonny Lee Miller. I rehearsed with the actors separately so that their whole physicality and entire journey was completely different to each other.

The progressions were based on discovering physical possibilities of each body part and incremental realizations that it has certain capacities in movement. I started with only the arms and legs, incorporating something else if we needed to go further. Then the spine came into play and the relationship between the head, the neck and back. Then the relationship with the pelvis, which then affected the legs. So, all those connections came into being. We would then experiment in those stages and slowly we built in realizations that the brain would very quickly 'learn' that if, for example, they painfully whacked their hand on the floor, they would slowly learn how to avoid such pain. It was trying to empty the brain of any generalized physical movement and bring it right back to scratch: to starting with nothing.

Like learning all of your physical skills as an adult without having had a childhood?
Exactly. So, I gave the actors an exercise to think of it as stages to pass through – going from one place to another – 'You're not going to arrive because you've no knowledge of direction'. 'You've got no thought process as yet'. I created a thought process, and the actors found that useful because then they could compartmentalize states and allow those states to build upon each other. Each stage accumulated the knowledge of the previous one, and it became a slow learning curve. At the beginning of the show you saw a body fall out of a 'womb' and go through a whole series of physical and psychological events up to the point where he was standing up.

A perfect example of taking a theme and turning it into movement is when Danny [Boyle] wanted the creature to experience a large image of the Industrial Revolution. You do all your research about the Industrial Revolution – what happened, how it changed the world, how it changed England – and then come up with images. A lot of my work is encapsulating an idea or creating a movement piece from an element that is almost outside of the main plot. On this occasion, I collaborated with the musicians, Underworld, who created a musical dynamic, and we worked together in finding a structure. I also collaborated with the designer Mark Tildesley, working out what actual tools we could use. Because it's theatre, everything has to be tangible, which is why it is powerful. We came up with a train on a track that would come through huge white doors and be projected forward, unstoppably, towards the creature and audience. Images of a mechanical world would explode off the train and then rejoin the train as it surged forward on the tracks, which extended into the audience of the Olivier Theatre. Out of our collaboration, I choreographed an entire piece that became a cinematic image of the Industrial Revolution, juxtaposing some very mundane movement with some automated movement which was influenced by the cinematic images of *Metropolis*.[5]

Lecoq's teaching is founded on an idea that everything that moves in the world is potentially a resource for movement – films, life, nature, materials.
Exactly, yes. There is movement in everything from which you can extrapolate different aspects, drawing on that to create images.

How do you prepare for a project?
It depends on the project; it's so specific to the job and what you've been asked to do. Obviously, you read the script, you think about where there might be any possibilities of expanding something. I brainstorm a lot very early on; so, I might have too many ideas. It's always better to have too many ideas than too few and maybe blurt out to the director, 'Oh maybe we could do this.' But then the second discussion would be, 'We're not going to have the time to do that,' or 'We want to get on with the plot.' Again, depending on what the piece is, I don't say, 'Oh, I must research this,' it's only if I feel that there's specific information that will spark movement ideas, and I'd like to learn more about that. I don't spend masses of time on a potential idea that might never happen; it's specific to what's required.

How did you prepare for the Olympic Games opening ceremony?
I was given an open book with much of the Olympics work, like Green and Pleasant Land.[6] I did a lot of brainstorming and then I'd come up with an idea. I'd practise on myself to see if it had potential and to see how it worked. It is about *feeling*. Basically, I always ask, 'Does it feel right? Does the story that your body is telling, work?' You set yourself up as an experiment. With the Olympics I had ten assistants, and having come up with the various ideas, we'd spend the day trying out them out.[7] I would try out simple things like an allotment choreography, and occasionally all the elements may have 'strange' aspects to them that the 80,000 audience members would see. For example, in the football field, at a certain point,

all the players would suddenly freeze for a short period of time and then carry on, as if nothing had happened. There was a large group of society ladies with umbrellas, like a little moving bubble troupe, and they all, at some point, went into a very simple choreography and then out again. Another was a group of farm workers, who would be out of sync and then suddenly they would slot into sync and do a movement sequence with their spades, rather beautiful, and then just go back to strolling along the pathway. So, there were just little elevations, little splashes that I wanted throughout the whole forty-five minutes. In the Industrial Revolution section, because we were teaching 1,000 people pieces of choreography and as they were not used to moving, the movements had to be very clear and precise. I was inspired by Victorian tools and machinery to create the movement, elements the participants would learn – evoking a changing world. What I wanted to do was to change the physicality, very simply, so that people would be moving quite differently from the very rural setting that had preceded it.

You often put yourself in the position of imagining the audience imagining the physicality.
My process often starts with a question: 'How do you create an image?' How to show an audience an image by selecting elements of movement that essentially will ignite the audience's imagination. I am not afraid to have a chorus or having an actor who may suddenly be talking while they're doing puppeteering or using objects with specific movement dynamics. And if the image is being made, the theatre will be ongoing.

Does the relationship between actors' bodies and materials explain how you worked on War Horse?
Yes, they very simply come into play. *War Horse* was particularly relevant because we were using puppets, and the audience's world would be tied up with their belief in the puppet.[8] If the horse looks like a horse moving, then you're not going to worry about the people inside the body. If it doesn't look like a horse as it walks, all you see is a carcass, a frame, and you will see the puppeteer's legs move; it's as simple as that. I was originally an actor for the R&D [research and development] of the show, and during that time I also started choreographing the movement of the horses, turning the puppets into horses. The other job was how to change the space, so I thought as we were using puppets we might as well use actors to become 'posts of space', to arrange the space so that within a farm you would see the confinement of an animal. So, we came up with the idea of poles and started by using some scaffolding that was lying around. The next stage was the design of custom-made poles with designer Rae Smith. Using various configurations and flow of movement with the poles meant that a confined space could then open up to create different environments and highlight different emotional states. It is

the quality of movement that's vital for any movement work because everything moves – but *how* do things move?

What do you draw upon to understand those movement qualities?
Just life – you look at what would be a calming motion like the wind, for example, so I started with a very airy feel, and then in the military stable the poles were used in a strong, structured way as if the characters were also holding guns. Then for the dynamic of confining an animal, the poles started off as farmer's staffs and then they turned into very sharp, defined lines that confined the foal. The dynamic can change but the poles, as objects, remain exactly the same; it's just the quality of movement that is very different. Changing the dynamic of that quality will tell a different story. Or a character may have a certain quality of movement, and if you change the dynamic they can change as well, for example from being aggressive to soft.

Movement of objects and motion of actors bleeds into design and design bleeds back into movement. Is that something you're aware of, or is that just how your mind works?
Whenever I'm given the opportunity to work on a piece, the first thing that you have to work out is what style you're working in and what is possible within the confines of the piece, because it's the language you are creating. So, once that's established in a simple way, it becomes clearer. For example, in *War Horse* the language was puppetry, and once you've established that style then puppetry is possible, animation is possible, projection is possible – lots of things suddenly open up when you begin to understand the language. The language becomes apparent either by creating a small bit of the piece, or a small idea can define the language for the whole piece – it can open a door on to the whole piece.

If you build the image with the body accurately, an imaginative and poetic door opens into the audience's mind.
Poetic gesture. It always stirs the audience's imagination, and as a movement director that's what gives me the biggest satisfaction, in any work that I do: if it inspires their imagination. If something works, they don't question whether it's good or bad. That's why you don't often get critics commenting on movement, because it's so embroiled in the style that they don't think of commenting on it. Sometimes that can be quite frustrating because you'll have worked for a long time on a piece. It was very lucky when I got the Olivier Award for *War Horse*, because that's one of the first times that a movement director has ever got one. I think it *was* the first time because it's always been a given to a choreographer – so when my name came up, I couldn't believe it, nor could Tom or Marianne [the directors].

A few years ago, you mentioned the power of observation, and you were telling me about being in a field watching a horse, getting to know its motion. That suggests that you've got an analytical eye.
Yes, I try to work out what someone means or what an animal means by moving in a certain way –

Marrying intention and physical expression?
Exactly, and that in turn will direct the quality of movement, and that quality of movement will be visualized by an audience into an understanding of their state of mind, so it all links back. I guess that's how I've worked, but I'm watching all the time – you watch body language and you get very attuned to that.

Yes, I recognize that, too. What's your process like with actors?
I've always gotten on well with actors, and they seem genuinely keen to help develop the creative ideas that I might suggest. I softly test them to try to find out their abilities if I don't know them that well.

Do you run a warm-up? How do you get to know them?
Yes, we'll do an energetic and fun warm-up to get their bodies moving and relaxed. I use the actors to play and to come up with an idea, or I'll give them something to rehearse; sometimes it'll be very specific. You have to be very careful and very observant about how they react to things. That's why I start off giving them little exercises. I'll try something out, I'll say, 'Why don't we try this and see how it feels?' And by doing that you can see who's comfortable and who's really *mal a droit* [clumsy or uncomfortable]. But I've always had an amazing rapport with the actors, and they've loved what they've been given to do because they get the same joy as I do having created it. They get the same joy having the audiences react to them doing that thing and them going, 'God that worked!'

That was great with *Stan and Ollie* when working with Steve [Coogan] and John [C. Reilly].[9] Big names are sometimes hard to work with because you have to gain their trust. And in this instance, it really evolved and was very satisfying for all three of us because we rehearsed for three weeks before we started shooting. I had to get them to *be* Stan and Ollie, and that took a long time. I had to teach them very complicated choreography, both slightly differently because Ollie used to get things wrong and so we had to also create all the mistakes. There was a sequence called the 'Two Door Sequence' which had never been written down and was something they did on stage. The film script on page fifty-six says, 'Then they do the Two Door Sequence' then a blank page, so John [S. Baird] said, 'Oh look, can you choreograph this, we need to do these two doors?' And so, I literally wrote an entire sequence, came in with John and Steve and all three of us developed this whole piece from one simple idea.

A physical storyboard? Was that you writing and notating it?
Yes, working it out, visualizing it on paper and rehearsing in *minimal* on a little table [*his hands enact a miniature duo on the table in front of us*].

Seeing your hands moving on the table, I'm reminded how you translate something epic into something in minor during some pantomime blanche tasks at the Lecoq school.[10]
A very important aspect of a lot of the Lecoq work that I certainly picked up was the expansion of something, the size of a gesture; whether it grows into melodrama or whether it's very, very small, what that means, or what that does, so a lot of things about using scale. It's like lockers in the back of your head and they're always there and then sometimes you'll just find yourself in a locker and going, 'Oh yes, you could do that!' A lot of the choices are inherently stored from experience.

And do you think your experience of being an actor gives you access to other actors?
Definitely, yes, because I'll try something first as an actor, and if it feels good as a performer it'll probably be good to pass that on to another actor and they'll like that. This often happens with a different aspect of movement when I'm directing movement which is actually specifically with the actors. For example, Pete Postlethwaite loved everything movement based, because I could talk to him about his body language and he was open to that.[11]

On which show?
On *The Tempest*. I did a lot of movement on that show, but I was also in it. In fact, half the shows, when I started doing movement, I was in them as well and so automatically I'd already gained the actors' trust.

You belong with them as well.
Yes, belong to them and to the creative team. In the first ten years I was also in lots of the pieces. As well as doing the movement, I was also an actor in the productions, for example, in *War Horse* playing the father, Ted Narracott.

And how did it work shuttling between the two groups?
It just gets a bit complicated, and because the actors fully understand that does work out.

And how do you work with directors?
Do you mean how do you start working? I tend to throw options out to them and suggest ideas, and based on their response, that will give me an insight into which

language they want to use or that they have an idea in their mind about what the journey of the piece will be stylistically; what style you can afford to have in it. So the first thing that I'll work out with the director is what their game plan is, and once I know that I tend to end up suggesting the right things.

And, and in the room, are you working alongside them, are you somewhere else or are you …?
It depends. Quite often I'll be given a certain amount of time, like if there's a theme, as there was in *Master and Margarita*.[12] I suggested to Steve Pimlott a physicalization of Moscow so that the audience could visualize where we were and what sort of world we were in. Steven said, 'I think that's a great idea, you go away and make it.' I went away with all the actors. I had bombarded myself with all the images that encapsulated the idea of Moscow like the cold, the clothes, the queues, the trams. Then by working with the actors, we got a whole sequence together that had a beginning, middle and end. When we showed it to Steven, he said, 'Fantastic, okay let's plot the Master in.' So we did that completed sequence and then just plopped Sam West into it. So, things like that.

I also really like this idea, that throwing in suggestions and actually letting some of them be batted out of the way brings you closer to what the world is.
When you start very wide, some of the ideas you know may not be right but are worth shoving in as it might just divert the director's idea towards a possibility. But it's always informative and it's always narrowing to a point.

Can you give an overview of your creative process? What's really important to you when you're working?
What I most enjoy and get most satisfaction out of is stretching the imagination, whether it be stretching the imagination of the director that I'm working with and/or of the actors, but most importantly of the audience. By stretching the possibilities of their imagination, they can understand and broaden a view of something that otherwise wouldn't be realized.

Looking more broadly at the field of movement and production, can you look outwards into the future? How do you see the field developing?
I have an inkling that there will be more fusion between dance and theatre, and that's what is already happening to a certain extent. And circus arts as well, it has already happened. For example I directed Ockham's Razor in *The Mill*, which was a theatrical concept put into circus skill. Already, there has been a growing amount of opera that is very theatre-like, very physical, even with 'danced' parts. So, styles are currently fusing more certainly than they were ten or fifteen years ago when there was a big separation.

Why has the field grown, do you think?
When I first started, the input of a movement director was quite large in depicting and enhancing the style that the director had already envisaged. I don't know how much of that is still happening. Maybe the movement director is being asked to do some quite specific work now, and maybe it's with the actors, so that's slightly different. There's a big difference in working with an actor on movement and creating a movement piece of theatre, not choreographing but creating a world. Sometimes, some pieces require both, so often I will suggest ideas to the director for the actors, and a lot of it can be spatial, such as where you say something on stage.

Are you teasing out some differences? Sometimes you've made an explicit movement-led section that exposes 'the world' of the work in some way. Then there's movement which goes into the actor's body that's integrated into movement in character. And then there is ...
... informing the dynamic. I think it's the dynamics of the stage and of the story – it's big, open space. The possibilities are endless, but it's always about the dynamic of the space and the actor in it.

I wonder whether it is also about directors being different; maybe there's a shift there as well, as we might be in an age of visual articulacy.
I do get the feeling that, certainly in some of the jobs I've done, the director has been very pleased that their work has been opened up and they're grateful for that.

Are there aspects to movement direction that you've not mentioned?
I'm often being asked how to go from one scene to another, how you move the story forward, and I've done that for so long it sometimes gets repetitive. But I do enjoy thinking that way as long as I'm not solely doing that in a piece. If all you are doing is moving furniture that is not great! It should be about the importance of creativity moving from 'here to there'. What I try to do is to understand the quality of the emotion and dynamic of the scene that you're coming from and the scene you're going to and reflect that in the movement of the objects. It's a classic Complicité technique[13] – the number of times we've done that neat little scene change from one thing to another! Then again, that will be reliant on understanding the concept of the whole story; you can't just do something completely out of style from one scene to another. It comes back to *tout bouge*; everything moves, when something is being moved, how it is being moved, what forces are upon it – everything basically returns to that - '*tout bouge*'.[14]

Notes

1 Toby Sedgwick's productions as a director of movement include *War Horse* (National Theatre 2007, West End 2009, Broadway 2011, Toronto 2012, United States tour 2012, Australia 2012); *Frankenstein* (National Theatre, 2011); *Swallows and Amazons* (Bristol Old Vic, 2010); *The 39 Steps* (West Yorkshire Playhouse 2005, West End 2006, Broadway 2008 and worldwide 2008); *A Dog's Heart* (2017) for De Nederland's Opera, La Scala, Lyon Opera and English National Opera; *Tintin* (Barbican Theatre 2005); and London 2012 Olympics opening ceremony, as Director of Movement and Choreographer for the Green and Pleasant Land and the Industrial Revolution sequences with Danny Boyle.

Movement direction and choreography for film includes *Stan and Ollie*, directed by Jon S. Baird (2018); *28 Days Later* (2002) and *Sunshine* (2007), directed by Danny Boyle; *Nanny McPhee*, directed by Kirk Jones (2005) and *The Big Bang* (2010), directed by Susannah White; *Victor Frankenstein* (2015), directed by Paul McGuigan.

As an actor, his work includes *War Horse* (National Theatre, 2007); *The Tempest* (Royal Exchange, Manchester, 2007); with Complicité, *The Master and Margarita* (2013), *A Dog's Heart* (2017), *The Noise of Time* (2000), *Light* (2000), *Out of a House Walked a Man* (1994) and *Help! I'm Alive* (1990).

Awards include 2008 Olivier Award – Best Theatre Choreographer for *War Horse*; 2011 Fred & Adele Astaire Awards nominee for Best Broadway Choreographer; 2012 Dora Mavor Moore Award, Canada, for outstanding choreography on *War Horse*.

As a director he worked with Ockham's Razor in *The Mill* at the Royal Opera House (2010) and *The Three Musketeers* for Mime Theatre Project (1991). He co-directed *Macbed* (2000) at the National Theatre with Ken Campbell and *The Hudsucker Proxy* with Simon Dormandy at the Nuffield Southampton and Liverpool Playhouse in 2015.

2 Moving Picture Mime Show was a mask-based physical theatre group founded by Paul Filipiak, David Gaines and Toby Sedgwick (1978–88).

3 See Chapter 1 for Claude Chagrin's movement work.

4 *Frankenstein* by Nick Dear, based on the novel by Mary Shelley, directed by Danny Boyle at the Royal National Theatre (2011), with Benedict Cumberbatch and Jonny Lee Miller alternating the roles of the Creature and Frankenstein.

5 *Metropolis* (1927), directed by Fritz Lang, is a silent German Expressionist film set in a twenty-first-century dystopia.

6 2012 Summer Olympic Games opening ceremony, Olympic Stadium, London directed by Danny Boyle. The whole event was entitled *Isle of Wonder* and widely praised as a 'love letter to Britain'.

7 See Diane Alison-Mitchell, Anna Morrissey and Polly Bennett in Chapter 15 – they were amongst the ten assistant movement directors.

8 This 2007 production is famous for the collaboration of all the creatives and actors in realizing the interconnected aspects of the theatrical language. *War Horse* was based on the novel by Michael Morpurgo, adaptation by Nick Stafford, with Handspring Puppet Company, directed by Marianne Elliot and Tom Morris, designed by Rae Smith, for the National Theatre.

9   *Stan and Ollie* (2018), feature film directed by J. S. Baird. Toby Sedgwick was Director of Movement and Choreographer; the Assistant Choreographer was Polly Bennett (see Chapter 15).

10 A teaching exercise by Lecoq to recount an epic film physically – action and narrative – using pantomime blanche, that is, descriptive mime that largely uses hand gestures.

11 Pete Postlethwaite OBE (1946–2011) was a British actor. He played Prospero in *The Tempest* by William Shakespeare in the 2007 production at Manchester Royal Exchange, directed by Greg Hersov. Sedgwick played Trinculo as well as directing movement.

12 A 2004 production of *The Master and Margarita*, adapted by Ed Kemp after the Bulgakov novel, for the Chichester Festival Theatre, directed by Steven Pimlott (1953–2007), a British theatre and opera director. Sam West played the lead character.

13 Toby is referring to a style of tackling scene changes that have a ludique aspect with objects being manipulated by actors in a heightened way and an ensemble working together closely to swirl in and out of a change of location.

14 *Tout bouge*, meaning 'everything moves', was a key phrase that underpinned Lecoq's pedagogy and was given to Toby Sedgwick as a 'commande', which is an individual stimulus to create your last piece of work as your departing performance from the school. No Lecoq graduate ever forgets their phrase, as it acts as a pedagogic push into the world of creation beyond the school.

7 SIÂN WILLIAMS

Inspire and encourage actors in their particular way of moving [2019][1]

Siân, how did you become a movement director?
It crept up on me, really, because I got asked to do movement for theatre directors who had seen the work of The Kosh – the company I started with Michael Merwitzer in 1982.[2] I was very fortunate to work with Greg Doran[3] at the RSC [Royal Shakespeare Company] on several productions, so I had an opportunity to develop an understanding of what was required of a movement person in theatre, and then even more so when I went to the Globe, where I worked with the director Tim Carroll several times.[4] We seemed to have an easy relationship with what was needed for the dances, and dance is quite a big requirement for the Globe, so this is the role I'm fulfilling now. There has been a fortunate, knock-on effect – you produce work and then somebody sees it and thinks they need somebody like that to do a production for them. In my very early days at the RSC, one of the actors asked me about how to get into movement directing – I thought, I don't know, because this happened totally by chance; I didn't really apply for the job. It's very elusive. I imagined it would just dry up as quickly as it came. Naturally, more people come along, and directors are hungry to have original thinking, so they get somebody else and that's it – there's no contract, other than the one you're doing for that six weeks, so it's a really strange, very privileged kind of moment that you have that role.

How do you describe what you do?
In terms of theatre work, my job most often is to fulfil a director's vision of the play and help to fulfil their vision of dance. They may have strong ideas but want somebody who is more specialized to draw physicality out. It is also my job to be

quite tentative and not start imposing great brushstrokes of ideas on it before I really understand what it is they want. My other job is to put actors at their ease, because dance sometimes makes hazard lights flash for actors – not all the time, but sometimes. It's important to make everybody feel that they're not going to be asked to do movement vocabulary that is in conflict with their idea of who they are in the play. I want to inspire and encourage actors in their particular way of moving. That's something they don't always think is going to be required, whereas I believe they will look great if they're moving from their heart. Albeit that I'm going to do it by going step-hop, step-hop, I still think it's got to feel connected to them. I suppose I'm there to promote the idea of going for things in physical terms. Movement specialists always see potential in drawing out more physical aspects of a play, and I feel it would be rich to offer that potential.

Do you mean movement that is outside of a 'dance'?
Yes. I don't know that I'm that persuasive in that direction. Directors are perfectly at liberty to resist your sense of that, because they've done all the work to have their overall vision of it, but I feel it's my duty to try and just get a little bit of an 'if you wanted. . .' notion in there. I firmly believe that even if some of the physical ideas that a movement person offers don't end up in the production itself, they're really informative, as exercises, improvisations. For example, getting a sense of the ensemble. It is a great way to remember that there are other moving bodies on stage and that physically, you're creating a huge impression, even though you might feel that the word is the most valuable communicator.

What are your skills and approaches?
Spontaneity is particularly important. The challenges of drama mean that the company come up against something in the rehearsal that they will want to unlock. It's very valuable to try something and not be afraid of coming up with something, an offer, in an instant. I've realized staying calm is also invaluable. You have to remain calm about discoveries that come up unexpectedly. For example, nobody told you there was a great big object just where you had planned a whole group of actors to be standing. The topography of the stage is really important, because you can imagine dynamics from early on and you can take it on board with your first plans. With experience, you don't get flustered by surprises in the same way. Another skill I've learned on the job is asking the right questions at the beginning of the project that will help me understand what it is that the director wants to achieve. When I first started working in theatre, I would accept all the information but realize afterwards that I should have asked this and this, to help me fulfil what they were wanting. I'm getting better at anticipating more, such as very basic things like, 'How many people do you want to be in that scene?' Sometimes I didn't used to ask and then found out that it would be significantly different to the plan I had made.

Could you expand on your movement skills?
A movement person like me can make something look authentic, so the actors do look like people from the 1950s doing a jive, for example, and they look at home as characters dancing in that way. I'm employed to make people feel comfortable with movements which might be alien to them. I have a firm grasp of coordinating numbers of people to dance to music, so that you can see it looks like a folk dance or it looks like a dance from a particular period. Social dance is a significant aspect of theatrical dance. I have a love of social dancing. I like watching how it works, the relaxed way that people can fall into a dance. I was lucky enough to do a training in which I had exposure to forms that I probably would have resisted if it wasn't on our curriculum, like Latin American dance.[5] In retrospect, I now feel at home with the detail of partner dances as I can help actors translate that. I'm really happy with working with music as well, and that's quite helpful not to feel alarmed by working out quick ways into a dance, that is, introductions. That very quick editing is something which actually I've learnt by having to do it, in the moment.

It's interesting, the parts I could have helped with I don't always get asked to do, like improvising. Maybe because it's an area that is dealt with by the director in their investigation of the play. But once you engage with a production for one reason, it can suddenly open up the door to other ways of contributing to staging, for example.

What other sorts of movement input do you find yourself doing?
Working at the Globe, where they did several productions that had all-male casts, with some of the men playing females, and I was asked to do sessions with them.[6] That work was very simple; I didn't particularly have a view on 'this is how you play a woman when you're a man', I was more interested in them considering the way that women might move in a way that was different to them. It was a laboratory of looking at each other and observing where the softness comes in a feminine movement. It didn't mean that they were impersonating women, but rather celebrating a kind of delicacy and femininity in themselves. I wasn't expecting to be asked to do that.

I've loved working with Mark Rylance as a performer because he really connects to movement and relishes dancing in the conventional sense of doing dances.[7] In the Globe production of *The Golden Ass*, for example, he was a man who turned into an ass, and he wanted an ass-like dance to do.[8] It was really productive working with such an amazing performer to explore ideas of a character-led dance. It has a lot to do with comedy within movement, actually; I've really enjoyed doing things like that over the years: in the Royal Shakespeare Theatre production of *The Winter's Tale*, for example, working on a comic scene where Autolycus is undressing the young shepherd by sleight of hand, getting him to give up all his worldly possessions without him realizing it.[9] That kind of physical dexterity where you've got to get clothing or props to work fluidly with the speech. Dramatically, the language has got to keep rolling, but in the course of that action you're working on very slick physical timing. So that is an area that movement people can make a big contribution.

What are you using from your background when you think about space?
When I am thinking spatially, I probably do use a lot of ballet references. I'm imagining that's because I saw a lot as a youngster, and I did a lot of ballet. Watching the way that ballet choreographers use bodies in space must have informed me. All the choreography of larger companies is an inspiration to me because of how they resolve geometric shapes – patterns that are constantly changing, and you realize that you don't remember how that happened, it just dissolved and suddenly they were all at the back, and when did that occur? I am also a complete sucker for 1950s musicals and Gene Kelly movies, in particular.[10] It's really captivating and thrilling to see this strange, stylized song and dance going on in a Manhattan Street. I really like storytelling in dance. Seeing a man in regular clothes, being able to look so elegant and light-footed, so that becomes a reference. I find fine art stimulating and visit galleries regularly. When I am imagining dancing, I can see everything moving from all sides, I'm imagining the actors like that and the way that movements are framed. When I first had an opportunity to work with movement on a film, I really enjoyed exploring all possibilities of locking off the frame and bringing movement in from all sides. There is a way of drawing movement into space that fascinates dancers, anyway: where they enter the space; the energy with which they enter and leave it – it's very much part of the thrill of dancing. That comes into your mind all the time, when you're trying to create something for other people. Even from your early dance training, when your ballet teacher is trying to teach you the concept of *croisé* and *ouverte*, you're in your square and I sometimes say it to the actors, 'You are in your square,' and then I turn around and see they are thinking, 'What the hell is she talking about?'[11] I think that there are imagined shapes all around us in dance. I don't think of it in quite the way that Laban specified, but I am inspired by the fact that he's got all these planes of movement.[12] Mine is much muddier I have to say, more like a swirling sketch. As a dancer you're always thinking that space is almost tactile, and it's rather a wonderful world we inhabit.

Do you think you've got a particular style?
In terms of the work on Shakespeare, my style is derived from what we understand existed for Shakespeare. When I'm asked to do work that is a homage to Elizabethan dance, it is on the whole very rhythmic and earthy. My natural gravitation tends towards peasant dancing with a lower centre of gravity, stompy, rustic. It seems to work well for actors; they feel earthed, connected and loosen up. My own devised work is often drawn from naturalism, but it's also quite cartoon-like. In theatre work, it is usual to be asked to produce social dances or a chorus of people that need to move in a certain way – movement of the crowd.

How do you set about preparing for work with a director?
I like to know if they've got thoughts about the physical side of a production early on. It can change, but following the changes can help me appreciate the development of the new direction.

    I read around the subject. If it's a play, I'm interested in the history and to get to know the play really well. It can happen that a director only realizes very late in the process that they need a dance, and then it's difficult to know much about it; in that case, you have to ask leading questions and offer something. You know there's something great about that instant response as well. My favourite way of working with my acrobatics mentor Johnny Hutch, when I'd be describing 'essence of this, and the something of that', he'd have a label for it and give you a taster.[13] There was a whole repertoire of work: a direct connection from music hall and circus from 'old-timers' with lots of knowledge. Maybe, sometimes that is what a director wants, someone who can come up with the goods for them in that way. With experience, I have come to relish both ends of the spectrum. By contrast, it can be good 'not to know' and to be asked to try to find it; when you experiment, you find the most wonderful rich vein that's coming from improvising with the actors, and they'll just draw on something inspirational in a moment and then you've got a really original idea.

What is important when you're working with actors?
I need to be prepared, and that doesn't mean I have to have it all worked out by any means, it's just I like to know enough. If it's going to be a dance to music or composed music, and quite understandably the composer hasn't yet composed the music, I like to ask them, 'Have you got a time signature in mind for that? Or even a tempo, a pulse?' and if not, 'can we try something and offer it to you?' Actors get unnerved if choreography changes drastically from session to session, so I always say, 'Look, we're just trying things out today and so don't hold on to any of this,' otherwise they invest a lot. Over time I have realized that some are so enthusiastic or anxious about dancing, they'll practise it in between rehearsals, and the next time you meet they'll say, 'I think I've got it.' I try to build on ideas from the previous session, so adjustments are easy to absorb and don't feel like big changes. It's that extraordinary thing where you can see that an actor can move just beautifully, when you ask them to step up on the right foot specifically, it throws them. I like to know enough to help them and ease them into the work and make them feel comfortable. It should be fun. Some people get brilliant results out of being quite challenging towards the actors, and I really admire that, but I find it very hard to work that way. I get better results just coaxing more and more out of them gradually, over time. Then you can start to say to people, 'You can extemporize,' because there are some people who are obviously much more familiar with moving and improvising. At the risk of it being potentially less fabulous choreography, it's important for the actors to look really at home with what they are doing. For the

most part, the dances are meant to be social dances that their characters would get up and do and know. I quite like that they look a little bit rough around the edges. Maybe directors are thinking, 'Why didn't we rehearse them better?' I like to draw on their own personality in the movement they are doing. Actors are wonderful at having their own quirky way of doing something. If they've got something to bring to it, it's great; you can make that happen in the piece as well. The way actors take it all on so thoroughly is why I enjoy working with them.

Can you describe the development of your process: before you start, in the rehearsal room, in the production week and on the first night?
I like to mull over it. It's valuable to let everything you see and do have some sort of connection. You let the notion of that play float in and out. It's a non-concrete way to savour, but that's definitely an important part of the preparation process. If movement ideas come to me, I like to think about that and start easing my way in. I really like that 'before' moment, because of the way that images pop into your head and you didn't really know you were thinking about it, and something suddenly offers itself up, and you think, 'Oh, I'll remember that.' It has taken me time to relax and not keep thinking, 'Oh, I've got to start writing loads of things down.' It's a really important time when you let ideas come and go, and then there is this moment when you realize, I can commit something to paper now, because lots of movements have formed in your head. Most people probably have a version of that when they're working on movement. I like to think about it when I'm doing my own practice, that's when I think about other people moving as well. Maybe there are little things along the way, like reading something significant, or going to see something that might have planted seeds. There's a crucial moment, when you put something down on the page, that you can go back to and think, I'm moving away from that, or I'm staying with that; again, like an anchor point to depart from or to stick with.

That first meeting with a director, when they sometimes speak very fast and you're scribbling just trying to get the information down, and then realize you didn't know that was all in the play: it's brilliant. That first meeting is really important. That's when I ask those critical questions that will help to take it on to another stage before I actually get into the rehearsal space. I like to sit in on a rehearsal, as it's really helpful to see the actors in action. If you only go to the meet-and-greet day, and you don't necessarily see them on the floor working, your first impression can mislead you as you think they're one thing and there turns out to be all sorts of other things that will make up that person's performance. It means that you don't underestimate what's possible with them. Some directors like you to be in a lot, and that's great, because it means that you can see the way that they are working the play as well, and that helps you feel that you're not making something that's completely away from the production.

I love the first session, because you haven't got to make the dance work, you've just got to get them all moving. With the second session I'm committing to it, rather than just dreaming about it. Now we are working on the dance officially, and when you come to do it you want at least another two of those sorts of sessions, but you know you don't necessarily have them. Then usually it is only one more session, where you're not quite finished yet but nearly 'there', and then the final session to get to the end and you steal other rehearsal moments to polish all of that. That seems to be the shape of my experience. When it gets to the technical week, I hope I don't have to make big changes, because the actors have so many other things to deal with. If the company know the dances well enough, adjustments or cuts are easy to make. It's that feeling that everybody's familiar enough for you to say, 'We're not doing that now,' and the actors are not thrown by that. I like to feel that I've brought them to a stage where they have ownership of the dance, and they can tell me something isn't working, and we can make a change quite easily. Then it's the same as notes that you'd give an actor to do with the play, to do with encouraging the performance of it, often a lot to do with extending it out to the audience, in anticipation of the first night where you really want it to be something that welcomes the audience in. The dances have so much power in that way, that they invite people in, but they will only do that if the performers are 'taking it out', so it's just reminding them about crossing their regard over to the audience. When they get that feedback from the audiences then you can really say, 'Do you see how it works?' We all appreciate the wonderful alchemy, and you start to let everything grow. Especially with dance, there is often such limited time to work on something which in some ways benefits from a bit of whittling. It's really important to see that certain moves may not be working and say, 'D'you know, actually I've made a mistake there ... should we try something else?', and find something that works on their bodies better. It's really interesting working with actors, because often you get really big guys, and you've made up some kind of twiddly little movement by yourself, something that works brilliantly on yourself, but you just need to find a translation of that for a bigger body and let them feel really good about it. I have found that really exciting, that way that you remould things; it's not that it has to change that much, but it's somehow letting them find their body shape in the steps. That's what those social dances would have been like – the people dancing them adapting them to make themselves feel great and look great doing them.

One of the best parts of working with acting companies is the diversity of ages and morphologies, and in these four or five sessions you have to put in a whole lifetime of habit.
I think that's very true. And you've got to feel really at home with the music, because the music is so important because dances often are interpreting strong elements in the music, so it is important that everybody feels really comfortable

with that as well. And sometimes the music is quite complicated; you've got to all find a common way of hearing that introduction. And then in tech we all go, 'Ah, there's not a trumpet there anymore,' because the composer has done something entirely different. All of those negotiations are really important – 'Hold hands everybody, this is the new version' – and what's great about that is it brings you all together.

And there's always one actor who knows when to start.
Yes, that's right … it's a good way to nominate a dance captain immediately!

How does the maintenance of work with the dance captain work?
I pop in to see how a show is going; if somebody's not well or has had an injury and then they've had to drop out of one of the big dances, I'll check on how we can refigure it. But the dance captains are also fantastic helping with things like that, and they keep the spirit going in the doing of it. What's great at the Globe is they make their fight calls and jig calls part of a warm-up – it's something that everybody is glad to come and take part in and you do the jig, which has everyone moving together before the show. It's good for morale.

How does working across genre, whether it's theatre genre or different mediums, affect what you do?
We came to film almost by lucky chance. I have found working with the editor fascinating, and very like choreography; very like the way I have found directors work in terms of editing moments, having an understanding of when that's enough of something, it's enough time to sustain a particular movement or a moment in a scene and move on. I think those crossovers are very interesting. I really like applying my sense of the physical to watching plays. I don't really follow a play if I don't follow it physically. If I didn't have that blessing of vision, I wouldn't have that to use, I'd have to draw on something else; but since I do, I'm watching carefully, and a lot of people do because I think the truth in movement is really important. Movement specialists always want to get to the nub of something physically, and I don't see why you can't do all sorts of experiments physically to find the answer to something. What is great is seeing how directors and movement specialists come together and end up collaborating over and over again. They start to form a relationship where those mediums cross over very intimately, and the production flourishes because of that.

It might be my one slightly contentious point about the creative dynamic between movement, composer and lighting designer. I don't know if other movement people have mentioned this, I've not really spoken to that many movement people, but with one I know well and in a very light-hearted way, we agree that there's a real hierarchy in theatre. The realm of lighting, set design and costume is up there with the director. And the movement person isn't up there in that kind of way. It is not to do with status, it's the fact that they're not included really early on and usually not involved in discussion about the concept of the production. And because you're not really 'in' on that stage, you have to make sure you understand the language that's been established and not tread on people's sensitivities at that point. It's often the job of a choreographer/ movement director to respond creatively to artistic decisions that are already made – that's the difference. You're asking people to interpret something physically, so it's a delicate thing. In some places, it is changing.

What do you think the future of the work of a movement director might be?
The immediate future will be that directors are more and more attracted to having a movement person doing more; they do find us appealing. I can see from lots of the productions that are being programmed now that are very exciting, that they are bringing choreographers in who have very distinctive approaches, they're bringing them in to work with them. I remember being in love with a production that Ballet Rambert did, *Cruel Garden* in the 1970s.[14] I loved that production, so I went several times, and I later read that it was quite a traumatic production period, perhaps because it was collaboration between Christopher Bruce, a choreographer, and Lindsay Kemp, a theatre director.[15] In the years ever since, I thought, I can bet it was two fantastic minds like that trying to find their common path, and they produced the most wonderful production, but I can really imagine that there were some difficult stages to get over. Although that's what the future will hold – it'll always be quite difficult to marry the two disciplines. What I think would be great, and what I can imagine happening, is that movement directors will emerge as directors of plays. I was thinking there are playwrights like Beckett and Chekhov, even Pinter, whose plays are really crying out for a focus on movement. The number of productions I've seen of *Waiting for Godot*, and I think you really need a good sense of physicality to do this, to steer people through this, so why not let a movement director have a go at that. For example, at the Globe, you get directors who've never worked with Shakespeare before being encouraged to direct and that's like another language, it's like another world that they're being asked to take on, and you have specialists to help support that – you could have somebody who had the skills of a theatre director to support you as a movement specialist. And there are enough performers around now who yearn for the opportunity to use a more studied physical language.

I see a balance coming: we call on specialists a lot, to do the song and do the dance and do the music. But drawing on Indian culture with their familiarity of all those areas; no dithering about whether or not to incorporate a song at that moment. I love that instinct, and if you thought, this should turn musical all of a sudden, stage it without fear, the more all those areas interweave; it would be the kind of the theatre I'd really love to see.

Notes

1 Siân Williams is a founder member of The Kosh dance theatre company. She has worked as a theatre choreographer for Shakespeare's Globe Theatre since 1999 and as Movement Director for the RSC and is a member of the Factory Theatre Company. She is an associate artist of Shakespeare's Globe. Movement and choreography productions include *Wolf Hall* (RSC, 2014); *Midsummer Night's Dream* (Royal Shakespeare Company, 2016); *Pride and Prejudice* (Regent's Park Open Air Theatre, 2012); *Café Chaos* (The Kosh, 2013); *The Mouse and His Child*, *The Merchant of Venice* (RSC, 2012); *Mother F* (Articulate Elbow, 2012); *Flash Mob Dance* (Mark Rylance's Pop Up Shakespeare, 2012); *The Glass Slipper* (Northern Stage, 2011); *Oh What A Lovely War* (Northern Stage, 2010); *The Snow Queen* (the Rose Theatre, Kingston, 2011); *You Can't Take It With You* (Royal Exchange, Manchester, 2011); *The Storeroom* (The Kosh, 2011); *Hamlet* (Globe, 2018); *Anne Boleyn* (Globe, 2012); *Henry V* (Globe, 2010); *The Taming of the Shrew* (Globe, 2003); *Richard III*, *Twelfth Night* (Shakespeare's Globe 2012 season); *Macbeth* (Globe, 2013); *A Midsummer Night's Dream* (Globe Education, 2012); *Adolph Hitler: My Part in His Downfall* (Rho Delta, 2009); *The Magic Flute* (Royal College of Music (RCM), 2009); *The Rake's Progress* (RCM, 2007). Direction includes productions for The Kosh, *The Handsomest Drowned Man* (Circus Space, 2006).

2 The Kosh is a dance and physical theatre company established in 1983 that was at its height during the 1980s and 1990s performing accessible, physically led works. Since 1997, the company has been producing documentary films with marginalized people, and it is undertaking a rural tour with a duet entitled *The Divided Self* in 2019.

3 Greg Doran is a British theatre director who became artistic director of the RSC in 2012. Williams directed the movement for Doran's productions of Shakespeare's *Macbeth* and *The Winter's Tale*, and for *Jubilee* by Peter Barnes.

4 Tim Carroll is a British theatre and opera director and founding member of the Factory Theatre Company. He has worked extensively at Shakespeare's Globe. In 2017, he was appointed Artistic Director of the Shaw Festival in Ontario, Canada. Shakespeare's Globe is a reconstruction of an Elizabethan theatre on the South Bank in London.

5 Williams trained from the age of eleven to eighteen in ballet at the Anna Christie School of Dance and then went on to the London College of Dance and Drama.

6 During its 2012 season, the Globe staged productions of *Richard III* and *Twelfth Night* with all-male casts.

7 Mark Rylance is an English actor and activist who was also the first artistic director of Shakespeare's Globe from 1995 to 2005.

8 A 2002 production of *The Golden Ass*, by Peter Oswald, directed by Tim Carroll.

9 A 2008 production of *The Winter's Tale*, by William Shakespeare, directed by John Dove.

10 Gene Kelly was a US actor, dancer and director. *Singin' in the Rain* (1952) is a musical comedy film. Here, Williams is referring to a musical number where Kelly is tap dancing with an umbrella through puddles of rain in a street.

11 *Ouvert* is a ballet term meaning 'open' and can refer to body position, alignment and limbs. *Effacé* and *croisé* are classical ballet terms for crossed leg positions (open and closed, respectively) on diagonals in relation to your personal square or kinesphere.

12 Rudolf von Laban was instrumental in describing space in relation to movement. He used a dimensional cross of three intersecting planes that pass through the centre of the human body, describing the cardinal directions: the sagittal – or wheel – plane, the door plane and the horizontal – or table – plane. He also developed the idea of the 'kinesphere', which might be most simply thought of as the reach of the body in all directions from the core to the peripheries. See Ewan with Sagovsky (2019: 36–9) for useful diagrams, as well as Chapter 1.

13 Johnny Hutch (1913–2006; born John Hutchinson) was a British acrobat whose long career involved performing and acting as an acrobatic consultant for a range of creative settings that included theatre, film and television.

14 Christopher Bruce and Lindsay Kemp co-directed *Cruel Garden* in 1977 for Ballet Rambert. It was revived in 1998. *Cruel Garden* is a dance piece about the poet and playwright Federico Garcia Lorca, set in a space evocative of a bull ring with music inspired by Spanish popular music. The original was filmed for BBC2. Available online: https://www.youtube.com/watch?v=duxtr1KFOfc (accessed 4 August 2019).

15 Lindsay Kemp (1938–2018) was a British dance teacher and movement artist who pursued ballet as a child and went on to study with Hilde Holger and Marcel Marceau. He became known for a flamboyant, queer approach to movement in a variety of forms – from pop to theatre. The author undertook a summer school with him in the 1980s and is indebted to his unforgettable use of imagery to ignite movement.

8   STRUAN LESLIE

Exchange of ideas relies on listening that is embodied [2018][1]

How would you describe what you do as a movement director?
I'm a collaborator within a creative team realizing the physical nature of the piece of work. That seems really broad, and that's because it is different in every project.

Can you trace your work history and what has led you to movement in theatre and opera?
Movement has always been there. A whole part of me *needs* to move. I've always been physically curious about other people. My journey begins with having a non-academic, non-analytical brain, and dance came about when I started doing community dance classes at home in Dundee with Royston Muldoom.[2] He was one of the first dance artist-in-residence in the community to be funded by the Scottish Arts Council.

Why did you decide to train as a dancer?
I was really inspired and encouraged by Royston, so my thoughts about choreography were really active. He made it clear that we could all make dances: we could all find a way of arranging movement. London Contemporary Dance School had just started doing auditions in Scotland in 1981, and in 1982, when I auditioned, I was accepted as a choreographer.

What did you learn at London Contemporary Dance School?
I learnt that my body was just not ready for the dance training they offered and actually wasn't made for it! I struggled with Graham technique, because it was designed by a woman on women's bodies.[3] The men who can do it have a real gift

for it. I became really frustrated wanting to be a dancer and not being chosen as a dancer. However, that changed with Viola Farber and Ernestine Stodelle, as I made a deep connection with both of these teachers and their movement and dance vocabulary.[4] Viola's teaching focused on economy of movement, a combination Cunningham technique[5] and ballet via Cecchetti[6] and an emphasis on musicality. And Ernestine taught the fundamentals of Humphrey's[7] technique of fall and recovery and a moving connection to breath that I found so difficult in the Graham technique. Another of my teachers was Nina Fonaroff, who led choreography classes with exercises and exploration.[8] She was the first person to make a connection between breath, movement and creativity, for me. Her classes were really important, as the exercises were really clear. She also introduced movements in art, such as abstract expressionism and the ideas of artists like Kandinsky, Klee and Miro. By looking at their paintings, I learnt to see structure, form, place, sense of space and an understanding of two-dimensional representation of movement or movement ideas. She actually began the process of me being able to see.

Can you expand on what you are seeing?
Seeing and reading are fundamental – whether it is in relation to the process of making choices about your own work or as a dramaturg to the work of others. It is not only about aesthetics; it also about specificity and rigour. We can only make those choices with information. Ideas of seeing and legibility are key to my work, as well as to the processes involved in all my work. An example might be understanding how the page works and how that relates to the stage. I have always taken for granted that, in the West, we look from left to right: as an audience member, we read the stage as we read the page. In our culture, if you enter somebody stage left, we have to physically work to get our head there. I learned that. As a result, I am able to freely place movement in space, such as the vertical arrangements of circus performers or the horizontal of a Greek chorus or the sectional interaction of an orchestra.

What specifically caused your shift towards theatre?
At the time, dance felt like it was isolated as a form. I was more interested in collaborating and had a growing sense that movement needed to come from somewhere – that movement needed something deeper as a stimulus. I was developing my collaborative capacities, which was combined with realizing and connecting to the work I had absorbed up to that point.

How did your contemporary dance background prepare you to work in other forms, for example in musicals?
Directly, it was the connection to music and the opportunity to explore making 'steps to music'. And musicals were on in our house growing up – Rodgers and Hammerstein era, mostly. And learning about the work of the great dancers

and, in particular, the men – Kelly, Astaire, Fosse, Kidd – and them also being choreographers.[9] So, I had always watched musicals on stage and in the movies. I was involved in the musical society at home and the Gang Show where you've got 120 scouts from the ages of eight to sixty in a show.[10] When it came to musicals I was prepared, because I knew how large groups of people are directed and managed from the inside out.

This then touches on *chorus* work that is so woven into my work and life. All these elements combined to form my preparation for what is choreography and musical staging when working in musicals.

What elements of your training were you developing?
Belinda Quirey had taught me historical dance at London Contemporary. She taught me minuets and pavanes in the early 1980s, and there's barely a dancer in the contemporary culture of that time who hadn't been taught by Belinda at some point.[11] Then, you take that information that you get from her and you move elements of it in to something else.

And how do you move it on to 'something else'?
By gathering the information from collaborators and teachers. So, on *Casanova* – a television series that I worked on – the costume brief was '1761 meets Vivienne Westwood', so that was what I did with the choreography.[12] I was combining historical dance ideas and steps from 1761 with contemporary movement to reflect the two periods. I turned the gestures of the period dance into a sexual thing, so that all the hand gestures were related to the genitals. There was a point where the choreography mimics masturbation, and choices like that emerge out of the character's biography – that all came out of the research about Casanova.

Can you explore that project a little bit more in terms of movement and actors?
It's important to create an environment in which people feel enabled, empowered, valued, and to work at that the whole time with actors and dancers. As a choreographer, it was very much about teaching the actors to move, and do these steps, and using dancers to balance the movement quality. You had performers with a whole range of processes, and the job is to blend it so within the dance there was a kind of *élan*, *éclat*. We had the whole breadth of a society embodied in the movement and an example of how everyone can be in the same situation together.

When an actor moves with intention, there is an impulse behind it. This is legible to the audience, who then have access to the material. Movement intentions lead my process, and that means that the choreographer in me and the movement director in me can work differently with actors and dancers. My aim is to be drawing the best from each and enabling each to communicate the same ideas. In this production, the actors and dancers working together in the same scene were existing in the same world. My work was to activate an inhabited dance and choreography that is specific to time, space and situation and in this case, a punk version of an eighteenth-century dance.

Can we move on to talk about the influence of Contact Improvisation of your work?
In 1986, I studied with Bob Rease, who was part of the US West Coast, contact-improvising movement in an all-male ensemble called *Mangrove* – very much part of the queer subculture in San Francisco at the time.[13] Contact Improvisation [CI] was at the time a new and experimental form.[14] My studies in Contact Improvisation were further developed in the United States with Nancy Stark Smith and Steve Paxton.[15] CI is an open-source form that relies on the practitioners sharing the work between them and thereby developing it.

Its influence is important to my way of working now because it is a movement style that has not been codified and has 'no failure' in the form. It presents an open structure that results in an environment of learning and that through movement we are able to create communities regardless of age or abilities. This is essential for the rehearsal room; the ideas of spherical space and a 360-degree connection to it through activation of the awareness of our skin.

CI's influence can be seen in many areas of my work, from architecture and urban design to developing training with actors and dancers, thinking about text and developing a sense of place/space as the stimulus for creation and to establish the same for productions of plays or devised work. It has a relationship for me to the work on Stanislavski and other theatre techniques where the exchange of ideas relies on listening that is embodied.

Bob's work also introduced me to the idea of the floor being the first partner in this work, and he did that through walking, which is now one of the fundamentals of my practice.

It is also worth saying that Bob was gay, and I made a really strong connection with him: partly through his sexuality, partly because as a young gay man I became politically more aware at that time. The politics of what it was to be gay was so potent in the mid-to-late 1980s with Clause 28 and AIDS.[16] I realized that my queerness put me outside the norm and that something else was happening creatively for me.

What was that?
Well, you're outside in memory; you're outside looking in. But I found myself searching for a language that allowed me to communicate about my identity. And growing up, as a gay boy, that vocabulary wasn't necessarily available to me. Something else, physically, was happening because of my sexuality; it feels like my body is allowed to be part of me, throughout my whole life, as opposed to just being a bit of my life. It's about identity. When I'm working on other people's shows, it allows me to be as open as I can to what I'm seeing. So that, in terms of not just my sexuality but also my gender awareness, I have a flexibility around what

I'm able to do and develop in people who are not the same gender as me. And also, to let people who are the same gender as me to broaden their own possibilities.

When did you start working with Neil Bartlett?
We did *Oliver Twist* in 2004, although I had known about his work since the mid-1980s and the centrality of the body and its queerness in his work.[17] It was also interesting as a young gay man watching a gay man be so clear about his sexuality in performance and recognize the body as political.

He does have a visual imagination. What happened in your collaboration in terms of movement?
He does, but I'd call it a physical imagination. My job was to create the visceral communication of the body in the space, such as realizing Artful Dodger's desperate running through the streets of London on Rae Smith's set and *point fixe* of the ensemble in the choric passages.[18] These are examples of the telling the story through the body.

What has prepared you to work with actors on movement?
All the work we have talked about has enabled that work: it's all adding up to a sense of the body in space, in relation to others – this then creating a process of preparation which enables the actor to have the body 'with' them. And really importantly, I have worked in a wide range of contexts as a teacher – with those movers who have other movement expertise such as PE [physical education] teachers and non-movers as well.

And how does that translate to the process with actors?
Teaching? Regularly preparing and facilitating this work with others. Developing a language that enables me to communicate movement and embodied ideas equipped me to teach fundamental skills. I had to find a vocabulary, and that helped me to clarify how to speak to actors.

How do you engage with their inner processes?
Contact Improvisation led me to understand the idea of physical dialogue – that the dialogue was between the performers, and between the performers and the audience. In both contexts, the actor responds in a particular manner to someone else. It's all about responding. And when you're trained highly enough you do that without thinking – it bypasses the cerebral process because it becomes part of the physical, non-conscious.

Do you use any Contact Improvisation in your theatre work directly?
If I do it is *touch* work between the performers that builds relationships akin to the ones of the characters within the play. I also bring in skeletal work and

anatomical work, asking the actor to 'just move off that touch'. That is to get them moving in relation to *actual* touch and also to the idea of responding to perceived touch between character across space. You can make contact in response to someone spatially as well as through direct contact. I could do Contact Improvisation on the opposite sides of the room. It's also a solo form. I really feel that your first partner is the floor and can be the room you find yourself in or imagine yourself to be in.

How does this translate to your work on a production?
Well, for example, Katie [Mitchell] and I worked together for fifteen years on over thirty productions.[19] I was responding in order to realize the physical world of the productions. As we came to know each other and the process well enough, I would be the one to prepare and start the day. With the actors, it was to bring a specificity – so they could be ready to be in *this world* in the play and *this process* with *this director*. I would begin by sensitizing the actors to their physicality, often through directed exercises using touch and building anatomical knowledge and 360-degree awareness. That then threads all the way through to performance preparation. As we often collaborated with the same actors, it became a vocabulary that we could return to and share with new actors as they joined the group.

This work then developed in collaboration with the designer Vicki Mortimer.[20] The design was always architecturally specific, and part of the early rehearsal process was to help to define the world beyond the set. What was through each door, rooms, outdoor space? I would gather materials for improvisations for the subsequent daily preparation – exploring the physical differences between the architectural forms and imaginative landscapes. In all of our shows there was an interplay between a three-dimensional space inside a fourth-wall design. For example, the chorus arriving at Agamemnon's headquarters in *Iphigenia* had to be very clear what the fourth wall looks like from the inside the room.[21] They had also arrived into this space from being outdoors, having been in the heat and sunshine watching the Greek heroes working out on the beach. The body has to contain heat and excitement as it arrives into the cool neoclassical interior. The audience can read this physical text.

How did the social dance-inspired movement language for **Iphigenia on Aulis** *come about?*
In preparation, we talked about which social dance forms to use, and Katie would ask, 'Is it tango?' and I'd say, 'No, tango is too angular, too on the front foot,' and actually difficult to do for a woman, without her man there. It was instinctive to go, 'It's foxtrot,' and I went off and relearnt it, because I had used it before, in a contemporary American play at the Donmar Warehouse.

What was the quality of the foxtrot that appealed to you?
The asymmetry of it. Like all ballroom dancing, but particularly with a foxtrot, there's a great control about it. And, in some ways, more than any other ballroom dance, it happens between the dancers, and by that I mean if you take a tango, there's lots of the movement going out into the space, you know, ochos, or leg-hooks.[22] They're flourishing out into the space, whereas the foxtrot is not very showy: it has that little hover with the feet underneath you, and the toe is leading.

And how did the actors approach that process?
I taught them it, and then we played with it. And they made it their own, and we developed it and played with it through different ideas, and then it became clear that it was a motif that would occur throughout the piece. But it was very much done in the rehearsal room. I did very little preparation on it before I had the bodies of the seven women in front of me. And also, I taught it to the whole company, and it became the means by which the whole company became a unit; though in the production it was performed without partners, thereby evoking the women's absent husbands. In this way, I am using the same fundamentals of touch and impulse as I had done in Contact Improvisation as a tool to develop the actor's movement language and as the basis for communication in the production between the actors, and between them and the audience.

How do you move from the physical building blocks to actually applying it?
Katie and I would talk for a long time about the bridges between movement work and the text. Sometimes it was very explicitly building blocks like in *Iphigenia*, and sometimes it's just general. There had to be a seamless progression. I developed a number of activities and exercises – such as grounding work, extension, control and transfer of weight, sense of place/space. These are then applied to establish a clear architectural and environmental sense of place. Katie would then do improvisation exercises, and then we'd do a scene.

Production-specific movement responds to the dimension, size, structure, décor [and] period of the building. Iphigenia was set in the 1940s. It had a very specific physical etiquette. And you can talk about it all you like in the rehearsal room, but until the actors put on their 1940s costume, where suddenly a lady's suit has four beautiful bits of darting on the back and a centre seam that you feel on your back, so you hold yourself differently. As a result, it's important to have these elements in the rehearsal room.

Do you feel that you're the holder of all of those elements around the body?
The holder of it in this process? No, I think we share it between us and in collaboration with Vicki Mortimer the designer, and the actors. As humans, we

exist within an environment, so when we walk into the space, we all have a place to exist within that environment – a kind of ecosystem.

And that collaboration is through lots of conversation?
This is something deep-seated; it's true collaboration.

I can see that movement was very integrated.
I have always said that my work should be invisible. Yet there needs to be some level of understanding of that work as being integrated and having an influence or a force within creative partnerships.

I completely agree. How do you prepare for a production?
I often read the script backwards. Literally, I start on the last page and then I'll read the second to last page and so on. I am very instinctive. Sometimes I'll do lists of all the movement words in the script. I'll go through to find the major themes. I am interested in rhythmic structures of language. If it is Shakespeare, I'll look at the structuring of the play and the language to get a sense of the rhythm of people, such as shifts from prose to verse. I often walk 'with' the text. This work utilizes ideas inspired by Cicely Berry's exercises for embodying aspects of the text, from structure to argument.[23] We had worked together at the RSC [Royal Shakespeare Company] prior to my post there. I also try to be specific about locations in the play, so may draw a map. Once I have taken that script and pulled out images and ideas, I will have early meetings with the director and the designer to talk about what we're doing – once we've met and exchanged ideas, we'll continue to exchange ideas until we hit the rehearsal room.

And what is that initial exchange with the director based on?
On the text and impressions, because in some contemporary plays there isn't very much to research, as such. But with a Greek text, for example, I will have done research and work on the Greeks.

And then how do you start with a company?
Movement is often about building ensemble and getting a connection between the performers. Developing a kind of playfulness means that we can have an open process; we can discover and keep exploring the physical life of the work together. I always start with walking, because everybody does it and it is a focusing exercise for me, too.[24] Walking is a great cleanser. My job as a movement director is to make people feel empowered and valued.

We haven't touched upon your work in in opera.
When you're in opera, it's dictated by the music. For example, I was able to ask a chorus recently, 'Can you move with the phrase, as opposed to the individual

word, the individual textual definition?' Immediately, there was a different response. Because they're musicians, my relationship with them is more fruitful when I relate to them with a musical language.

What's interesting about the potential of all of those bodies? The chorus in opera, for example?
Identifying a mass of bodies in space as individuals is essential. I know the chorus's names on day one. It's like at a concert, a football stadium, Trafalgar Square and protests – to see those numbers of people is to be elated by it. And not always elated in a positive way, but also be scared of it, to recognize yourself as part of that herding animal. It's primal. I remember the first time I went to one of the big Native American dance events in Colorado and seeing hundreds of people dancing – individuals bound by situation and purpose. The same is also true of the body in many styles of performance.

And the fantastic thing about a chorus is that the audience doesn't consciously know it, but it completely connects with this community that reflects them on stage. Choruses also shift the space. They change the room – they become 'space' shifters. That's the interesting thing about movement work – ensuring that they are hearing, seeing and experiencing the truth through their physicality. We have this decoder inside our bodies that tell us whether someone's physicality is true or matches what they're saying. We read them as text.

That is also the case in psychological realism as well, when you're working on Chekhov or Ibsen or Strindberg, for example; a good Chekhov is good physical theatre – it's all there, together, enhancing what's going on.

How do you see movement direction evolving?
There is still work to be done in all areas of training and creating. I think as a distinct job it might die out for me. Application of those skills is becoming more broadly recognized, though there are still a lot of directors out there who would benefit from the skills we bring to the room to balance the sometimes static nature of theatre making.

Notes

1 This interview emerged out of a series of conversations held in London in 2018 and 2019.
   Struan Leslie is a director, movement director and choreographer. He was Head of Movement at the Royal Shakespeare Company from 2009 to 2014, where his movement direction included *Macbeth* (2011) and *As You Like* (2009) It, directed by Michael Boyd; *Twelfth Night* (2009) and *Morte d'Arthur* (2011), directed by Gregory

Doran; and *Life of Galileo* (2013), directed by Roxana Silbert. He also devised and directed *Song of Songs* (2012) as part of the King James Bible Season. Other work includes directing and choreographing *Illuminations* (Aldeburgh Music Festival, 2016); *Guys and Dolls* (Theatre Bielefeld, Germany, 2008); movement direction on James MacMillan's opera *The Sacrifice* (Welsh National Opera, 2007) and *Much Ado About Nothing* (National Theatre, 2007); *Women of Troy* (National Theatre, 2007); *Tale Of Two* Cities (National Theatre, 2014); *The Hook* (Royal Derngate, Northampton and national tour, 2015). He has also worked at the Teatro Piccolo, Milan; at the American Repertory Theatre and Berkeley Repertory Theatre, United States; and at Welsh National Opera and English National Opera. Film and television credits include *Casanova* (BBC, 2005), the remake of *Sleuth* (2010) and *Babs* (BBC, 2017). Leslie co-devised and choreographed *Everybody Loves a Winner* with Neil Bartlett for the Manchester International Festival (2009) and was the director of Edinburgh's Hogmanay Street Party 2017 and 2018.

2 Royston Muldoom OBE (born 1943) is an English choreographer who studied under the auspices of Hilde Holger in the 1960s in London. In the early 1980s he was dance artist-in-residence in Fife and Tayside. He founded Scottish Dance Theatre in 1986, a dance company that mixed professional and community dancers in creative collaboration, based in Dundee. His career spans many decades of activism and transformation through participatory dance events. The documentary film *Rhythm is It!* (2004) tracks the collaboration between conductor Sir Simon Rattle and Muldoom where his philosophy of transformation, 'You can change your life in a dance class', is clearly articulated in his work with 250 young Berliners dancing in Stravinsky's *Rite of Spring*.

3 See Chapter 5.

4 Viola Farber (1931–98) was a German-born American dancer, teacher, choreographer and pianist. She was a key performer in Merce Cunningham's company. In 1968, she left to form her own dance company. She became artistic director of the Centre National de la Danse Contemporaine in Angers, France, from 1981 to 1983. From 1984 to 1987, she was part of the teaching faculty of the London School of Contemporary Dance. In 1988, she took up a post as Director of Dance at Sarah Lawrence College, NY, United States.

Ernestine Stodelle (1912–2008) was an American dancer, writer and teacher. In 1929, she joined Doris Humphrey company as a dancer. She was frequently to help dance academics reconstruct works by Humphrey such as *The Shakers* (1931) and *Water Study* (1928). She often taught out of the techniques developed by Humphrey. She also authored *Deep Song: The Dance Story of Martha Graham* (1984).

5 See Chapter 5.

6 Italian dance teacher and dancer Enrico Cecchetti (1850–1928) was the creator of the Cecchetti method – an enduring and influential ballet training technique. He taught many renowned dancers including Olga Preobrajenska, Tamara Karsavina and Vaslav Nijinsky. From 1910 to 1918, Cecchetti was the lead teacher of Serge Diaghilev's Ballets Russes but left to tour with his pupil, Anna Pavlova. In 1918, he and his wife opened a school in London where he was to influence Alicia Markova, George Balanchine and Serge Lifar. Many of his students later taught the Cecchetti method, including Ninette de Valois and Marie Rambert (see Chapter 1). From 1925, he directed the ballet school at La Scala, Italy. Cecchetti 'had a method of training where every day of the week nothing was left untouched. … It

was all meticulously worked out, and therefore trained the dancer to be totally in control, co-ordinated and in time with the music', suggests Ursula Hageli, Royal Ballet Mistress. See *Ballet Evolved – Enrico Cecchetti 1850-1928*, Royal Opera House Insights, 17 June 2014 (https://www.youtube.com/watch?v=mG1WuZViibU [accessed 28 March 2020]). In this Royal Opera House Insight, the reader can watch an adage demonstrated by Royal Ballet dancer Nicol Edmonds as an example of Cecchetti's training with an emphasis on flow and effortlessness in performance underpinned by exactitude of technique.

7   Doris Humphrey (1895–1958) was an American dancer and choreographer, and is considered a key figure in the emergence of Modern Dance in America in the 1920s and one of the 'Four Pioneers' (Martha Graham, Hanya Holm and Charles Weidman). Humphrey, like her contemporary Martha Graham, sought a language for emotional expression within dance or moving 'from the inside out' (Au 1988: 125). She was less interested, however, in dance as an act of self-expression but rather as an expression of an idea. Her works frequently explored relationships between an individual and a group. After eleven years with the Denishawn Company, Humphrey left in 1928 and created dance works such as the *Colour Harmony* and *Water Study* (1928) and *Drama of Motion* (1930), progressively abandoning music in favour of phrasing created by breath and exploring underlying themes of the natural world. Her famous work of 1931, *The Shakers*, was inspired by the rituals and gender segregation of the Christian communities of Shakers. She developed a dance technique of fall and recovery or the 'arc between two deaths' (Au 1988: 120), which navigates the extremes of full release into gravity and to the regaining of stability at the other end. She was to influence her pupil José Limón (1908–72), who developed his own incarnation of fall and recovery. Humphrey authored *The Art of Making Dances* (1958) which lays out her thoughts on the craft of choreography. Her list of common mistakes has been subsequently challenged but can offer the movement director food for thought and debate:

> Symmetry is lifeless
> Two-dimensional design is lifeless
> The eye is faster than the ear [this has been since disproved, the ear is faster than the eye]
> Movement looks slower and weaker on the stage
> All dances are too long
> A good ending is forty percent of the dance
> Monotony is fatal; look for contrasts
> Don't be a slave to, or a mutilator of, the music
> Don't intellectualize; motivate the movement
> Don't leave the ending to the end.
>
> (Humphrey 2002: 229).

8   Nina Fonaroff (1914–2003) was a choreographer and teacher from the United States and a Martha Graham Company dancer (1936–46) – see Chapter 5.

9   Gene Kelly, Fred Astaire, Bob Fosse and Michael Kidd are all American dancers who between them have worked across musicals on stage and screen as performers and choreographers.

10 Gang Shows are musical and dance revues mounted by Guides and Scouts organizations, with large casts of boys and girls.

11   See Chapter 3 for Jane Gibson, Chapter 4 for Sue Lefton, and Chapter 5 for Kate Flatt, all of whom were also taught by Belinda Quirey.

12   *Casanova* was a BBC television series (2005).

13   Mangrove was a performance ensemble based in San Francisco, California, who performed intensively in the five years up to 1980 and taught Contact Improvisation (Novack 1990: 98).

14   Contact Improvisation was developed and disseminated by Nancy Stark Smith and Steve Paxton.

15   Nancy Stark Smith (born 1952) is an American dancer, writer and teacher. Before joining Steve Paxton in 1972 for the earliest performed contact dances, she had trained as a gymnast and athlete. She is one of the founders of the dance journal *Contact Quarterly* and continues to lead the field in thinking about and practicing Contact Improvisation. In the film *The Poetics of Touch*, by Pozzoli and Siciliani (2013), Stark Smith highlights the novelty of this way of dancing in the '70s, redefining the use of weight bearing, and touch in movement dialogues that were neither a social form nor combative/martial in dynamic. Looking back to the early days, Paxton recollects that 'mutuality' was 'inherent in the dance in the way that we defined it ... there was to be a mutual listening to the movement'. He continues, 'There was to be the creation of a third entity in the dance, which was the mutual movement paths and timing and all of that. That's the way it was defined. So, what we were doing was essentially defining power as not applicable' (Paxton 2018: 37–8).

16   Clause 28, as it was commonly known, was Section 28 of the Local Government Act 1988, a highly contentious piece of legislation introduced by the Conservative government, which banned local authorities from 'promoting' homosexuality, in particular in British schools. Margaret Thatcher, prime minister at the time, is remembered for her homophobic views. Section 28 was repealed in Scotland in 2001 and in the rest of the UK in 2003. In 2009, David Cameron, then leader of the Conservative Party, apologized for Section 28, calling it a 'mistake'.

17   Neil Bartlett OBE (1958) is a British director, writer and performer. Leslie is referring to a 2004 production of *Oliver*, adapted and directed by Neil Bartlett and designed by Rae Smith, for the Lyric Hammersmith and UK tour.

18   *Point fixe* is a term that originates in mime technique but was repurposed by Jacques Lecoq. Lecoq defines several characteristics of the fixed point in his 'laws of motion': '5. There is no motion without a fixed point; 6. Motion highlights the fixed point; 7. The fixed point, too is in motion' (Lecoq et al. 2000: 98).

19   Katie Mitchell (born 1964) is a British theatre and opera director. Also see Kate Flatt, Chapter 5.

20   Vicki Mortimer is a notable British theatre designer who works across theatre and opera.

21   *Iphigenia at Aulis* by Euripides, translated by Don Taylor, directed by Katie Mitchell for Abbey Theatre, Dublin (2003); subsequently staged at the National Theatre, London in 2004.

22   'Ocho' is a tango dance term used to describe a set of moves comprising steps and pivots in a figure-of-eight pattern for the follower.

23   Cicely Berry (1926–2018) was a world-renowned British voice practitioner who shaped the field of actor voice on stage and voice teaching in the UK. She trained

at Central School of Speech and Drama (1943–6) and then later taught there, overlapping with Litz Pisk (see Chapter 1). In 1969, Berry started her lifelong journey with voice work at the RSC as company voice director. She authored *The Actor and the Text* (1987), a classic text for teachers and actors alike. In 2016, Berry was still very much part of the life of the company, asking, 'How do we make the language of Shakespeare sound as it is being spoken for now and honour all the sound and rhythm in the text that is integral to the meaning?' (Berry, unpublished conversation with author, 2016).

24 Leslie explained the origins of walking as being a melding of, among other elements, Rease's practice, reading Chatwin's *The Songlines* (where he posits an equation, in which you walk as a Sufi until the point where you are no longer the wayfarer but you become the way), and Julia Cameron's the *Artist's Way*, where she suggests that you should walk for fifteen minutes a day to develop you 'Imagic-nation'. These sit alongside Leslie's own passion for long walks in the countryside, wherever in the world he finds himself.

9   ELLEN KANE

It felt like a really good collaboration with the actors as they felt so rooted inside it – it was very home-grown [2018][1]

Would you mind describing what you do?
I have come through quite a varied route. I began as a contemporary dancer. I then became associate choreographer to Peter Darling [Chapter 10] and we then moved into a co-choreographing realm. And more recently, I've gone off in my own direction: within that I've done a couple of movement directing jobs to understand my own process a little bit more, and musical staging too. I am also very much excited by, and interested in, choreographing big dance numbers. I would like to able to be functional in all of those things, really. So, I'm not sure what I would call myself. Choreographer, movement director, musical staging by … any of those will work a treat.

I understand that navigation – feeling your way through what a job is and what's required.
That's exactly right. What I enjoy most is looking at fundamentally what kind of movement the show needs to drive. I've learnt to not paste anything on top of something where it doesn't feel like it really has roots to live properly. That is an important factor in describing what I do on each job, what my function in that job is, because if a show doesn't need choreography, even if it's labelled a musical then I won't put that in. I would much rather tell the story through a conceptual idea of how they would move in space and relate to each other; I would physically represent that rather than to try and load dancing in there.

Could you talk about why you made that transition from training as a contemporary dancer – which takes you, potentially, down one route – to working in theatre and musical theatre in a very different role?
Well, I started really late, so I didn't start training until I was sixteen, and I trained at Lewisham College, which was a passionate place full of people who were very hungry but came to things very late.² I was trained in isolation technique and contemporary dance and ballet.³ I then got a scholarship to London Studio Centre and so I was trained in all sorts of areas, but my passion was always contemporary dance.⁴ Once I left, I then worked in very small companies and ended up dancing for Richard Alston Company.⁵ As much as I loved him and the company, I found that I'd lost the very passion that I had always had, and it had become a very theoretical practice in a very strange way. Even though I was having to physically do it, I was completely analytical about my process of dancing and so I left and started teaching at The Place.⁶ Then, by coincidence, Peter Darling was looking for an associate for *Billy Elliot*, and that was how I started working with him.⁷ At that time, I had no idea about musicals, I had no idea about the structure; I had no knowledge – it was like learning a language. That really was my transition. Of course, I count myself as very fortunate, as I believe Peter to be one of the most skilled theatre makers that I've ever come across. And so, learning and growing just kept going. That was how I ended up transitioning from a world that was very much about contemporary dance and company life to being thrown into the musical theatre world. And actually, it was a brilliant time because it was like starting over, and my skill at that time was exactly what was needed for that sort of a musical – working with children and classical technique. Having the right complementary skills to Peter was incredibly rare.

And how would you describe that skill?
My skill at that point? Well, I was a neoclassical dancer, but I'm also trained to teach isolation technique, so before I met Peter and before I'd gone into Richard's company, I used to tour to all the RAD international teaching schools to teach isolation technique and it's always been very fun.⁸ I used to dance for a company called Jazz Xchange, which was very rhythmic and fundamentally about dance and passion.⁹ My skill, in terms of what was needed then, was knowledge of how to teach children, because I came to dance so late myself, and I had to learn as an adult. This meant that my learning involved 'telling' my body at that late age, and that gave me so many skills. I was able to pass that on to the children. I had enough classical ability to teach children who really had very little experience with that technique. You can't underestimate how complex the material [in *Billy Elliot*] was for these children, for example, how to execute standing on one leg. Due to starting so late, I've had to analyse it and analyse it and analyse it – so I could help

them. I've always had a kind of mathematical brain. Peter doesn't – he's not really a 'rememberer' of things – and so my brain absolutely does that. I can remember steps and counts for all the shows. It seemed like it was a 'fitting' that was almost meant to be.

How do you prepare for a show?
Now?

Yes.
It depends. If it's a musical, I read the script a lot, and then I tend to ask myself a series of questions: what role does the movement, or the dance, have within the play or within the piece? And then inside that, answering that question, I would go through each musical number and look at the characters. And this I've learnt from people, which is a really clear way of looking at things, that you analyse the objective. What does the character want in that scene? Where is it located? What does the location do to the characters? What is the A and how do we get to B? And then all of those structural things: how to split the song up so that you are building to deliver the end. I study the script/score like that really, and a lot of the time, depending on the piece, I break it down like a scene. So that you're working out the action, the objective, the character relationships and the narrative that you're aiming to tell.

What about the music within that?
The music of course is key, and if you are lucky enough to work with brilliant people inevitably you don't really question the music because they've already asked those questions themselves. Therefore, what I do is ask how I best enhance the story that's needing to be told from the characters and highlight the qualities in the music that are obviously *there* to be highlighted.

How do you prepare ahead of time? What do you make in the rehearsal room?
When I worked with Peter, we used to prepare everything, because the projects were always so big. From an outside point of view, you'd think there's a huge amount of rehearsal time, but on those juggernaut musicals there really is not that much time. It really depends on skill levels. There are incredible gifts to be had inside the musical theatre realm – for example, some people are incredible singers, and amazing actors, but can be actually quite fearful of movement. To create those big sequences, if you haven't got a vocabulary ready to present, it is actually quite frightening for them. I try to prepare the structure ahead of time so it will guide me through the storytelling. Then everything else that might happen in the rehearsal room can be an addition to the structure underneath. Then I know that the story is being covered. And depending on the people you're going to use,

if they're confident movers I'd maybe wait until I come into the room. However, if they're less confident I might go, 'actually this is the vocabulary', so you can at least give that to them to adapt and feel confident.

Can you talk about working with actors, dancers and directors? How would you work with an actor?
I can't really comment in terms of a straight play as I haven't done one, so for me that would be a new experience. I haven't done movement direction within a play so it's hard for me to comment on that. I would say the project I've recently done is the closest to working with people who fundamentally would call themselves actor-singers. It was brilliant, because it made me question myself and have a whole, almost project-worth of information in order to explain why I was asking them to do certain things. So, in terms of the actor, I guess we sat a lot, and I would go through the song with them. I would explain how I saw it and ask how they saw it, explain what I thought the movement was meant to do within the whole piece and how it pertained to that specific song. I talked to them about their relationship within it, their relationship within the space. I gave them a huge amount of understanding of how I saw it and I broke it down into sections, so it's not a generic wash. So that would be for the actor, and I felt that was very successful because it was really empowering for them.

So that they have a voice within it –
They have a voice, and actually it was more a communal way of working; it was a real collaboration, even though I had a very clear initial idea which I would say probably stayed pretty much as I thought it would be, it felt like a really good collaboration with the actors as they felt so rooted inside it – it was very home-grown. So that was the actor.

The dancer, that's interesting, as it's a really different set of skills. How you approach a dancer is so different. The questions you are asked by actors inform actually, I think as a practitioner, how much work you have to do in order to approach the work, so in terms of evolving – it's brilliant. On a dancer front, what's interesting is that we were trained never really to ask questions, or I was trained never to ask questions, you just 'do' it. So, intention … it didn't really work like that. What's fascinating is on the bigger shows, like on *Charlie*, on *Billy* and on *Matilda*, what has been incredible to do is to be able to work with incredibly talented dancers, some *mover* people, and to find a universal language that everybody can tap into and everybody can somehow be challenged by.[10] It's actually very different: you could come into a room full of dancers and you can teach them an audition sequence very quickly. But if you try to do that process with a group of actor/movers who might also be very capable, if you approach it in the same way it will be a catastrophe – you have to know how to feed the mind and I love that.

You like having the mix?
I really do, and it's valuable for us all to be surrounded by people who are different.

How do you work with a director?
Well, directors are all different, aren't they? Some directors are very much, 'You get on and do what you're doing,' and other directors are much more hands-on. The last show I did the director was really hands-on and wanted to talk about his concept right from the beginning and talk about all of the numbers, the ideas and how that was really going to work. It felt quite odd, because I'm used to doing that process but in a less collaborative way. Usually it's *you* who has to know what you're doing, and then you go off and do it. And then the director comes in and says, 'I like it' or 'I don't like it', and then you have to go off and change it. So, I think it really varies. It varies because of their relationship with movement. People that obviously really enjoy movement and appreciate what it can do to a piece and how it can really hold a piece are very collaborative. But that in itself is sometimes challenging, because you go, 'Well I really see it like that,' and that person's going, 'Well I don't really understand that,' and you're going, 'Argh … but I really want it to do that!' Yes – what I've learnt, and only recently, is that you have to take each project – and, in turn, each director – and understand how it is *they* work.

With directors you have to be able to talk about an idea and then put that idea into …
… practice …

… real bodies, real time and real rhythm. I guess for them it's a difference between seeing and imagining.
Yes, that's absolutely right. And I personally struggle with the 'in-between place', because I would say that it is the detail. The attention to the detail is actually what makes the work clear – so when you try to 'rough something up', inevitably it doesn't quite represent the fullness of the idea, so it's tricky. I'm trying to learn to be more articulate in what the idea hopefully will do and therefore, allowing the director to have trust in that. Also, to be quick enough to be able to do it in a good amount of time, so that you leave yourself time if it isn't right, you can change it.

Maybe directors could become better at imagining it, too? And lastly, how do you work with Peter Darling?
Peter and I, we've changed as the years have gone by. We met – probably fourteen years ago, and he is, fundamentally, a choreographer of ideas; he has the most incredible mind. Originally, when I first met him, he used to do a lot of task-based work, so he'd give you the idea – because Peter comes from an acting background, and so we're very different – and so it used to be exploring ideas

through movement, by responding to tasks. As we moved forward in time and our relationship became stronger, it very much became a balancing of minds, really. I could almost finish his sentences. I would also be the person who would be able to put into practice what he saw in his head, maybe no one else could understand what he was saying, but I knew so I would be able to go, 'Oh okay, so you mean like this.' Interestingly I could 'rough it up' for him to see that, 'Do you mean like that?' And he would go, 'Yes and this, this, this and this.' But that's because I understand him probably better than I understand anyone else that I've worked with, really. And we see things very similarly, and I don't know whether it's because I've always been like that or because essentially I've learnt this work through his eyes, and so it's tricky to know which is which really, so that sums us up in a short way, really.

Can you give an overview of the phases of a production, so right from receiving the script or score through to realization?
That's a hard one, as it's so varied. In working with Peter, it would always start in a workshop environment, so you would always be part of that initial trying to scratch away for the ideas and casting the right people for the show. Sometimes we'd create the work with other people and then go about casting the show. When I am in the associate role, I play a very different role to when I am working alone. As an associate, I guess I pride myself in being able to clean the quality of the numbers in the show. Each number has a different emotion and a different feel, so rather than clean the steps I would clean *the feel* and *the quality*. So that the audience are feeling something different from everything that they're watching and trying to enhance the narrative of the world of that location – I really enjoy that. And then I've been very fortunate in my role working with Peter in that a lot of the shows have moved to other places, and we initially started moving them ourselves and we'd go to Australia or New York or Chicago and set them up. That's actually quite tricky, the recreating of the show. First off, it's incredibly challenging, because I had to write these huge bibles – books – in order to be able to recreate it, so that's without anything else. As it became more global, I did less of the recreating because for me personally, it wasn't challenging anymore. It was more interesting to enable someone else to do it. Now I keep an eye on the shows, more generally, and make sure that I support everybody that works for us as best as I can. I try to inspire and give new ideas to the movement so that they feel like they're changing all the time. I see that as quite an important job, actually.

And then in my own process, I'm learning all the time, and I feel so fortunate to have had the experience that I've had because I feel like now I have such a rich foundation in order to ask myself lots of questions. My process is trying to navigate *everything* at the moment. I am trying to do that [enabling others] and still read new scripts and find projects that I'm really interested in, alongside keeping all of that going too. So, it's quite a mixed bag.

Each creative process raises questions and makes one expand –
It really does, and for that I am incredibly grateful, I am in a position in my life where I feel like I've been exposed to some incredibly creative people, and I'm still fortunate enough to be inspired and learn from the things that I do all the time. As well as being able, now to start to really investigate what I really think or where I'm going.

Just thinking about the wider field now. When did you notice you were doing what you were doing?
What do you mean?

Sometimes you find yourself working instinctively in a certain way and then have to define it or start labelling it, and then you start noticing who else is doing it.
That's an interesting one. I had some experience with the jazz company at my old college and had been really interested in structure and the 'cleaning' part of assisting. So, on graduating I had an instinct that I could do that, even before dancing in Richard's company. Because I was thinking that I'd love to be an assistant to a choreographer, I wrote to Antony Van Laast.[11] I didn't hear back from him, but strangely, a year after that, maybe two, he came to the Jazz Company to make a piece, and I assisted him. He then asked me to do some work in Berlin with him and for the BBC, and then we did a big show called *Sister Act*.[12] Over that period, I had already begun working with Peter and was also dancing, too. To be honest, what's interesting is that I never really *saw* myself as *anything*, and it's only when you start realizing that other people see you as that. I just used to go to work; I used to get up and go and do what I was doing and because once they started, they never stopped, there was very little time – you'd just go, 'What am I doing today?' And I've got a child, so my life is quite busy, so I never really took the time, if you like, to think, 'Oh, I'm doing this', or, 'I'm doing something that I always wanted to do'. I knew I always wanted to be a dancer, and I feel like as a dancer I absolutely did everything I wanted to do and beyond that – I've always been so lucky, so incredibly grateful.

Is there a question that I haven't asked you that you would have liked me to ask you?
No, I don't think there is. I'm very fortunate and I'm really keen to learn and happy that I'm in a position to keep going, it's brilliant.

Notes

1   This interview was conducted at the Royal Shakespeare Company's Clapham Rehearsal Rooms, 3 May 2018.
    Ellen Kane trained as a dancer at Lewisham College and London Studio Centre. She was a founder member of the Henri Oguike Dance Company. She also danced

with Richard Alston Company. Her credits include Movement Director on *Pieces of String* (Mercury Theatre, Colchester, 2018); Choreographer on *Women on the Verge of a Nervous Breakdown* (Playhouse Theatre, 2014); Co-choreographer on *Groundhog Day* (Old Vic and New York, 2017 – Tony-nominated in 2017); Associate Choreographer on *Matilda the Musical* (Royal Shakespeare Company, Stratford upon Avon 2010, West End 2011, Broadway 2013, US tour 2015, Australia 2015); *Charlie and the Chocolate Factory* (Theatre Royal, Drury Lane, 2013); *Billy Elliot the Musical* (West End 2005, Australia 2007, United States 2008, the Netherlands 2014); *Sister Act* (London Palladium, 2009); *The Lord of the Rings* (Theatre Royal, Drury Lane, 2007); *The Three Musketeers* (Germany, 2004).

2   Lewisham Southwark College, London, is a further education college with a notable dance training that has had considerable success in nurturing dancers to progress to full-time and professional dance training.

3   Isolations exist in a huge variety of dance forms. It is useful to draw attention to the African American roots of jazz dance, which was to influence a wide variety of teachers and choreographers across film, musical theatre and modern dance in the United States. The influence of Katherine Dunham (1909–2006) as a pioneering anthropologist and dancer was through her choreographic works and through the Dunham technique (anchored in Haitian forms and rituals; and Caribbean dance, comprising undulations, isolations, the use of the pelvis, breathing techniques; and a through line of ballet). She was influential in many spheres of dance and can be said to offer the underpinnings of American jazz in the 1930s. Jack Cole was considered to be a leader of modern jazz dance in the twentieth century in the United States – he is remembered for developing a unique style borne out of Cecchetti ballet method, modern dance influences from Denishawn and Humphrey, and Indian dance, in particular bharata nātyam. Matt Mattox was considered to be his inheritor and developed a variation of American jazz style. The YouTube video 'Matt Mattox Real Jazz' (2017) gives a good insight into the systematic preparation of the body and then an example of the techniques at play in a short choreography (available online: https://www.youtube.com/watch?v=wzsNimr6mJk). The Matt Mattox lineage of teaching in Lewisham Southwark College is a jazz technique that is acknowledged as having a place within the Imperial Society of Teachers of Dancing (ISTD) curriculum (Modern Theatre Dance). In the early twenty-first century, it might be useful to draw parallels between jazz and hip-hop – some dance academics draw a direct line. However, for the purpose of this study, the development of hyper dexterity in isolation of body parts, polyphonic rhythmic combinations, counter rhythms, a variety of points of contact with the floor and use of the whole body, including the pelvis, that feature in this style of dance is what becomes relevant to Kane's work.

4   London Studio Centre founded in 1978 is a dance school that prepares and trains dancers for a broad application of dance in professional theatre and dance settings.

5   Richard Alston Company was founded in 1994 is notable for its emphasis on movement over theatricality and dance creation with emphasis on line, curve and musicality. Dance critic Alastair Macauley, writing in the *New York Times*, said of Alston's work, 'Other British choreographers have been more theatrically exciting, but it is Mr Alston who, over the last 30 years, has made most of Britain's best dances' (Macauley 2008).

6 The Place is home to London Contemporary Dance School and Richard Alston Dance Company.

7 On *Billy Elliot the Musical*, see Chapter 10.

8 Royal Academy of Dance (RAD) is an organization dedicated to the training of dance teachers and the continued professional development of teachers, as well as running examinations in a variety of dance styles.

9 Jazz Xchange Music and Dance Company was formed in 1992 by dancer, teacher and choreographer Sheron Wray.

10 Kane was associate choreographer with Peter Darling on productions of *Billy Elliot* and *Matilda*; see Chapter 10. *Charlie and the Chocolate* Factory was the stage adaptation of the Roald Dahl story of the same name. The book was by David Greig, music by Marc Shaiman, lyrics by Shaiman and Scott Wittman, and direction by Sam Mendes. The show ran from 2013 to 2017 in the West End.

11 Anthony Van Laast MBE and Nicola Treherne are theatre, opera, concert and film choreographers.

12 *Sister Act*, stage musical with score by Alan Menken, lyrics by Glenn Slater, book by Bill and Cheri Steinkellner, choreographed by Anthony Van Laast in the West End (2009) and on Broadway (2011).

10 PETER DARLING

No form is better or worse than another: It's all human beings moving [2018][1]

How would you describe what you do?
What do I do? I create movement sequences for musicals, by which I mean I choreograph the musical numbers. My overarching attempt is to *always* make sure that I'm telling a story so that the story doesn't stop the moment the scene ends, and the song begins, and then the story continues until the baton is taken up again by the scene. My other attempt is to make something as interesting or surprising for the audience as I possibly, possibly can. What I love is to combine drama and story with unabashed entertainment. However, whilst I spend many, many months in preparation and coming up with the sequences in my head, I have always had help in the realization of these imagined sequences. I believe it is better to work openly and collaboratively, but that may simply be because I don't have the skills to do it all myself!

How do you prepare for a project?
My preparation is perhaps the most arduous part of the whole process, and for the likes of *Billy Elliot* or *Matilda* it took roughly two years on each project.[2] I start by reading all the material again and again in an attempt to work out what the themes of the show are, so that my work will reflect that of the authors. It's a process of thinking and allowing ideas to emerge, marinate and join together in one's head.

My real training was watching my father's variety shows every night until the images were burned into my brain and I could remember the routines. My training as a choreographer is essentially non-existent, as I was an actor, and I learnt everything from other people: I learnt by watching and truly studying the work of other choreographers I admired. Most importantly, I had the greatest privilege of working with Lloyd Newson (DV8) as a performer.[3] Lloyd imprinted on my psyche the belief that all movement had to be about something and should not be decoration. This chimed with the belief that Stephen Daldry held that the narrative should never stop.[4]

Having got a sense of what the show is truly about, I begin to read the lyrics of the songs endlessly; this is an attempt to find out what the individual song is about so that everything in the staging reflects that central premise. It's a bit like detective work: finding out about who the characters are who are singing, what their characteristics are, where the action is taking place and what is happening. Once I discover what is happening, then I have physical action and can begin to choreographically depict that action in a way that is fitting to the place and illustrates character. I also look at what the objective is for each character involved in the musical number – somehow a physical objective is a shortcut to having ideas about choreography, for me. All the while, I keep my eyes, ears open to everything around me for any idea that might help me create a specific choreographic style for the whole show and thus best illustrate the material. Matthew Warchus asked me, when I choreographed *Our House*, to come up with a style that would be particular to that show, and it is advice that has always stayed with me – to the extent that I began to want to create my own choreographic style as opposed to imitating other people, which I did initially, but that is part of the learning process before one finds any originality within oneself.[5]

The next step in the creative process, for me, is to get in a room with an associate as I did at the beginning of my career to try out material. As I became a bit more successful, I was able to have a few dancers and my associates to try and workshop sequences. Stephen Daldry said, 'Start with the number you understand and feel confident about.' I have always followed this. Stephen also believed that the big sequences should have been fully workshopped before embarking on a rehearsal period. As somebody from America has said, 'Once the ship sets sail you can't turn it around.' And some sequences in musicals are like big ships in themselves, so they have to be headed in the right direction as early as possible.

In terms of preparation for a project, I do a huge amount of research and reading with regard to the time period, the context, the setting, etc. For instance, on *Matilda*, I spent a week at a primary school, sitting in on all lessons after school clubs, standing in the playground, etc. I went to Roald Dahl's house, studied the drawings of Quentin Blake, etc. Research invariably gives you ideas you could never come up with on your own. I also always talk through the sequence with my associate, so I understand if it's clear and to get invaluable feedback, as has been the case with my friend and collaborator, Ellen Kane [see Chapter 9]. In my opinion, sharing really helps the creative process.

Can you talk about your process with actors? And with dancers?
It's harder for me to talk about my process with actors, simply because I haven't done movement on a play for a very long time. When I started, I worked with

actors a great deal, so perhaps if I describe the kind of process I would go through it might be helpful.

Invariably, I was asked to provide a dance in a play; I was less comfortable telling an actor how he should walk or sit, etc. I think this stemmed from having been an actor myself and feeling that was somehow a part of the actor's process. However, as an actor I might well have benefited from somebody helping me in this regard. Personally, I have never felt greatly skilled at this.

Invariably, when I did a dance in a play I used to try and find an idea that would 'frame' the actor, often using a prop, so the audience's eye is taken by the prop rather than needing sophisticated movement from the actor. For instance, in a play called *Power* about Louis XIV, I did a dance for an actor whose character was a philanderer; the dance itself was somehow supposed to woo his upcoming conquest.[6] I decided he should dance with a costume mannequin on wheels; this mannequin was dressed in full seventeenth-century costume. As he danced with this mannequin, he gradually disrobed it, almost puppeteering 'her' – thus bringing the mannequin to life. It was a courtship/seduction in itself. My sole purpose was to tell the right story and make the actor look good. Before starting, I explained the idea to the actor and showed him different moves so he could see what he might achieve with lots of application.

My overriding objective whenever working with actors was, anything that the actor looked awkward doing I would change, regardless of how attached to the idea or movement I was. The only thing I have ever needed from the actor was willingness and application; it's hard for actors not used to moving/dancing and therefore feeling outside their comfort zone. I choreographed three musicals early on entirely with actors who could move or wanted to move; those were *Oh! What a Lovely War*, *Candide* and *Merrily We Roll Along*. Generally, the movement was defined by large blocky energetic moves! It was not sophisticated, it was not subtle, it was rough! But the narrative idea was always prominent. Ironically, I came to realize that I treated actors like dancers, in the sense that I would push them to exceed their expectations of themselves and discover that anybody who can walk, run, jump and fall can indeed dance, as that was essentially the extent of much of the movement. What I didn't really possess early on was a process that would help actors to create complex choreography for themselves and thus 'own' the material – and I regret this.

Ironically, I did create this kind of process so that I could get dancers to create narrative choreography for themselves. In this respect, I treat dancers like actors and even more so when coming to create material with them. Now, I work very differently with dancers as a result of having created my own process to create choreography. However, even when I was coming up with the movement myself and with my associate, I would always make sure that the dancer understood the reason *why* we were doing each movement, what the intention of each movement was and the overall story they were telling at each point.

I longed for the process to be more democratic and use the incredible skill that all dancers have. I often felt in musicals the contribution of the dancer was undervalued, not least because somehow they were not seen as creative. Whereas I knew from having worked with Lloyd Newson and his extraordinary dancers and studying the work of people like Pina Bausch that dancers were astonishingly creative and always part of the creative process.[7] For some reason in musicals this did not happen (though I think it's very different now), and for a long time I worked with contemporary dancers first, workshopping ideas because they were used to improvising and creating movement based on task-related exercises. However, I was determined to work with musical theatre performers and have them create the movement, and so I spent a long time creating a process that I felt could unlock their creative potential and work in the style that I suppose I have developed for myself and like watching.

As a general overview, if you discover the setting/the place and what's going on in the song (that is, the action), then – combined with the objective of the characters – you have everything you need to create a musical sequence.

For instance, in the opening number 'Miracle' in *Matilda*, I realized from reading and analysing the lyrics that I had to have a location that both children and adults/parents would be present. The action mostly consists of children behaving badly and their parents refusing to acknowledge the bad behaviour in their child. I chose a children's birthday party as the setting, as it involves both children and their parents and often the children behave very badly! The overarching idea was a birthday party celebrating birth, which in itself is a miracle, thus illustrating the central theme in that song.

Going into a bit more detail, nowadays I usually split the song into a beginning, middle and end trying to build excitement as the song develops. Within each unit (that is, beginning, middle and end), I look at what the objective is for each unit: what is the physical objective of each character, and what is the relationship between each character. For instance, in *Matilda* there is a song called 'Loud': Miss Honey is very nervous of Mrs Wormwood, and her objective is to get away; Mrs Wormwood's objective is to teach Miss Honey, a woman she sees as her inferior, to dance; Rodolfo, a Latin lover, is attempting to woo both women, and his objective is to dance with both of them.

Can you give an overview of your creative process? What are the important ways of working for you?
I'm not sure I can describe my process as I think it would be unclear and has several permutations. But now I always start by discussing character situation, place and time. I ask the performers what has just happened before the song starts, what the character wants, the age of the characters, the rhythm/weight of the characters. 'What is the space like?', for example. Is it familiar or unfamiliar, light or dark? And then essentially, I use 'actions' (in the Joint Stock sense[8]) combined with mime to

create movement phrases, which then – with my associate Ellen – we restructure, reorder, adjust and pattern.

Has your background as an actor influenced how you create movement? Are there any other influences?
My background as an actor I used to think of as a handicap, and that somehow, I would never be able to choreograph at the level I deeply wanted to. However, as in all things, it is limitation that often turns out to be one's greatest strength. So, for instance, I realized that I could never create jazz choreography at the level of some of my musical theatre heroes, simply because I did not have that training. Gradually, I realized my knowledge of acting and that process could become a cornerstone of the choreography, and indeed it is central to the 'process' I created: a strange mix of different directors' techniques like 'actioning',[9] improvisational ideas from Joan Littlewood's Theatre Workshop,[10] or those of Declan Donellan,[11] combined with improvisation techniques from William Forsythe[12] or task-based exercises from Pina Bausch. I suppose it is clear that my only discrimination in terms of taste is, do I like it or not? Do I feel something or not? Hence, I get as much of a thrill watching Pina Bausch as I do the work of Susan Stroman[13] or Jiří Kylián[14] – I just keep my eyes open watching and learning, excited by great work regardless of the label.

It's all movement, and that was my driving purpose for *Billy Elliot* – that there should be a democracy to dance. No form is better or worse than another, it's all human beings moving. My only attempt has been to try and make sure it means something so that those watching might feel something; my mantra to the performers is that if you feel it, I, the audience, will feel it, and therefore we will connect.

How do you work with directors?
How do I work with directors? I have worked with relatively few, probably due to the length of time musicals take in their creation. However, I have one overriding principle. I am not the director, and therefore if the work that I produce does not fit the director's vision then invariably I will change it. This does not mean to say I won't argue my case and have been known to do this quite vociferously. However, as I think every director I have worked with would attest, I force myself to try and accommodate an alternative and always to try it out; maybe it is because of this that I have returned again and again to work with the same directors and they with me.

As a result of having listened to the director talk about the material, and my research into it, I work hard to come up with my own vision for the piece in terms of the musical numbers. Although it is the director's vision that is ultimately being presented, I hope a director will always value my addition. On a musical, nobody can do it all themselves, and it is the greatest lesson in collaboration. I have always likened it to an aeroplane which needs several 'engines' to keep it in the air – be it music, design, script or choreography, it is only when all these things come together that a really good piece of work comes to life. We all need help, and the wisest learn to accept help; I learnt this over the years from watching people I have had the good fortune to work with.

How do you see the field developing in the future?
Your final question is perhaps the hardest of all for me, but in brief, I would say from what I see around me movement/choreography seems to be more prevalent in theatrical work than ever before. I imagine this will only increase in a world where our eye is so used to moving and following very fast imagery, finding it very hard to be still; who knows if this is a good or bad thing? We live in a moving world so very different from that of the previous generation, and inevitably theatre is going to reflect this. One very brilliant director said to me, 'The only way I know how to focus "the moment" is through stillness'; I suspect for myself it's a combination: the movement isolates stillness in the same way that pauses work in music. In musicals, it seems that great contemporary dance choreographers are now exploring the form and are bringing new and interesting ways of telling story and entertaining through dance, so to me that would seem to be the future.

Thank you so much Peter, this has been so interesting.
The only thing I would want to add is how grateful I am to the associate choreographers that have worked with me and helped me along the way: Ellen Kane for giving my work a precision and clarity I longed for, Katherine Dunn for her balletic knowledge and ideas, Nikki Belcher for her glorious tap dancing, Tom Hodgson for his physical imagination and Lynne Page for her daring and bravery.

Notes

1 This interview was conducted in July 2018.
   Peter Darling is an award-winning British choreographer. In his early years, he undertook a variety of dance forms but switched to training as an actor. He read Drama at the University of Bristol (1985) and trained as an actor at the Royal Central School of Speech and Drama (1988). He went on to work as an actor for a decade, performing at the National Theatre with Cheek by Jowl and notably with DV8 in *MSM* in 1993. In other interviews, the creative and collaborative experience of working with Lloyd Newson appears to have marked the start of a career shift from actor to movement practitioner and then to choreographer. Choreography in theatre work includes *Groundhog Day* with Ellen Kane, see Chapter 9 (Old Vic, 2017); *Matilda the Musical* (Courtyard Theatre, Royal Shakespeare Company (RSC) 2010, West End 2011, Broadway 2013), for which Darling received an Olivier Award and a WhatsOnStage Award for Best Choreography); *Charlie and the Chocolate*

Factory (Theatre Royal, Drury Lane, 2013); *Billy Elliot* (West End 2005, Broadway 2008, Australia tour 2007), for which Darling received an Olivier Award for Best Choreographer and a Tony Award for Best Choreographer; *The Lord of the Rings* (Toronto 2006, West End 2007); *Power* (National Theatre, 2003); *A Midsummer Night's Dream* (Bristol Old Vic, 2003); *Our House* (West End, 2002); *Closer to Heaven* (Arts Theatre, 2001), for which Darling received Theatregoer's Choice Award for Best Choreographer; *Sunset Boulevard* (UK Tour 2001); *The Tempest* (RSC The Pit 2000 and International Tour 2001); *Merrily We Roll Along* (Donmar Warehouse, 2000); *Candide* (National Theatre, 1999); *Oh! What a Lovely War* (UK tour 1998). His film work includes *Plots with a View*, directed by Nick Hurran (2002); *Trauma*, directed by Marc Evans (2004); *The Phantom of the Opera*, directed by Joel Schumacher (2004); and *Billy Elliot*, directed by Stephen Daldry (2000).

2 *Billy Elliot* was originally a film (2000). Darling won an MTV Best Dance Sequence Award for his work on the film. *Billy Elliot the Musical*, book and lyrics by Lee Hall, music by Elton John, directed by Stephen Daldry, opened in the West End in 2005.

    Matilda the Musical was based on the original story by Roald Dahl, adapted for stage by Dennis Kelly, with music and lyrics by Tim Minchin, directed by Matthew Warchus. It opened at the Royal Shakespeare Company's Stratford upon Avon theatre, The Other Place, Courtyard Theatre in 2010 and transferred to the West End in 2011.

3 Lloyd Newson is the artistic director of dance theatre company DV8, founded in 1986. The company's work has engaged with themes of sexual politics, otherly-abled dancers and queer experience using vocabularies of contact work, spoken word, text and physical prowess (forms as diverse as hula-hooping, ballet and club dance).

4 Stephen Daldry CBE is a British theatre director. He has collaborated with Darling repeatedly and notably on *Billy Elliot*, the film and stage musical.

5 Matthew Warchus is a British theatre director, currently the artistic director of the Old Vic Theatre. He has collaborated with Peter Darling on several shows, including *Groundhog Day*, *Matilda*, *The Lord of the Rings* and *Our House*.

    Our House is a musical with songs and lyrics by the band, Madness. The first staged production was in 2002, and the production won Best New Musical at the 2003 Olivier Awards, where Peter Darling was nominated for Best Choreographer.

6 *Power* by Nick Dear, directed by Lindsay Posner, National Theatre (2003).

7 Pina Bausch (1940–2009) was the artistic director of Tanztheater Wuppertal and one of the most influential dancers and choreographers of the twentieth century. Throughout her prolific career she worked with a core group of dancers over most of their working lives, often creating material from their memories and performance personas. She created pieces fuelled by gender relationships, memory and place through the poetry of movement and emotion.

8 Joint Stock Theatre Company was a British theatre collective that ran from 1973/4 to 1989, driven by socialist aims, collective research and experiences in the creation of play texts.

9 Actioning is a method of analysing a play text with the aim of inscribing a character-led objective to text. This is a negotiated process of turning written text into doable actions that interact with the world of the character, scene partners and sometimes audience. It is attributed to the early days of Joint Stock Theatre's working methods.

10 Theatre Workshop was a radical, innovative theatre collective directed by Joan Littlewood. Political subjects formed the heart of collective research and creation. Training of movement and voice was embedded into the rehearsal process. Movement director Jean Newlove was a Laban-trained practitioner who became the company Movement Practitioner (see Chapter 1).

11 Declan Donnellan is a British theatre director and the founder of Cheek by Jowl theatre company. Also see Jane Gibson Chapter 3.

12 William Forsythe is a US-born choreographer based in Germany. He was Artistic Director of Frankfurt Ballet for twenty years, and then formed the Forsythe Company (2005–15). He is a prolific creator who works in a variety of settings from dance to installations to architecture. His creative techniques were articulated and disseminated in DVD form in a series of movement lectures, *William Forsythe Improvisation Technologies: A Tool for the Analytical Dance Eye* (2003).

13 Susan Stroman is an American choreographer and theatre director and has many musical theatre productions to her name.

14 Jiří Kylián is a prolific Czech contemporary dance choreographer.

11 STEVEN HOGGETT

The answers are in the bodies of the people in the room [2019][1]

How do you describe what you do?
The definition does seem to shift. There are various moments in your life where you do change the description. I think of it as bringing to the fore that which exists in every piece of theatre: inherent in every actor and scene is physicality happening in front of a live audience. I am taking what is extant and drawing focus to it. I am trying to meet the demands of the play, or scene, or character by letting that physicality be a conduit. Movement direction or choreography, for want of better terms, is a joyous work experience because it's about bringing inherent qualities out of peoples' bodies. We don't conjure out of nothing. I don't feel like I'm building from zero, which is the joy of movement. I'm sometimes surprised that people are not aware of what they have in front of them or within them.

There are tricky aspects in movement direction and choreography which start at a contractual level and go right through to awards. It has become 'a thing' a couple of times – in fact, last month. I didn't personally have an issue, but a show became ineligible because I class myself as a Movement Director. Right now, it's a term in flux. What's interesting is that the nominating panel are going to change the way they award that category next year to include movement direction. Movement direction is really muddying the waters for people who want to give out gongs at ridiculous ceremonies. I quite like that, as it feels a little bit anarchic. If certain sections of the world outside are having issues with that, then I'm happy with that for now; but it's time for change, and change is happening. 'Movement direction' as a term is coming into focus, and it's about time. I don't feel frustrated; change is on its way and it's healthy.

In the room, whichever area of movement direction or choreography you're spilling into, you're just doing your job. It's what we do, and how we see a room full of people; how we behave with performers and with a creative team, and how we respond to text or music. That's really simple to me.

What is your background?
I studied English Literature at Swansea University and while I was there I went to see *Medea: Sex War* by Volcano Theatre Company.[2] I'd only been to the theatre about four times in my life before that. I'd never seen anything like it – the most visceral thing I'd ever sat in front of, I couldn't believe that *that* was what theatre *was*. I knew *why* it did *what* it did: I understood it. The week after, Volcano were looking for student performers to work on developing a project, so that was the start for me. I was twenty, I went to a workshop, it was incredibly physical and everything about it made sense! I started late. I joined *Volcano* after I left university and then the *Featherstonehaughs*.[3] For my first job I was choreographed by Nigel Charnock and then my second by Lea Anderson, so between those two people I really got a great start.[4] And then we started *Frantic*.[5]

You really learnt by doing?
Absolutely practically – yes. For our first run of Frantic shows we were bringing in a different choreographer to direct and choreograph, because choreographers make great directors. Each show we'd make we would learn from a different choreographer; different values, qualities, warm-ups. Every year we got to learn, make, tour and perform following a different style of choreography.

During that phase, were you in the performer role? Were you on the receiving end?
Yes. I just had to listen and watch and then *do*.

Do you think that experience as a performer affects how you work now?
It makes me brave in the room, as in what I will ask, and it makes me thoughtful and caring in a way that maybe I wouldn't be. I do have to care because I do know what that feels like, but also just in pragmatic terms; with something like *Harry Potter* where I know it's going to play for a year, I *have* to take responsibility for certain sequences, knowing that that's something they'll do eight times a week.[6]

Repeatedly and sustainably.
Yes, I know what my warm-up will afford them so I know what I can push for, because all of that lines up. Just in terms of how I felt as a performer being taught by the people that I was gifted with for those first eight years. I learnt from people that just have such a beautiful way of guiding, who took people that didn't have the traditional dance background, if at all, and used language in a certain way

to elicit responses that then became ideas, that became physicality, that became sequences.[7] Just rolling tasks forward in ways that were very articulate and easy for us to respond to but also really hard, challenging and provocative. It's quite a big thing for me – that nobody ever gets it 'wrong' in a rehearsal room. Even if it's down to something we do in a warm-up, something needs to have moved forward – even if it was a small step. That's really important because we were 'wrong' a lot of the time with early Frantic material, particularly. We were never made to feel that way: we've been corrected and given challenges, but we were never made to feel that we were getting it 'wrong'. It's worth every moment of your life to make your mouth come out with the language that encourages. With movement direction I think you should be pulling from the front or pushing from the back, and in any given moment you are bouncing between the two things. Sometimes you push from the back so as not be the gobby person at the front, saying, 'No no no no', and then to pull from the front is to say, 'Come with me.'

Language is a big thing for me. I feel very comfortable taking a piece of text as the place where ideas come from. I like to read to get inspiration for how people might move. I'm also very happy looking at a score seeing what the dynamics are rhythmically, because I can see where the notes bunch and where they have space.

How do you prepare for a project?

I will prepare myself, so I watch films and read books, but I won't make many notes about them. I'll have a firm knowledge in my head that gets me to the first day, and my big point to a company in the room is, 'It's *your* bodies in this space and the tasks I'll give you – this is all we need.' At the beginning of any project, I'll say, 'I've got a page of ideas in here but that's all I've got,' and I'll literally show one page from my notebook and then I'll turn the page over and there's nothing there; as long as I have some exercises and some tasks. I didn't come through ballet or contemporary dance training. I definitely had a career choosing projects where the language is not something that I can just take from dance forms.

Does that mean that you are inventing everything?

Yes, that is why I don't have all the answers, or barely any, because the answers are in the bodies of the people in the room. I've got plenty of tasks, and I've had enough experience now to throw exercises at the group and adapt them to whatever the project is. I always know how to start something. Even today, the performers made this very beautiful movement just from thinking about airline flight paths, and last week they made some work based on a video which was directed by Chris Cunningham and we watched the qualities of a cloak on a performer.[8] So I will use starting points like that. I know what I want, but I want the actors to launch themselves, too. So, I would never have a movement phrase that I would teach or show. I'm not interested in the aesthetic as much as the internal that becomes the aesthetic.

I can see how a company might really respond to that open terrain.
I use the word 'ensemble' and I use the word 'collaborate' and I *mean* those words. As a movement director, I really pushed to be in the room quite a lot. That's what I ask for because I really want to see them, and it's not just observing them; it's also a commitment to the project and to say to the director, 'I'm threading through the entire thing for you.' I don't like dropping in and being given, 'Oh, can you just look at some physical character work.' I find that an impossible situation. I did try it about ten years ago. The danger is that you drop something in, in week one, and then the rest of the production really develops through the next three weeks, but the movement doesn't develop because you are only back right at the end. There's a lot of problems with just dropping in, for me.

That said, two years ago, I was asked if I wanted to work with Ivo van Hove.[9] I've wanted to work with him for a long time, so when the producers suggested just two days I was shocked but said yes. For me to be in my first room with him was a big thing, but I didn't know what I was doing until the night before, and just when I was thinking that it was unsalvageable he called with one question: 'What is it that makes the adults in the room so afraid of these girls in these scenes in *The Crucible*?' It was the most beautiful thing: I knew exactly what my job was, and it was two days. I don't like dropping in unless you give me the Ivo method, which is so rich. So, there are exceptions, like with anything.

Is there a difference in working on plays and musicals?
Yes. They're incredibly different beasts. Musicals are the ones that seem to have the most lateral drift. You can treat a musical like a play with songs. *Once* was a play where the songs lifted out and fell back into it, so they didn't kick off or lift as much as they just opened out like a big, long breath that then folded back in.[10] That felt like we could use actors that were phenomenal musicians. I hadn't worked with musicians on stage before, and being in there early during the music week when they were learning their music was invaluable. I used to sit behind them to take notes of where they would move when they were playing their instruments – even when they were getting things wrong – how they'd arc round between cello and banjo and violin players. I used the way their frames fitted around an instrument and tried to create a general language from that. It was everything I needed for choreographing *Once*, which is all based on the physical shapes of musicians and musicianship and what it is to play music. So that's a musical where you're using musicians, not dancers, but you can end up pushing that towards a form of choreography.

Musicals with dancers become a very different prospect. Your responsibility is to music and with dancers – that can feel amazing, and I don't mean it's simple, and you do make lots of work very quickly. It is the most comfortable in terms of why you do what you do; it's the fullest expression of movement.

And then a play, it depends what the play is – is it character physicality with the occasional moments of enhancement? Across the board there's just as much work that can go into a play as into a play with music. Musicals will always take a lot more prep because you're going to make so much material. My first musical was all choreography as there was no 'book' to speak of, so it became ninety minutes of full choreography. I had a very extreme entrance into musicals.

And are you weighting theatre and musical theatre equally in your process?
Certainly, in the States, the musicals I tend to get are actor-led. I will get the jobs with a full cast of working-class, older men 'facing unemployment in a shipyard', or I will get an autistic boy and his brain, or I will get the one that's got boxing at the end of it.

It's another kind of register, isn't it?
Yes, I do like that.

Can you articulate your process with actors?
Yes, even this week we're working on a new adaptation of a Neil Gaiman novel with a room full of actors. What I do love about actors is that they will not consider the aesthetic of their movement; they won't have a reserve of instinct of how to move physically, and if you set a task correctly, you'll get some beautifully lateral choices. If you're smart about how you link them, they absolutely go to the heart of the task, and sometimes that's exactly what you would want. There's a fine balance; you sometimes have to say, 'Stop signalling, I want you to get in your bodies a bit more,' and that's okay. In a room of actors, you can say that and they don't suddenly feel like they're watching their body and have to then become dancers. Sometimes you do have to say, 'You don't need to dance; I'd like you to move.' I do say that fairly regularly.

Their expertise lies in understanding human behaviour and charting emotional journeys; is that something you work with?
Yes, completely. I'm always cautious of letting actors give me results quickly. Sometimes actors, because they're actors – and it's even more so with dancers – they will, if you ask, give *it* to you, and sometimes it needs to be more measured. Layering in qualities so that material can grow and build. Genuine exploration will produce the more unexpected material. In lots of ways, in theatre, you will always get by presenting what that perceived wisdom is about that moment or about those people in those circumstances; I like being a bit more playful. To achieve that, it's about giving actors slightly less than you should, because otherwise you'll get exactly what you asked for. But there's the risk of it becoming nebulous and not getting what you want. Again, that's *my* job, that's *my* responsibility. I often get everybody in the room to make material and then cross-pollinate. I love watching the cross-pollination of bodies; that is gorgeous. We did an exercise today which was making you move in ways that you would never normally move, just unlocking

ourselves physically and particularly actors – it's amazing watching actors just suddenly go, 'Oh my god, I've just moved and I definitely moved and it's not dance and it's not regular movement.'

Your building process is following a logic that actors have in discovering the character's logic?
Yes, I did a job very recently with an actor who had to play somebody who started at the age of seventy and who became 400, and so we developed anatomical triggers so that when he's 200 we'll say he's going to connect or pull or sink from the sternum; when he's 300 he's going to connect and fail around his kneecaps. That's the inverse of what I would normally do, but the actor wanted to go on to the set and be able to play with these things over the duration of the shoot. I don't necessarily want the movement to be the forerunner, because then it feels like it's the part that doesn't get any better or any worse.

Actors and dancers can be very reverential, so as a movement director you have to make sure that they still feel like they're operating within the realms of a sequential event. I did a piece at the Royal Court where the actors have two movement sequences in a kitchen, and each sequence takes them forward through ten years and it's only two and a half minutes long.[11] From day one, I was very clear that they should try to 'let your performance pass through from the end of the scene and into the physical sequence – the minute you become anything _other_, I will spot it'. I often ask performers to bury the choreography, not to change what they do but the quality of it can become heightened or slightly spelt out.

It's a constant negotiation between the actor's experience and the audience's experience for a movement director?
My whole theory with movement in this country is that we've had TV viewers on Saturday watching _Strictly_ [_Come Dancing_] with four people talking about forms of choreography: what's it's doing, what's it's saying, what it's not, how it's failing, what it should be.[12] The judges use technical terms and language that's heard every Saturday by millions of people. I used to have the fear that movement, if you don't present it correctly, is the bit where the audience would sit back. Or if it was within the scene or sequence, you're 'making strange'. And this is why it is the golden period for movement directors, and that is because audiences now _do_ understand; everybody knows what choreography means. It's a language now that audiences will now not necessarily have to sit back from – they will sit in and towards and invest and look within it. Our job now is a lot easier, but also, we need to be smart about that. Certainly, when I worked on _Black Watch_, I had learnt just enough to know I had to be very careful with soldiers doing any kind of movement that went beyond regimental material.[13] Which is bizarre, as real soldiers do loads of choreography. In the structure of _Black Watch_, I made sure I informed the audience that movement was an element, and it started at a low level and there were flickers

of movement and then it built, and built, and built. We got to the last third of the show where I could kick out two massive sequences. I was very mindful of blokes who were in the military coming to see *Black Watch*.

You introduce a movement vocabulary progressively to the audience.
You make it palatable –

Give an audience a way in –
Or to not to sit back in that bit. I do feel a responsibility, as with actors, is to just open it out and declare it, but not to make it a challenge for them. Then you can really push, go for it but don't 'make strange' – it doesn't help, particularly with plays. You can be 'other' and 'lift it off and out', but to be mindful that to 'make strange' feels alienating.

How do you work with directors?
I've probably got the easiest career in that sense, because Scott [Graham] and myself were co-directors on every Frantic show and so I've always been very happy being half of a room, half of a directorship. That was very helpful for me.

In America, I've had a career which has happened in my late thirties where I'm in rooms with incredibly smart, brilliant directors who would never let me be in there as a fellow director, so I'm there as a choreographer.[14]

Most directors, when they start to really let their movement director do their 'thing', they realize that they will always benefit from letting the movement director have a thought or a take or a pass or even a session before rehearsing a scene. John Tiffany will quite often say, 'The blocking of this scene just doesn't seem right,' and I'll go, 'Okay' and sort it out.[15] We can use an aesthetic, a logic and our instinct about how the audience are seeing the image – it is a big thing for movement directors, and sometimes we are just the best people to ask.

Directors often ask me, 'How do I get good results?' I'll tell them that I need an hour's warm-up every day, no matter how physical the show is, and after a point there's some shows you don't need that. But if you really want a *Curious Incident of the Dog in the Night-Time*-type show, a real ensemble, then you'll give me an hour every single morning all the way through the rehearsals, through tech, and for the duration of the show the actors will also warm up for an hour – that's the deal breaker.[16] Ultimately, every day starts with people's physicality, with their bodies, and starts with a sense of their body. It's not just for the director to have a better group of people; it's for *me* to have tools that are warm and good. Most directors that I've worked with, who have seen work that they've liked, that's what I've declared: we had an hour's warm-up every day and I had some time every morning *to make* some material – that's really quite straightforward.

That's such a clear approach, and then are most of the directors you work with watching that as well, or do they come in with fresh eyes?
It depends who they are, really; I worked with John Tiffany a lot and so he does the warm-up with me, and on *Harry Potter* we had most of the creatives in the warm-up. It is very democratic for me. I had a followspot operator recently who did all my warm-ups, so there's something about that that gets them 'in' that way. I like a director being right on my shoulder, to be honest; it feels good … I like the bounce of it. Maybe it's because of my experience with Frantic, that the two of us watching the same thing shoulder to shoulder, that literal physical relationship is one that I know best. I can sometimes feel a bit lonely without it. Even Ivo, on the second day, actually came in halfway through and watched. So, after a while it's just healthy.

I would agree. What is the most important part of the process for you?
I have two thoughts. One is about what the show is on its last day in the rehearsal room and launching that into a tech. A tech ostensibly is where that delicate thing you've *just* put together, you shatter it and you hope what gets pulled back together is something like the same. I've actually been in a rehearsal process where at the end of the rehearsals we had something beautiful that felt ready, and when it got shattered, when we got it back, it was like Frankenstein. I've also been in rehearsals where it wasn't quite ready, and when that gets shattered you've got no chance. In terms of processes, there's something about my job in looking at that rehearsal period and making sure that that final day there, I have to know what that needs to be in an incredibly detailed way, because even if it's beautiful, it still might not live or breathe ever again. The company might never know about my sense of time, but I have to know that that's what I have to do in that transition.

The second [thought] is that my relationship with the performers is absolutely vital. I can't afford for anybody in that ensemble to feel that I don't have an overview of what they're about to do. I certainly can never have undermined them, and I can never have made them feel like they didn't have agency in a creative process, and if I've said 'ensemble', I better deliver ensemble. That thing [*hand gestures indicating the space in front of him, referring to the actors on stage*], but that, that's your work on stage, and I don't mean that in terms of 'Oh, you better look good for my credibility', but that [*indicates the stage space*] doesn't work without everything being absolutely as it should, which is creative, creative, creative, creative and creative.

If you look out to the wider field, how do you see movement in production, movement direction, direction and choreography developing?
The blend is going to come together even closer, and the two terms will always have to exist; I think people are going to say 'choreography' for musicals and they're going to say 'movement direction' for plays, but people are constantly going to mess with that, because shows that I've worked on, it was choreography and it

was in a play and I've done musicals where it was movement direction and so – I'm good. It will matter less.

The big change has been for directors, realizing just what a movement director might bring to that room. And they can look at a bog-standard play and there still might be things where a movement director could lift their vision. It's a great period of time that we're stepping into now, with directors who do realize that any kind of performance is a physical event as well as cerebral. An acting event and lighting event is a physical experience for the performers and certainly a physical, storytelling experience for the audience. The minute you get a movement director in the room who starts to say, 'Well, you know if they've got proximity there then that line is really going for nothing'. When I'm watching a play, things that are obvious to me, when you start to let a director in on *that* process, they're very quick to learn that as well. Then there's going to be an incredibly rich period of time between movement directors and pure choreographers, who will start to get pulled in there as well. It's going to start to bring everybody into those rooms and then it becomes much more interesting and exciting. We're going to see more actors being less scared, and certainly in Scotland now, because *Black Watch* kept going for years, we always needed ten new boys, so their physical training is getting much more robust. Frantic's Ignition program is getting people early.

It's so interesting to hear about the principles that you can see clearly on the stage.
A lot of the time you don't think you have principles; you're just having to get the work up and on, so you forget that there's something other than the task. You are always looking at a room where you are outnumbered. And there is a sense that I have to be other than myself, I have got to be public. That's the thing about movement directors – you really *are* bigger, it's a bigger room for you. What I have realized as I am getting older is that I might be on the outside edges of the room a lot more, and that is something I am not looking forward to. At the moment I am in the middle of the room, and I talk from there where I want to see it, that is, from the ground. And as my job gets clearer, I didn't know what it might be like, coming towards fifty and doing all the warm-ups, being in the middle, and it's going to shift again. The ecology of movement direction is shifting and so am I, and we are not necessarily doing the same thing.

Notes

1   This interview took place on 8 July 2019 at the National Theatre studio, London.
    As Movement Director/Choreographer, Hoggett's theatre credits include *Harry Potter and the Cursed Child* (Palace Theatre, 2016), *The Twits* (Royal Court, 2015*), Let the Right One In* (National Theatre of Scotland, West End, St Ann's, NYC 2015); *The Last Ship* (Broadway, 2014); *The Glass Menagerie* (Broadway, 2013), *The Curious*

Incident of the Dog in the Night-Time (National Theatre, 2012, West End, 2013); *Once* (Broadway, 2011, 2012 and West End, 2013); *Rocky: The Musical* (Broadway 2012), *American Idiot* (Broadway, 2010), *Peter & the Starcatcher* (Broadway, 2012); *The Light Princess* (National Theatre, 2013); *365* (Lyric Hammersmith, 2008); *The Bacchae* (also Associate Director, National Theatre of Scotland, 2008), *The Wolves in the Wall* and *Improbable* (National Theatre of Scotland, 2006), *Black Watch* (also Associate Director, National Theatre of Scotland, 2006); *Mercury Fur* (Plymouth Theatre Royal, 2005); *The Straits* (Paines Plough, UK tour 2004). As Choreographer, Hoggett's opera credits include *Rigoletto* (Met, NYC 2019); *Dr Dee* (English National Opera/Manchester International Festival, 2012). As Director, theatre credits include *Truth* (Birmingham Repertory Theatre with Helen Chadwick, 2018); *War Correspondents* (UK tour with Helen Chadwick, 2018); *What's It All About/Close to You: Bacharach Reimagined* (New York Theatre Workshop/West End, 2015). Other opera credits include *Dalston Songs* (Royal Opera House, 2010). Film credits include *How to Train Your Dragon 2* (DeBlois, 2014). Hoggett has also created choreography for Prada, Radio One and Selfridges and the award-winning 'Harmonious Dance' TV commercial for Orange, as well as music promotion videos for artists including Goldfrapp, Calvin Harris, Wiley, Bat for Lashes and Franz Ferdinand. Steven was founder and Co-Artistic Director of Frantic Assembly. For Frantic Assembly, his credits include *Little Dogs* (National Theatre Wales, 2012); *Lovesong* (Drum Theatre, Plymouth, 2011*), Beautiful Burnout* (National Theatre of Scotland, 2010); *Stockholm* (Drum Theatre, Plymouth, 2007); *Othello* (Theatre Royal Plymouth, 2008)). Awards include Olivier Award for Best Theatre Choreographer for *Black Watch*; Lortel, Obie and Calloway Awards for Best Choreography for *Once*; Lortel Award for Outstanding Choreography for *Peter and the Starcatcher*; Theatre Managers Award Best Director for *Othello*. With Scott Graham, he co-wrote *The Frantic Assembly Book of Devising Theatre* (2014).

2   A 1991 production by Volcano Theatre Company, a Swansea-based theatre company founded by Fern Smith and Paul Davies in 1987. Available online: http://www.volcanotheatre.co.uk/about-us (accessed 9 August 2019).

3   The Cholmondeleys, an all-female dance company, and Featherstonehaughs, a male counterpart, were founded by Lea Anderson MBE in 1984 and 1988, respectively. According to the 2016 Arts Council report by Susanne Burns and Sue Harrison, the period 1979–89 was one of growth, diversity and expansion, with 'the advent of the choreographer-led company model' and the following companies established: Second Stride in 1981; Siobhan Davies Company in 1981; Lloyd Newson DV8 in 1986; Michael Clark Company in 1984. Matthew Bourne formed Adventures in Motion Pictures in 1987, which would become New Adventures in 2002. Anderson and Lloyd Newson of DV8 are seen jointly as significant influences on British dance and dance theatre. In their varied ways, they accessed new audiences and reshaped the content and action of dance works.

4   Nigel Charnock (1960–2012) was a British performer, choreographer and director. He was founder member of DV8. He started Nigel Charnock and Company in 1995. For more information on Charnock, see Houston 2012.

5   Frantic Assembly was formed by Vicki Middleton, Steven Hoggett and Scott Graham in 1994. The current artistic director is Scott Graham. They have created works that frequently overlap new text, heightened physical style and music. Their training scheme, Ignition aims to 'seek out talent in unexpected places' and was

originally established to develop male performers. In 2020, they will be running Ignition for Women.

6   The 2016 production of *Harry Potter and the Cursed Child* was written by Jack Thorne, from an original story by J. K. Rowling, directed by John Tiffany. Hoggett was movement director, the associate movement director was Delphine Gaborit and the international associate movement director was Neil Bettles. Since its premiere in London (2016), it has played on Broadway (2018), Melbourne (2019) and San Francisco (2019).

7   Stephen Kirkham is a movement director and choreographer; T. C. Howard is a performer and choreographer who is currently part of Vincent Dance Theatre; Christine Devaney is Artistic Director of Curious Seed.

8   We met during a research and development phase for a forthcoming production of Neil Gaiman's novel *The Ocean at the End of the Lane*, adapted by Joel Horwood for the National Theatre, directed by Katy Rudd. Hoggett is referring to Chris Cunningham, a British video artist who creates short films and music videos.

9   The 2016 production of *The Crucible*, by Arthur Miller, was directed by Ivo van Hove for the Walter Kerr Theatre.

10 *Once* is a musical based on the 2007 film directed by John Carney. The book is by Enda Walsh, music and lyrics by Glen Hansard and Marketa Irglova. It premiered in New York in 2011 and has subsequently played on Broadway (2012), in London (2013) and in many more locations.

11 The 2019 production *End of History* at the Royal Court was written by Jack Thorne and directed by John Tiffany, with movement direction by Hoggett.

12 *Strictly Come Dancing* is a televised dancing competition. A variety of performers from the field of light entertainment, acting, music, politics and sport are each paired with a professional ballroom dancer to compete by performing short danced extracts from the competitive ballroom canon. It is not surprising that many movement directors watch to see how non-professionals adapt their movement skills in the pursuit of pressurized performance – steps, styles, lifts, partnering – because there is overlap between their work with actors on core transferable skills.

13 The 2006 production *Black Watch* was written by Gregory Burke and directed by John Tiffany. It premiered at the National Theatre of Scotland during the Edinburgh Festival. For an overview of this production, see Jack 2008.

14 Hoggett was referring to examples of directors which included Michael Mayer, a US theatre director who works across opera, musicals, film and plays. He directed *American Idiot* (premiered in 2009, and subsequently played on Broadway 2010). Music was by Green Day, lyrics by Billie Joe Armstrong and book by Billie Joe Armstrong and Michael Mayer. Hoggett was the choreographer.

15 John Tiffany is an award-winning British theatre director who has a long-standing collaboration with Hoggett.

16 *The Curious Incident of the Dog in the Night-Time* was based on the novel by Mark Heddon, adapted by Simon Stephens, directed by Marianne Elliot and movement directed by Scott Graham and Steven Hoggett of Frantic. The production premiered at the National Theatre and was transferred to the West End in 2013, and subsequently played on Broadway in 2014; it had a UK tour in 2014 and 2017, and a US tour in 2016.

12 ANN YEE

The body has its own way of speaking [2018][1]

Could you describe what you do?
I'm a theatre maker. It's the easiest way to describe all the different hats from choreographer to movement director to director.

Choreography is perhaps clear, as it is usually related to the dance aspect of a piece, but what is movement direction for you?
My job as a movement director is three-fold. One aspect is to facilitate the experience of the performer to achieve their best physicality for what is required of them. A second aspect is to create and build any physical sequences or sections of choreography in the piece, choose and direct the movement vocabulary of the piece and to support the ensemble with a warm-up to sustain them for however long and gruelling that run is. And a third aspect is to be in tune with the vision of my collaborators – the director, the writer, the composer, the designer … the list goes on.

Recently, a theatre asked me to choose my billing. Their suggestions were 'movement director', 'movement', 'director of movement' or 'choreographer', and I didn't know what to choose. I had recently seen a billing: 'Movement Direction and Choreography by …' When I read that, I asked myself, 'Where's the line drawn between the two?' I consider choreography as quite broad.

All movement directors work differently, as do the directors who are helming the piece. Sometimes we are involved in the initial design and dramaturgy conversations and sometimes we aren't. Sometimes we come into the dialogue last minute, when the director or lead collaborator sees a need for more nuanced or bold movement choices that can't be achieved without someone with more expertise on board. What we are always responsible for is the body. I talk about the body having its own intelligence ... that there is a physical instinct we can tap into without 'thinking' about it first.

In the production of *Julie* at the National Theatre, there was a sequence that we were working on when the director turned to me and wondered aloud whether or not I had given the actors enough information to head into an improvisation.[2] At that point, I didn't have any more words for them, and thought to myself, 'We're going to have to start and see what happens.' Once it started, more words came, more prompts came, I got up, I was in it, I was out of it, and it just happened. If you don't have the right words to say, trust that the body has its own way of speaking. I was working with an ensemble that had developed a phenomenal kinaesthetic connection: we had cultivated it together. They came into the project with their own individual histories; I provided them with tools and a structure. Within that structure, we shared our histories and we created our own shared intelligence. You can't underestimate that. When I started to be affected then I was able to affect them, and we created something that we knew was special and exactly what needed to be made. That was the vital step along the way within the process – trust – without which we could not get to where we needed to go. They trusted me to sculpt. What is that? Is that movement direction, is that choreography, is that direction? How does that work? I don't know. But I do know that it requires a lot of tools.

Can you articulate what those tools are?
I have an undergraduate degree in dance from Boston Conservatory at Berklee, where the training was both varied and challenging: we worked long hours.[3] It was sophisticated and hard.

Where was your graduate programme?
I received my MFA in Dance from the Ohio State University in Columbus. I moved from Ohio to London, a pit-stop towards Europe and the proverbial dream of Pina [Bausch], and I never got out of England: I got stopped here. My movement direction started with Daniel Kramer on *Woyzeck* at the Gate in Notting Hill.[4] It was a moment of luck, a moment of meeting, and from there things happened. I started working with different directors and different actors, all who came with incredible knowledge and physical theatre practices. I was a sponge, soaking up all of their practices, which were so similar to contemporary dance but so different.

How might you start to prepare for a project? Could you step me through what might be a process, from a first encounter with a script or a score or an idea?
My first point of contact is usually the director; sometimes it can be a producer sending you a script or score or pitching an idea to you. Once I'm in a conversation with the director, I pay attention to what excites them visually, conceptually, and how passionate they are about aspects of the work.

Then I read the material to see if I have an affinity for it, or at least, I find points of contact with the material so I can be excited about it. Sometimes I'm more excited about working with the director than the material. Sometimes I'm more excited about the material than the director. Sometimes the venue is relevant or whether I've worked in that space before, or it's the offer to work with eighty or 200 chorus members. Sometimes it doesn't matter what the project is, because that event is going to teach me and give me an opportunity to become a better artist.

Different directors prepare differently, and I try to fit my prep around and within theirs. Some directors can talk to you twice before you show up on the first day of rehearsal. With others, you storyboard the entire show before you set foot in a rehearsal room or a workshop space. The prep work is as much about cultivating the ability to communicate as it is about doing the research. Even though I've been doing this for fifteen years, I am always attentive to how the communication between me and a new director is going to go.

For *Julie*, I talked to Carrie a couple of times; I already had an established relationship with her. I knew we were devising the movement work, and I knew that the material I needed to work with was 'in the room'. It was about creating two different vocabularies: one that we could work with within the room so that we could create structured improvisations that created narrative, and then the actual vocabulary of what ended up on stage – and that went through quite a few changes. Carrie and I communicated about aesthetics; we would send songs ... almost like a mood board of songs, YouTube references and Pinterest images. You begin to understand what intrigues you and what doesn't, what lives in this world, this design world and what doesn't. The designer and writer, Tom Scutt and Polly Stenham, were part of the conversation as well.

I recognize this, as I do it too – a type of visual and aural conversation ahead of rehearsal.

Yes. And then if it's a musical we do all of this, and I go into a pre-production rehearsal space with one or two or three associates and assistants. We listen to the songs, break down the structure and try to understand the narrative that they need to tell and we build it. Musicals require a different type of clarity. In the *Julie* room were contemporary dancers and actors who move, that is, makers. They want to be part of that creation and they want to 'own' it. Sometimes on big musicals you have incredibly skilful human beings who want to be told what to do in a vocabulary they've trained in. Neither's right or wrong, and both need to be looked after.

In addition to the vision and vocabulary for the piece, the prep is also about how to best look after and provide for the performers to make their best work. That's why my prep has to change with each project. For instance, at Oregon Shakespeare Festival [OSF] I was working with a wonderful rep company of actors and singers and dancers.[5] I had to insert myself into their already incredibly articulate and familiar system that was foreign to me. There was a turning point through one of my warm-ups when we keyed into one another … it was as if the room started humming. It was joyful.

Can you expand on how warm-ups function within your work?
Warm-ups are simultaneously simple and complex. In that particular situation at OSF, because I didn't audition or know the actors, I needed the warm-ups to teach me what the company could do. Via the warm-up, I could drop in movement language or exercises without triggering fear or anxiety. An actor who does not identify as a dancer can be terrified of dancing, a singer who does not identify as a dancer can be terrified of dancing, and so it is my responsibility to take the fear away so that they can attempt it without thinking about it, so they can find out what they are capable of and then want to use their body to explore the work.

I think we do a lot within warm-up.
The warm-up is about muscles, blood, breath, joints, tendons, ligaments, all the tangible, technical stuff we've been trained to do. In addition to the somatic aspects, I also believe it's about creating the invisible lines to each other so that what exists on the stage has that magical spider web between everybody on it, that can be so dramatic when it's cut and absolutely delicate as you see it rethreaded. We introduce that in the warm-ups, we start making that in the ensemble, we start saying, 'You are a company, a unit, a unique organism.'

I create a new warm-up for each project, for each specific challenge – with a 100-strong chorus or a project that wants to keep the actors apart until tech, I think, 'Let's figure it out, let's find a way through this.' That's one of the reasons I love my job: there is always something different and challenging on the horizon.

This is the warm-up that I've been able to do in a couple of places, and I did with *Julie*: before you start, you need to recognize boundaries and make sure everyone's okay being touched; you need to make sure everybody who has injuries has shared them with the group.[6] I'm huge on responsibility within the room; once you let the people know you have an injury, you are responsible for that self-management and communication.[7] Then we begin with a standing massage. This is the first communication between two people, how much do you have to hold your own weight in order to receive pressure on your shoulders. Then I go into a system of hugs. I talk about the language of weight, heart, pelvis, head, power, lack of power. Observing without judgement is the key to moving freely while being present and connected. Immediately, I introduce the idea that there is 'no right' and 'no wrong': this is creativity, right now we're observing without judgement because what just happened was a real moment so let's just observe it. We observe that this is 'the *first time* that on this day that all these creative bodies are in this space and therefore it's *new*' – the who, what, when and where that is impossible to repeat. It is our responsibility as storytellers to hold that and know that a 'first time' is an extraordinary event and will happen every single performance because of the live exchange between the actors and the audience.

On some projects, this evolves into 'big dance, little dance'. It's a simple way to access improvisation, story and relationship. We evolve from the contact of the hug to the exchange of motion. I explain: 'I'm going to take some movement information from you, and I'm going to give it back to you. If your eyebrows are going to go up, I might put a movement response in my shoulders. My shoulders might trigger a response in your knees, your shoulders or somewhere else. It's a physical exchange, and the only thing you need is the person across from you and their physical offer. I'm letting you change me and you're letting me change you. It's a scene. The only difference is that it's through the physical response of the body which is different to the response of the brain (one could consider this text) which is different to the response of the heart (one could consider this emotion).' The experiential aspect of theatre is when all of these parts work together. I'm constantly trying to free the actors without exposing them, release them without dictating 'how' and find more movement 'keys' to unlock their physical expression. We eventually move from partners into groups and then gradually build ensemble improvisations. We begin with music that is very accessible and then journey it closer to the mood board of the piece. There is a constant truth: the work is *never* the same from show to show, because the individuals bring their histories, and it changes the work.

I sometimes use an old analogy about ballet teachers that actors have told me is useful. In San Francisco, the teacher would come to you with an adjustment and start with, 'Ah, how was that, how did that feel? I know, just drop your weight, breathe in and do that again.' And in New York they'd go, 'Higher, faster, harder, higher, faster, there's twenty-five people outside that door that want your job.' Even though it's exaggeration, it's a useful framework to use to put different ways of working in perspective. The process starts in San Francisco; the actors can feed back to me what they learn, they tell me what they observe, they tell me what they're seeing and feeling. This crucial exchange starts creating the point of view of the piece from *the inside of the ensemble*. 'New York' within the analogy is about being consistent, reliable and representing with discipline and rigor as well as creating an awareness of consequence and responsibility.

And do you think the ensemble work that emerges also affects the director too?
Yes. Without a doubt. I've already mentioned Carrie. I remember when Dominic Cooke and I did *The Comedy of Errors* at The National.[8] We built the entire chase scene this way, which dictated when we would end up spinning Bunnie Christie's set. Dominic and I would see opportunity when it happened, name it and sculpt it. *Mr Burns* with Rob Icke and Anne Washburn was such a wonderful experience.[9] Before we would stage a scene, I got everyone moving into huge improvisations. Rob was by my side soaking it all up, 100 per cent supportive; he could see all the

actors changing and he could see the ensemble becoming a tribe, he could see them accessing the spontaneous, the immediate, the feral, the ability to change the space without telling each other that they were going to change the space. The most epic example of this work is Phyllida Lloyd's *Shakespeare Trilogy*.[10] We worked together over five years, mostly with the same core company and a few new additions, depending on people's availability. The range of experience and ability between the actors was immense. With such a vast vision from the director, the movement work was crucial to creating a hive mind – an equal mind with equal voices within the ensemble. Phyllida was voracious in her interrogation of the material. The movement work's power to access spontaneity and change while scrambling on the skeleton of the text was a bedrock to her constant exploration. It's wonderful when directors and writers are as entranced by the work as you are. That's when you know they're going to take it somewhere special.

What do you think is particular to actors when you're working with movement with them?

Actors are amazing creatures, and it's a joy watching them interpret material and discover character and story. Some of them are so keyed in to imagination and immediacy of response that in working with them, I understand more and more what the word 'art' means. However, sometimes they don't think their body is their first point of call. It just doesn't feel like their 'go to' place for confidence, even though that's their instrument they just don't look at it that way. They say, 'It's my psychology' or 'I have access to my emotional life, but I don't know what to do with my body.' Not every actor struggles with it; loads of actors thrive on the movement work. But I would say when there's a challenge it's because they don't think that their body is as much of an instrument as it actually is, or there's a fear in it. All of us understand fear that sits in our bodies – that is universal and human. Even though there is psychology and emotion involved, all of it is housed in the body. I separate emotional, intellectual and physical intelligences into categories, but that's more for me to be able to talk about them. All of it lives in the body, and it's much more complicated than categories or even the word 'intelligence'. It's not about having the answers for an actor – in every situation I genuinely feel like I have to make a discovery I've never made before in order to guide the actor to their performance.[11] That's how it feels, like my job is brand new with each production.[12]

I recognize that. Each company and each work does necessitate its own response.

At the Oregon Shakespeare Festival, on a show that a lot of people will remember as a 'gender-inclusive *Oklahoma*', the Rogers and Hammerstein estate had okayed this ground-breaking leap into redefining who gets to do what. In a traditional *Oklahoma!*, Laurey is female, Curly is male, Ado Annie is female, Will Parker is male. In Bill Rauch's *Oklahoma!*, Laurey is female, Curly is female, Ado Andy is male and Will Parker is male; our two main love stories were same-sex love stories, and Aunt Eller was performed by a trans actress.

Myself, who identifies as a member of the LGBTQI community,[13] who identifies as a multiracial person, who identifies as an immigrant, who (clearly!) has a lot of identifiers – I thought I was pretty aware, and yet I wasn't. There's a whole world where words that I was used to using I had to stop getting used to using. You couldn't call a room together going, 'Hey guys and gals', or 'Hey ladies and gentlemen', because not all people could respond to those gender identifiers. I struggled with it, opened myself to feedback about it, and nobody had a really good offering. One day I said, 'Humans! Gather around here!' And it happened. It was a joke and it was kind of funny, but it wasn't, it was natural and it worked. Suddenly stage management and the rest of the company were using the same language. Awareness, mindfulness and the ability to truly communicate through awareness and mindfulness is a lesson from the word *humans*, which is poetic and speaks to our need to keep evolving – I can imagine lots of other practitioners are speaking to this.

There's a relationship between having a toolbox and being present in the moment to know how to respond.
Absolutely true. I actually feel like I'm in a constant 'big dance, little dance'. In that exercise, your partner will *change you* and that is a real, honest thing – to be changed. That's what making theatre is, that's what acting is; we change each other on stage, which is why it's so exciting. If we're playing the end of the scene at the top of the scene or playing the end of the play at the top of the play, nobody's going to want to watch the next two hours.

What do you think you respond to, or activate, within the creative dialogue with directors?
I consider what they're curious about and if I'm curious about it too, and what they want to make. A fundamental creative aspect for me is their fearlessness in interrogating the piece: I value vision and courage. As far as what I activate within that dialogue for them … one director I work with often said this to me: 'I'm working with you because you will make this the best piece it can possibly be.' That was very nice to hear.

I was having a conversation with a music director and a producer who said, 'There are two things that you need in a director: one, they need an artistic vision, and two, they need an ability to read a room, assess a room and lead the room.' I'm still navigating this to find out what rings true for me. Artistic vision is subjective; it's not for me to decide if someone else is an artist, but I can decide how I think and feel about their art. The second pre-requisite – 'read a room, assess the room and lead the room' – that three-fold list is an example of clear leadership. However, what I've learnt is that it isn't solely about leadership in the rehearsal room, it's also the way that director works with their collaborators and the stage management. It's also about how that piece exists within the building, whether it's the National Theatre or the Old Vic or the Lincoln Center or Oregon Shakespeare Festival. I really respond to directors who respect and understand that they, and their project, are part of a much bigger picture and that there are many, many people facilitating the vision. They manage to do this in a way that never compromises the work but brings out the best in everyone involved and therefore makes the most interesting work.

What is interesting is how different directors manage this or inhabit this differently.
True. I respect my collaborators. I think that's the joy of letting someone change you, I think that's the joy of sharing an experience, cultivating and growing something together. I love them for creating a space where we can tell a story, for leading it, for guiding it, for contributing to it. I love the lighting designers, sound designers, the composers, and they all have all of these skills I don't have, and they all bring it; I see the magic in them, and I want to be around it.

Do you think that, over the fifteen years you've been working, you have seen a growth in dialogue and collaboration?
I think so, I do. As social media and AI [artificial intelligence] and interpersonal physical relationships and our relationship to our planet and our environment continue to change, quickly and vastly, I am very curious to see how live theatre will evolve in this world. I guess we can go back to the idea of being changed by someone. I have gained skills and the directors have gained skills and the work has changed. We are all hungry to move forward, to cultivate new culture, ask bigger and harder questions and therefore the dialogue and collaboration must reflect that. How is theatre going to meet all of those new needs, as well as continue to respond to the eternal questions we can't stop asking? All of this will shape the ever-evolving dialogue of collaboration; we are in a crucial stage of our evolution where we must be brave and vulnerable and bold as theatre makers.

Notes

1 This interview took place on 30 May 2018 in the National Theatre and 8 June 2018 at the British Film Institute Southbank, London.
    Ann Yee's credits include *American Clock* (Old Vic, 2019); *War Requiem* (English National Opera, 2018); *Caroline, or Change* (Chichester Festival Theatre, 2017); *Sunday in the Park with George* (Hudson Theater, New York, 2017); *Shakespeare Trilogy* (Donmar at King's Cross and St Ann's Warehouse, New York, 2012, 2014, 2016); *Threepenny Opera* (Salzburg Opera Festival, 2015); *Queen Anne* (Royal Shakespeare

Company, 2015); *Anita and Me* (Birmingham Repertory Theatre, 2015); *Urinetown* (St James' Theatre and Apollo Theatre, 2014); *Blurred Lines* (NT Shed, 2014); *Mr Burns* (Almeida Theatre, 2014); *How to Hold Your Breath* (Royal Court Theatre, 2015); *Birdland* (Royal Court Theatre, 2014); *The Commitments* (Palace Theatre, 2013); *The Color Purple* (Menier Chocolate Factory, European premiere, 2013); *Torch Song Trilogy* (Menier Chocolate Factory, 2012); *Wozzeck* (ENO, 2013); *Macbeth* (Trafalgar Studios, 2013); *Berenice* and *Philadelphia, Here I Come* (Donmar Warehouse, 2012); *The Accrington Pals* (2013) and *The Country Wife* (2012) (Royal Exchange Theatre); *The Duchess of Malfi* (Old Vic, 2012); *After Miss Julie* (Young Vic, 2012); *She Stoops to Conquer* (National Theatre, 2012*)*. Other credits include *The 25th Annual Putnam County Spelling Bee: The Musical* (Donmar, UK premiere, 2011); *Salome* (Headlong, 2010); *Romeo and Juliet* (Middle Temple Hall, 2008); *Oxford Street* (Royal Court, 2007); *The Lion, The Witch and the Wardrobe* (WYP/Birmingham Rep Theatre, 2008); *Bad Girls: The Musical* (Garrick Theatre, 2007); Angels in America (Lyric Hammersmith/UK tour, 2007); *Bent* (Trafalgar Studios, 2006); *Hair* (Gate Theatre, 2005); *Woyzeck* (St Ann's Warehouse New York/Gate Theatre, 2005); and *Food* (Traverse Theatre/UK tour 2006).

2   *Julie* by Polly Stenham after Strindberg, directed by Carrie Cracknell, National Theatre production (2018).

3   Yee trained at Boston Conservatory at Berklee, Harvard Summer Dance Center and Ohio State University. Her training included *pointe* work; *pas de deux*, contemporary; Graham; Cunningham; Nikolai; Contact Improvisation; Alexander classes; kinesiology, choreography, history of dance, history of choreography; rhythm tap, acapella, and music classes.

4   Daniel Kramer, originally from Ohio, is a theatre director working in Britain. He is currently the artistic director of English National Opera.

5   *Oklahoma!* (2018) at the Oregon Shakespeare Festival, Angus Bowmer Theatre, directed by Bill Rauch, was billed as the '75th Anniversary production of the classic musical that breaks new ground with LGBTQ2+ affirmation' through the choices of casting. Jaclyn Miller was the Associate Choreographer.

6   For many years, the fields of dance and movement direction have been using touch as a creative tool for generating choreographic material or establishing character rapport. This creative approach must be supported by an ethical and practical skillset. The movement director must navigate what both actors and dancers have in common, that is, bodies as a professional resource as well as the site of lived experience.

7   Rehearsal rooms are often intergenerational, so working with bodies with a variety of capacities and aptitudes often characterizes the work of the movement director. Equally, there is sometimes a culture of actors internalizing injuries and conditions, as they are worried that declaring their injuries might act as a hurdle to casting. A welcome shift in this culture seems to be in progress.

8   *Comedy of Errors* by William Shakespeare, directed by Dominic Cooke, Royal National Theatre (2011).

9   This 2014 production of *Mr Burns*, by Anne Washburn, was directed by Robert Icke for the Almeida.

10 Yee is referring to productions of William Shakespeare's *Julius Caesar, Henry IV* and *The Tempest* that were directed by Phyllida Lloyd for Donmar Warehouse and staged in 2012, 2014 and 2016, respectively. This trilogy had all-female casts.

11 Filmmaker Luca Guadagnino described Yee's approach as 'psychoanalytic choreography ... trying to pull out things ... it was a great collaboration' when working on *A Bigger Splash* (2015). The film's star, Ralph Fiennes, said Yee 'gave me a language of movement ... it wasn't choreographed as such'. Fiennes had seen Andrew Scott in *Birdland* and had sought Yee out as he identified an actor-focused approach (Jays 2016).

12 Movement directors often invisibly deal with actors' relationships to movement and to their own feelings about moving. There is a recognizable phenomenon – a type of self-consciousness or a privacy of process that can be played out on the terrain of movement, and that manifests as reticence or fear of moving freely or experimentally. Resistance to movement in the profession is rare, but somehow the profession can close down certain actors' capacity to be a novice or to play. Yee spoke of accompanying actors carefully, quietly, privately and practically to enable the work to occur.

13 Lesbian, Gay, Bisexual, Transgender, Queer and Intersex.

13 IMOGEN KNIGHT

Everything is in the body [2019][1]

Where did you train?
Northern School of Contemporary Dance[2] and London Contemporary Dance School.[3]

How did you become a movement director, when your background is in dance?
I have always been interested in the human condition, which is why theatre appealed to me perhaps more than conventional contemporary dance at that time. Towards the end of my training as a dancer, I found a great deal more creativity and freedom when I was improvising and finding movement through a thought, feeling or situation. I felt quite constricted in a purely dance form. It took time to learn this, though. For a long time, I felt I wasn't creative because I couldn't choreograph more conventional-looking dance. I've now come to realize that, for me, movement comes from a deeper, more subconscious place. My dance training gave me rigour and a strong work ethic. My training was brutal, but I learnt what I was capable of and what I was willing to sacrifice. If you train in something so intensely, with that single focus and obsessive attention to detail, there is more of a desire to shake it up and reconfigure it later: a rebellion, so to speak. I've found this in my recent work with orchestras, for example; there is a defined form that adheres to quite strict traditions, and I like working with those, turning them on their head and finding new ways.[4] Making musicians move whilst playing is not only a real technical challenge for them but also a radical presentation of structure to an often conventional audience.

Dance definitely gave me the rigour of training and precision. If you do something over and over, you can refine your understanding of your body. So, I try to instil something that is repetitious when I am working with actors, even if it's in a warm-up.

As a child, I did a dance training run by Pat Woodall at a school called Chantraine in a church hall in Kilburn.[5] It was an incredible practice where she taught whole generations. I remember dancing around free-form, no technique – but you had to have an understanding about the feeling behind each dance, what it was about. It was very inspiring, like a rite of passage – I just remember running around the space. It was very limitless. This was the kernel of my interest and practice. I think that has probably instilled in me an interest in people moving in a way that is unguarded, unrefined and moving together. It also instilled an interest in people who don't come from a movement background. That has fed itself into why I find actors so interesting to work with, because you get this kind of rawness and humanity.

How would you describe what you do as a movement person?
In theatre, it really varies from project to project, so I think it's quite hard to define as one thing. Within any theatre production, a great deal of my work is about supporting the director's vision and creating a physical language with the company and the director that can be drawn upon throughout the process. It's about the relationship and the offering up of ideas, ways of telling the story, physically. I listen … I think that's the most valuable thing and the basis of how I then work within the room.

And then on a movement scale, it's really to do with the project and what is required: it can be movement, work with the energies or choreography; it really varies with me. It all comes from the same place. Sometimes this is clearly visible in the finished project; sometimes it is much more fundamental in the construction of the company and the characters which can stay in the process rather than what is necessarily seen in performance at the end.

Movement directors develop their own approaches. Do you get a sense of what those are in your work?
One skill is to be really clear and be yourself. Movement can be daunting for some people and bring up insecurities, so it's important to be aware of this and make it accessible for each individual. It's about giving information and using a language that they're going to understand. Not being too abstract. The more we work the more trust builds, and that is key. I'll ask a group to explore some movement and then explain why I've asked them to do it or what my thoughts are. I like actors to feel they have ownership over what they are creating, and there is a skill in making them have ownership by creating material together. I very rarely demonstrate, because I think if they watch me, they'll think that that's how it should look. How a group interpret an instruction is so much more interesting to me. I don't want a room full of 'me'; I want a room full of individuals.

Where did you develop your capacity to guide actors in a non-abstract way and offer very concrete tasks?
I learned my core skills and techniques teaching in my early career for various drama schools and theatre companies, either individual workshops or across educational programs. Fundamentally, the key is to be as enthusiastic and open to the room as possible, to feed from how the participants in a session respond to your initial direction and be responsive to that, much in the way a DJ might shape their set to a crowd. Also, from making mistakes, talking too much or too little! Teaching large groups in these environments gives you more margin for experimentation with instructional language and to craft your technique before working in closer proximity to actors.

When watching rehearsal, I ask myself questions: 'Why is that not as impactful or as interesting as it could be?' 'What does it need?' 'What do the actors need?' 'What does it make me feel?' 'Do they understand why they are doing it?' I need the space in between the instruction and the actor's exploration to be alive, spontaneous and from the inside out. That space is the unknown, and it's where you have no idea what might unfold in front of you. It's very exciting.

When you're thinking more dramaturgically about movement, what do you think about?
For any project it's about if I can map my feelings from one action to the next. These actions can come out of nowhere and be a sudden change of gear, but you have to know why. I work through the play or beats listening to my body and building the dramaturgy from there. You can trust your body. What is right for this moment and what drives it forward? Movement needs to drive the story forward; it's not there for decoration.

I'll often listen to a certain composer for months or search out a genre of music or feed from visual art. Anything that I feel connects me and the project to my imagination. Sometimes it can be just one image or piece of music that unlocks it all: something epic and that has its own dramaturgy. I keep hold of this in my mind during a process. I think it helps bring me back to the core of something, the bare bones of a story or a feeling.

Composition is often a consequence of a movement process and based on what is emerging in a rehearsal.
For me, any movement is meaningless without a centre; with a sense of why it's happening, or why performers are doing it. Even if they're walking, I need to know the reason – it's never just walking. If you have the feeling located in the right place, the movement that emerges is usually pretty close to what you need and what the work needs. You may shorten, lengthen or change movement in some way, but in its essence it's in the right ballpark because the actor is connecting emotion with the action.

Do you think you've got a style? When people engage you, do you get a sense of why it's you?
I think I have a style in the way I like to work, which is fundamentally based in the psychology of a character and actor. I very rarely come into a room with a set of instructions to teach performers. It is entirely an evolution, and direction of and initial position from my base feeling about the piece or specific area of text. Working collaboratively is where I work best; I prefer working in rooms where there is a live conversation. When I am asked to be involved in projects it is usually for my ability to see the whole picture, as well as the movement – I consider myself a collaborative artist, specialising in movement and choreography.

How do you start preparing for work with a director?
I mainly listen. I take a lot of inspiration from sound and music. Visual art is also hugely important to me; I try to have the broadest approach with these in terms of both period and location. The natural world informs much of my thinking. I walk a lot, both in the city and in nature, and the simple shapes and energy of any environment inspire me continuously. These are the initial stages. Then there is the more conventional part of the preparation, including talking with the director about different aspects they are interested in. I then think of ways to marry those initial explorations with these creative conversations.

The first session with a group of performers can be the most daunting for me and them, but it can actually be hugely illuminating and inspiring. Sometimes, ideas that are explored in that first session are the very bones of what will be in the final piece of work. People are at their most vulnerable but also at their most brave; this is where the building of trust begins. Actors throw themselves into ideas because more factual thoughts and ideas about character, setting, etc. are so embryonic that there is a freedom at this first stage. It's a heady concoction but a brilliant one.

Creative relationships are always different from director to director and from project to project, and navigating the differences is what shapes the work. The relationship with the director is key, and it's incredible how different people are and how different their processes are, too. I think our job is to be incredible navigators, and that's a real skill that I think people probably overlook.

There's something additionally complex about movement, because there's a privacy to some of the creatives' roles, which isn't actually afforded to movement because you are sharing the same bodies and the same space.
It's really important that you confidently build a process with a company and that a director trusts you. Then you can feel less inhibited about the open nature of your work. You are working very closely with the company and often exploring intimate and abstract concepts, which can feel quite exposing for everyone. When a director shares and holds space for you within this, it creates a very open and

brave working environment. I'm also a strong believer in trying to break down the privacy of other creative roles and for creatives to be as present as frequently as possible. When this happens, other creatives are often able to highlight something that I've not seen, and it can evolve what happens in the room. Equally, I like this to be reciprocal with their work, so we create something as a whole.

And do you have an instinct for when movement ideas will settle, as well?
Yes, I'm getting there. And sometimes it's good when the director goes, 'No – it does make sense: leave it for a bit', and that's great. Sometimes directors see the wider picture, which I'm not able to do at that point. When a director understands that movement, just like text, needs time to bed in, time to develop throughout the process, it's a real gift. It's easy for me to cut my own work too quickly. It can come from a feeling of being exposed or work looking too choreographed, too demonstrative. I, too, have to learn to allow some things to 'bed in'.

What really works for you when you are working with actors?
Being myself. I sometimes describe what I'm interested in exploring. I never describe what I want to see because I don't know. What is far more interesting is how that is interpreted and realized through someone else's imagination and experience. Bringing a group together through movement, dance, rhythm or breath work is of huge importance to me. My main aim is to encourage freedom of movement and a willingness to be open to the possibility of going somewhere different. Warm-up is essential, whether it's coming together in some form or whether it's doing something very physical. I'm really conscious that all movement needs to include people of all ages and all body types. My sessions involve continuous movement and improvisation. There is an element of endurance in my practice. Improvisations can be between one and three hours without stopping. This is where the group can gradually drop deeper into their bodies and be more led by instinct and imagination rather than from a cerebral place. During these improvisations I observe a lot of material that I later use and develop. They don't have to be big actions, but sometimes it's just a quality somebody is bringing in that can be very arresting. I watch, collect and create an image/movement collage in my head.

This kind of moving endurance work can be done with any group of people and at any stage. For some groups they might benefit from a long-form improvisation, and for other groups, perhaps younger or more vulnerable groups, shorter time frames are better and just as challenging and rewarding. It's really important to read the room and see where the focus is and if they are with you. You are responsible for the well-being of the group within the movement, and ideally the working culture of the rehearsal room is supporting them and their creativity, too. Moving can feel very risky and exposing for a lot of people. I encourage people to be aware of the voices in our heads that tell us what we are doing is silly or not good enough and to try and keep going anyway. Move with it and through the discomfort.

Could you talk about the shape of your process over a whole production?
In the beginning, I like to work frequently with the performers and bring the group together, create an ensemble and look at central ideas or themes. Once the piece begins to gain some context I start to create more focused approaches to certain areas, refine some of those initial ideas and give clarity. After that, we start and get the physical work deeper with clearer intentions. Towards the latter stages, editing of the work to clarify is very important.

How do you use the tech and previews?
I find tech and previews a very creative time, as often this is when the work really transforms. Something that might have felt great in the intimacy of the rehearsal room can fall flat in a bigger space. It's very illuminating because you have to reconstruct it, and it's always stronger as a result. It is quite normal to restage the whole show in tech. It's the process of learning over time what a piece is about. It takes time – you need to be patient, work quickly and have an open mind.

What sort of changes would you make in preview, for example?
Previews can be like tech, and there are often big changes which I find really exciting, usually. You've got to be brave, to switch material around, to reimagine, to re-find, to cut, to refine. I try and listen to the work like a piece of music – where the rhythm of it is and how each moment needs to be necessary to earn its place. This doesn't mean that all the movement has to run with pace, but one should feel that whatever you are watching has a life span – everything only has a certain amount of breaths.

Can you talk about how the presence of the audience effects the dynamic between performer and audience in terms of movement during previews?
Often during previews, certain elements or actors become clearer and everything takes on a greater meaning and context, so you need to be responsive. An audience also needs to feel connected consciously or subconsciously to the movement we have created, and it's a key part of my job to make sure that still transmits in performance from rehearsal. I'm very much of the view that the movement should charge the work and how the audience is receiving it. You also need to watch the work through the audience's eyes for the first time. You need to see what they see and what they feel as this may change the context of how we propose or deliver evolving direction. We have a responsibility to the audience to take them on a journey, to challenge expectations and to present in an original and unexpected way. Also, as creative teams we have a responsibility to take care of an audience. As an audience member, I've seen work where violent and abusive things happen to a

character on stage, and there appears to be no awareness of the impact this might have on an audience. It's important for me to really interrogate the representation of intimate and violent acts and to have open conversations in the process and to consider *all* the bodies involved.

You are holding three spaces, aren't you? You're holding the space of the rehearsal room; the imaginative space; plus, the space of the eventual auditorium as well, so it's quite a complicated space, isn't it?
The rehearsal room is my favourite place: it's raw. It is where everything is possible, there is incredible bravery and exploration and most people are in their socks! However, you need to work with the auditorium or space in mind, you can't forget that. I think an auditorium can swallow a realism that I love. I try to keep a lot of the initial feelings in mind so as to remind myself and the performers where something originated from so as they can connect to it as the production becomes more staged.

You have had a real range of projects – from new and classical plays, work with orchestras, choreographing your own pieces and movement directing on screen. How have you managed such a range of differing mediums?
I choose projects carefully and dynamically. It is important to me to have a range of work I apply myself to; I'm not interested in just working in one strand. The approach I use can be readily changed to apply to any of these areas.

Are you working on two pieces at the same time?
Frequently. Sometimes I can be working on a number of different projects and with very different requirements, so I need to work with a different kind of eye and presence for each project. Those projects are often at different stages of development too, some immediate, some as much as a year away but still need initial conversations. This isn't always that easy as I like to have time to think, and sometimes when it's a very busy period you don't get much of that. Being freelance, it is a real art to judge how much you can do and what time you have for things. You have to be realistic in every sense. Why are you doing something? Does it have a hook for you? I always need a hook. Nowadays I try to be really discerning about my work, I am fortunate to get a number of offers at this point in my career so it's about how they shape together and what new thing they ask of me. I have also become better at setting out some boundaries, which has meant I can harness my creative energy and focus.

Creative relationships that repeat have a different energy, don't they? With new directors it's all about finding out, whereas with collaborators you know you're on a shared terrain, aren't you?
Absolutely. Directors who I have had a long-standing working relationship with, it's very often a very fluid conversation throughout the whole process. You need

to talk less about the fundamentals and more about the detail, because there is a shared language and understanding already in place. When there is a history between you, this communication can also take place in a number of informal ways because you already have a shorthand. This is less suitable with new collaborators. With new directors it's about trust that is only really gained by what you do in the room and how you are with the company.

Do you think you have a style or a particular movement 'taste' or tendency? Can you describe that taste?

I'm interested in the psychological messiness of being a human being. Life isn't easy for anybody, so maybe I lean towards this. I'm also interested in nature, how it organizes itself and how it takes no prisoners. Somehow, I will find ways that work connects to nature in some way, invisibly or visibly. I think it inspires me because it is so vast, so much bigger than us. It has a quiet yet unpredictable presence; I like the tension in that.

In parallel, my process is always about encouraging people to explore their creativity, celebrate their physical freedom and learn and trust their bodies. I can only ask people to go to the more unknown vulnerable places if they feel safe and are in a place of openness which comes from trust – trust of me, themselves and a process.

My tendency will always be about what the body knows, what is stored in the body memory. We have everything we need in there. I often say to performers, 'The body knows what to do', 'All the answers are inside'. It takes the pressure off of the idea that there is something they need to 'get' from outside; it stops a sense of working from the outside in. When actors are able to work without watching themselves, they make remarkable discoveries.

It lets your imagination pour in and out?

Yes, exactly, it is a bit like a trance state. Everything is felt and expressed with complete presence. Then I can see things and interpret the work into something.

Looking more broadly at the field of movement, when were you first aware of other movement directors?

Probably on one of my first jobs, when I assisted Steven Hoggett [see Chapter 11] in tech on *Dido, Queen of Carthage* at the National.[6] I was terrified every day because I didn't really know what I was doing, and I didn't really understand how everything worked in theatre. I then learnt that Steven had these specific sections that he had made, movement sections. I saw a production by Cheek by Jowl, and in the programme, Jane Gibson [see Chapter 3] was credited as the Movement Director and I remember thinking that was really interesting because it felt like the movement was an integral part of the work. I then did a workshop with Jane Gibson, and that's where I realized that that kind of practice is a real art, has a specific style, and she had a real confidence in what she did and a deep belief in the importance of movement. Something about the group coming together, moving slowly in a circle, walking in space, doing very straightforward steps, all made so much sense to me. Maybe because it felt more like a human connection than dance? It was powerful. I remember feeling like movement didn't need to be difficult or complicated to be considered movement.

What do you think the future developments of the movement director might be?
It has grown a lot in the last decade; it feels like a really expanding discipline. Movement directors are doing more varied work in theatre, art, performance installation, music, making their own work and, of course, for screen. Movement direction in film and TV work can be just as varied as it is for theatre. There seems to be a lot of film work where choreography is a huge part of the story or aesthetic. So, working on large set pieces or on a more intimate scale, one-on-one sessions are required in equal measure. For example, I recently helped an actor find how they might have a stroke – how it would feel in their body, not just the generic pattern of how these things happen in our bodies. Or recently, I worked with a group of actors helping them find a joint physicality specific to a point and location in history. In the sessions the actors and I discussed the politics of the time, the culture and class structure. All these areas have a huge effect on how a society moves. We are products of our environment and of our collective and personal history. Everything is in the body.

Actors have very little time to rehearse for screen work, so sessions away from camera can be hugely beneficial for them and build confidence. They want to feel connected to what they are doing emotionally and physically, and working one on one means they can go on set feeling physically and psychologically prepared.

I haven't asked you yet: what do you like to be called? What do you think describes what you do best?
It changes each time depending on what the project requires. I think of myself as a collaborative artist; the specific title can then come depending on what the project requires. Quite often my specific role on a project is not apparent until the end as it really does evolve with what any piece requires. This means I could be a Movement Director, Co-Director, Intimacy Consultant, Movement Consultant, Movement Coach and Choreographer.

Do you think choreography is something that's identifiable to an audience and movement is broader?
Yes, I think choreography can be defined as 'people all dancing/moving in time' or something where there are noticeable choreographic elements such as steps. Movement is much broader and can be invisible in some cases. Movement work can be more sprawling, perhaps. Musicals have very clear choreography most of

the time. You know when you are watching it: it has music or a song and a start, middle and end.

Are you saying that doesn't interest you?
It's not that it doesn't interest me; it just, generally, doesn't come from the psychological place that the rest of my work and practice does. In terms of traditional musical choreography, it's therefore not of a really strong interest. I have done choreography for less conventional musical plays, and that was great, as it asked something new of me. Fundamentally, I have to be interested in what I make. I have to be able to say, 'That's interesting to me', 'What I'm watching has originality, truth, courage and vulnerability.'

Notes

1 Imogen Knight is a choreographer, director and movement director. The range of her movement work reaches from film and television to art installations and opera. Theatre credits include *Macbeth* (National Theatre, 2018); *The Birthday Party* (West End, 2018); *The Last Testament of Lillian Bilocca* (Co-Director and Choreographer, Hull City of Culture 2017); *Belleville, Knives in Hens* and *The Lady from the Sea* (Donmar Warehouse, 2017); *Our Ladies of Perpetual Succour* (National Theatre of Scotland, National Theatre, UK tour and West End, 2016); *Nuclear War* (as director, Royal Theatre Upstairs Court, 2017); *OMG!* (Sadler's Wells, Company of Angels and The Place; Winner of the Choreography for Children Award 2012). Opera credits include *Rush Hour 10: Motion* (Southbank Sinfonia, 2017); *The Winter's Tale* (English National Opera, 2017); *Powder Her Face* (English National Opera, 2014); *How to Make* and *Opera, The Little Sweep* (Malmo Opera, 2013). Television credits include *Chernobyl* (HBO, 2019); *Patrick Melrose* (Sky Atlantic, 2018); *The Innocents* (Netflix, 2018); *Harlots* (ITV, 2017); *Call the Midwife* (BBC, 2014), *The Hollow Crown* (BBC, 2012). Film credits include *Swan Song*, directed by Guy Mansfield (2018); *On Chesil Beach*, directed by Dominic Cooke (2017); *My Name is Ruthie Segal*; *Hear me Roar*, directed by Minkie Spiro (Jewish Film Festival, 2009). Knight is choreographer for filmmaker and animator Jasmin Jordy, and on commercials for Age UK and Childline.

2 Northern School of Contemporary Dance is a vocational dance conservatoire established in 1985 in Leeds and affiliated to the University of Kent. Its alumni include Akram Khan (choreographer), Tom Roden (of New Art Club), Robert Hylton (who works across street dance and film), Benji Reid (a 'Choreo-Photolist', who unites theatricality, choreography and photography in a single image or series of images) and Fleur Darkin (choreographer and former Artistic Director of Scottish Dance Theatre).

3 London Contemporary Dance School was founded by Robin Howard in 1966 in London. It offers dance education programmes validated by the University of Kent. This influential conservatoire dedicated to contemporary dance methods of Graham, Cunningham and Limone. Its alumni have populated the British dance scene, and is the birthplace of many notable dance companies. Also see Kate Flatt (Chapter 5) and Struan Leslie (Chapter 8) for an insight into their training at the School. For information on London Contemporary Dance School, see the V&A archive. Available

online: http://www.vam.ac.uk/content/articles/l/london-contemporary-dance-theatre/ (accessed 15 August 2019).

4   Orchestras such as Southbank Sinfonia Concert Lab.
5   The Chantraine School of Dance, run by Pat Woodall, was a school of expressive, developmental dance teaching a method originated by Alain and Francoise Chantraine.
6   This 2009 production of Christopher Marlow's *Dido, Queen of Carthage* was directed by James MacDonald for the National Theatre, with movement by Steven Hoggett and Imogen Knight for Frantic.

14 SHELLEY MAXWELL

The beauty is you don't think, you just do, you have impulses you follow [2019][1]

Shelley, we are continuing a conversation that we started quite a few years ago. What were you working on at that time?
I was working on *Hamlet* with Simon Godwin, as assistant movement director.[2] I'm from Jamaica, so it was my first official movement gig on this side of the pond. I felt that the role of movement director was really the right fit for me, so I dove in headfirst.

Could you talk me through your background and your training?
It's a rich, higgledy-piggledy training. In Jamaica, I started dancing at the age of five. Formal dance classes from the age of six were in modern dance, folk forms, social dances in a Caribbean setting, dance hall, it was street and jazz, so I had this big world of different dance forms that I was trained in.[3] As a kid I would also enter dance competitions with my dance group. So, I learnt the craft of performing and stage skills. I was in a teenage dance group from age thirteen, where I started to choreograph. As I had a pull to create movement, I went to the director to suggest that I created some work for the season.[4] From then on, I was just a fixture. Technically advanced training started when I was fifteen, and then on to dance school in Cuba aged nineteen.[5]

How was the shift from Jamaica to Cuba?
In Jamaican culture, dance holds a spiritual and ritual relevance, and like Cuba everything feeds back within music and dance. It's a lifestyle; it's a way of living;

it's a way of breathing; it's a way of being.[6] It feels like a spiritual embodiment, like something that's bigger than self. So, it was similar from a cultural perspective but very different from a dance training perspective. The major difference being that at that time, in Cuba, training carried more weight, and more importance was placed on dance as a profession. The major shift was the focus I felt when I went to dance school. The training itself from a technical perspective is very disciplined and very effective – they have some of the best dancers globally.[7] I trained in ballet, which I'd done in Jamaica as well, modern, and their folk forms and styles. Coming out of the experience, I was completely changed: mentally, physically. I felt technically solid in my dance prowess. I had expanded my mind with a different artistic realm, doing choreography and improvisation. Coming back to Jamaica after my training, I was thinking, 'This is my love, this is what I want to do, its choreography and it's dancing.' But I suffered an injury during my training in Cuba.

I returned to Jamaica to re-evaluate and it was the best thing that I could have done, because I produced a festival where I gathered young, up-and-coming choreographers who weren't being given a platform. Eventually, I went back into dancing for the National Dance Company in Jamaica as well as choreographing for them and for the other companies in Jamaica.[8] I felt that I needed to grow more, so I decided that London was the space to do that and came to do my master's in choreography at Laban in 2006.[9] It was quite a hard year: I felt myself shut down creatively. At the end of it, I shut aside my choreographic voice and went into performing in the contemporary dance world and ended up in musical theatre. Thankfully, while I was there I was a *swing*, so I had to use my brain in a different way which encompassed thinking from a choreographic perspective, so I learnt a lot.[10] As a swing you're seeing everything: the way that the actors were being worked with and the way that theatre functioned behind the scenes. Then I decided it was time to start a family and that point was time to pull back from the stage. Dancers' Career Development provided someone to help me through the time after the birth of my child.[11] That led to me eventually working on *Hamlet*, which was a pivotal point, because I was in that rehearsal room, not knowing what to expect. I ended up working closely with the director, learning immensely. I felt it was something I could do. That brings us to being in London and becoming a movement director.

Would you describe what you do now?
I'm a movement director and choreographer. But what does that mean? The formal title is movement director and choreographer. I always say that what I do is 80 per cent psychology and 20 per cent movement.

How has your background as a dancer and choreographer influenced how you create movement with actors and directors?
As a dancer, my training is brilliant from the standpoint of understanding your body and anatomy; understanding how things move and work, and how to tie in

emotional connection with the physical. But the way that we are trained, the way that we receive the information, is very different to how an actor would be able to receive and interpret that movement information. Even though I had this wealth of information from a training perspective, I realized that I couldn't put that on to an actor. I wanted to be able to translate my understanding of how my body works, how 'the' body works, in a way that's amenable to an actor's needs. That was the first challenge of using the dance training. Every project is different, every director is different, the actors and energy in the room and what is *needed* is different.

How do you start to indentify what is needed?
Generally, the first thing to determine is the *feel* of the room. What's the world of the rehearsal room, and where do I fit? The key for me is to build trust across the board: with the directors, actors and the creative team. Once I've figured out what that is, my approach tends to be not a dance one, because sometimes there is a trepidation about the word 'dance' in a rehearsal room. I always say to people that 'we move, dance is movement', and if you get up in the morning out of your bed and you have a shower and put your clothes on you are already moving because we *are* movement. I try to get them to move with me in a 'non-dancer' way. I'm seeing how they feel about movement, what their confidence level is and if there's anyone who has a special skillset. I approach it from more of a fitness perspective, versus a dance one, so with aerobics or yoga or a boot camp feel, just to determine what people are able to do physically and what they feel comfortable doing. We create a baseline and from that we can then work. The dance training, it's very much there informing me, more so than the work outwardly. It's informing me in a *way* that I can make choices and how I'd like to *translate* something. I like to establish a two-way communication, more like conversations with the acting bodies. I don't like to impose – so, to impose movement on someone is not a very good thing. With theatre you want the world to come across organically, and to make the organic happen it has to be a two-way communication between the movement person and the actor. I devise a language with the company that makes sense to them through observation. I place a lot of value on observing people in the rehearsal space, not in a way that is judgemental, none of that! I am actually observing so that I can find *a way in* with the company. I am seeing how you move naturally, how you walk, how you hold your weight, where you place your emphasis on your sway or your gait. When you are laughing, what is your body doing when you are tired, physically, what collapses, what relaxes, where do you hold your tension? So, if I do a one-on-one session, I already have a working process – a type of base line. And we go from there. People don't actually think about what they're capable of doing with their bodies, because the beauty is you don't think, you just do; you have impulses you follow. My job is to see what you can do and to then work creating something that makes you feel comfortable, confident and enriches your character and that is within the narrative of what we're trying to create.

How do you think your approach developed?
The world of movement direction is a very practical one for me. I was learning as I was practising; pulling on different elements but also being guided by instinct. Everything for me became instinctual. It is actor-centric because I realized from being a performer in the past that it is a very sensitive thing, you are in a very vulnerable place, and as an actor it's the same. Once you get someone to be confident you have a wider scope. I had a strong instinct that I had to be guided by the actors as much as they were being guided by me. I followed that from day one.

There's no space for ego in the room, and as a creative if you come in with your own agenda that's not going to be helpful. As a movement director we facilitate. I always refer to myself as a facilitator; we facilitate a vision. Sometimes you will be asked to collaborate a lot more than other times, and then you can go from being a facilitator to a collaborator, but by finding out what that balance is and shifting with the people in the room.

I need to harness the aptitudes and the tendencies of the actors in the room. What's lovely in doing my analysis and assessing what's in the room is finding out about injuries, ailments, anything that I should be aware of. At the same time finding out about their natural, physical abilities. People tell you, 'Oh, I am doing rock wall climbing,' 'Oh, I'm an avid swimmer and I run marathons' or 'I love going on trapeze because I do circus.' The bodies in the room are not just acting bodies, they're human beings who have different facets, and sometimes that is very helpful to the story and to embodiment. I translate that understanding from one area to another, if I need to work with an actor on embodying something specific for their character, a nuanced movement or the way that they have to be held or weighted. For example, I was doing *Tartuffe* for the RSC [Royal Shakespeare Company], working with one of the younger actors who had decided for his character, he was going to have a basketball and he also had to rap.[12] The way he was moving with the basketball was going to help him with his rapping, because when he was rapping, he got very tense, so I thought, 'Okay, let's not look the movement of the rap, let's just do some basketball.' In a one-on-one session, we were moving around the room with the basketball and I was pointing out, 'Do you see how low you are?' 'Do you see how you're bending your knees, how you're moving your body?' 'Where's your centre?' And so, we took the ball out of it and I was able to say, 'That's what you need for the rap, that's that feel' – so, transferring his skills from one area to another. By chance, the actor playing Tartuffe took the basketball up and started spinning it.[13] He had been a good basketball player as a teenager. When I told the director this, he picked up on it, and it became thread in the show because this actor also had the same skillset.

How do you prepare for a project?
Every project is completely different, so I am fluid, and I don't have a blueprint. Some projects need a lot of research. I like to really understand the plays by

reading the play and books on the play, researching the era, what was happening in the world at the time around it; so, understanding the environment and social structures, politics behind it as well. So, when I get into the room, I have a great understanding of what the world is 'within' it and 'without' it. How many plays have you read where you see 'and they break into a dance'? And then you ask, 'Is it a social dance? Do I need to go to do some research on that?' With *Equus*, it was different because you're being asked to do a characterization of a human as a horse, so then that became about looking at the animal instead and deciphering what my approach was going to be.[14] It's dependent on the project, and I'm always guided by the need. And after doing all of the research, it's important then to walk into the room just being a blank slate. It's just having the knowledge that is the key, so you have all this knowledge that you can pull on.

Directors are all different. Some directors love meeting beforehand and speaking, which I find invaluable. Reading the play doesn't tell you anything. The important part is what is the world of the play according to the director. Meeting them and sharing the vision, hearing what they think it will be. You know it will change in the room, but at least you walk in and have some footing. Some creative teams work quite tightly, and that comes from the director beforehand. I've been in scenarios – like *Equus* – where we've had lots of pre-production meetings because the director wanted everyone to be on board with this new vision. That worked extremely well, because then we came in the room and it was fully collaborative.

Some directors send video references or images that help me comprehend *the feel* that they are going for, and these inform what I create. I also explore outside of the rehearsal room to create a pool of ideas that I can then take into the rehearsal studio. Working through movement ideas on my own and exploring concepts within my own physicality is a way of playing around with a range of ideas by figuring out and sensing things through. This allows me to become a better translator for the actors later on.

Then there are times when you meet with the director maybe once before, and you don't meet the team until model box sharing. Then I love walking in with nothing but myself: knowing that what the room will require is you to come with a very open mind. It's just us; our eyes our brain, our bodies, that's it – and from that we're going to breathe all this movement in, it's so beautiful.

What are the things that galvanize you when you interact with a director?
In that first meeting, I'll try to ascertain what their practice is like and how they work. I'm very honest about how I work to see if that marries, because you're going into a marriage for eight weeks. I am identifying what their needs might be in the room beforehand. That tells me what my role is and helps in determining what kind of person they are in regards to their vision; whether they are looking for someone who's going to feed in ideas to them or if they're looking for someone who

is going to hear what they're saying and respond creatively. They are quite different across the board. I happily work with everyone. I always say that I can be a mouse or a lion – so, I can be the quiet movement director who is just reserved and in the corner until called. I'm also observing the director and the actors and what the vision is so that when I am called upon, I will come out and I will be just around the room, doing my bit, and then I'll go back into my corner. A lion being more vocal and being called upon to be more leadership-oriented and being a bigger part of the process where your voice can be heard. The most important thing is to learn the director's process so you can learn where you fit into the mix. It's about creating a good working relationship which creates a good working environment.

Because you are actively sharing in the moment in the rehearsal space – your collaboration is part of the fabric of the rehearsal room.
I'm able to decipher from that meeting where I sit on that, and when you work with a director on more than one project you start to develop that relationship. There are directors if they are working on a scene I know when to just put my voice in because they want to hear it; there are other directors where the approach would be that they work the scene and then you speak to them after and then you go, 'Oh, when I was watching this I saw …'

I flourish more in an environment where my voice is able to be heard. We see things in a very different way, and projects become really enriched by a collaborative approach and this is from all aspects. I love working with the designers and composers because I ask, 'How can I feed into their world, how does their world feed into me?' If everything is in tune and there's a synergy across the board then it becomes a piece of art and it lifts off that stage to the audience, and the audience can feel the difference. That is my preference, but I get just as much working in different capacities. I learn from every experience, and directors to me are brilliant people; their minds are so complex.

I do know that with repeat collaborations you start to create a shared vocabulary.
I don't know if you've found this: I don't have a blueprint, but directors do have one. Have you found that?

Some certainly have their way of leading a creative team, and some are creatively organized, which can be helpful for movement.
A director might have a blueprint that can start to develop a useful shorthand in repeat working relationships. I will also want to bring new energy to each process. I'll always be investigating my craft. I find it exciting because it's always a challenge; how can I translate this idea so it's understood in such a way that the actor feels it is organic, lived, real, a truthful embodiment, and they feel comfortable doing it.

Can you talk about what a typical production process might be; what are the recognizable phases of creative development?
Let's say an eight-week production process. In week one, the room is a gigantic puzzle with all these pieces lying down and figuring out how the pieces fit together. Week two is tearing the puzzle apart and asking, 'But can't we cut the pieces a little bit more and have it fit in a different way?' – opening up the mind to the possibilities. Weeks three and four is crunch time, where things *have* to be happening and we have to get movement made. You can feel the shift with the actors; there's the pressure of learning text and building the scene. So, I give freedom to the director and the actors getting things up and going and on its feet. If I need to be up and on my feet, helping a lot more, I am as well. It's about layers and seeing – seeing a scene that could benefit from having a different shape. From a movement perspective it's spatial, gestural, blocking: it's the concrete side of it. Its dependent on the needs of a character as well. There are instances where I'm giving one-on-one sessions with actors to help develop a specific type of embodiment for their characters or a dance routine, like I did in *Twelfth Night*.[15] When I was working with Tamsin [Greig], she had a task with the mustard stockings moment that we had to create together.[16] We delved into movement, finding that right fit. *Twelfth Night* was a beautiful process where often, Simon Godwin and I worked in parallel.

By week five everything is up on its feet and running, and you have a show. It's good again to think of day one of the rehearsal room when you approach the final day of rehearsal, because this is just a show in the making, and my favourite part of the process is tech week. My orientation has always been a logical mind; seeing things and breaking them down and restructuring, and that's creative – they work well together somehow. I love tech week because now we go into the theatre. There is a misconception that the job is done, but quite the opposite – it's just begun because now you're in the realm of the actual set, which comes with different issues. You are negotiating with the actors, who are also negotiating the space and costumes; they feel different. Things that worked in the rehearsal room that don't work here as well become apparent. The director changing their vision; working with music, sound and making it all make sense. From a movement perspective, the worst thing that I could do is to see when something is not working and to not fix it, regardless of whether it looks beautiful. If it's not feeding in in the right way, it needs to be looked at. Tech week is the week, as a movement person, you are going from the director to the stage management to the actors. You're like the stage magician; I'm trying to find the right word for it. You are doing your 'list' while the team are doing something else, and you find that you have a pocket of time and you're trying to do the 'fixes' so that when the scene goes up on stage it just flies.

In previews, you get to see what works and what doesn't, and you get to look forward to the production team meetings where you say, 'We need to fix this, what should we do?'¹⁷ And this is why I love it, because you can go, 'What if, what if, what if', and you are able actually to go from a creative perspective, offering up all these different solutions to fix what's not working. When someone does hit the nail on the head, you have the joy of the next morning, trying to do it in a practical way; the adrenaline of that week is so exciting.

Is it because the audience is there that you're also finding out what is not reading and what could be improved?*¹⁸ *What's the difference between something not working in tech and something not working in previews?
Having the audience there, you see movement in a different way. Things are read differently. When you have the live audience there you can sense the full journey from start to end. That's when you know what parts aren't really 'clicking' yet. In the rehearsal room everyone has that shared consciousness of what it became, and sometimes you lose track of what it might feel like to watch it for the first time. I find myself sitting down in previews – generally about four shows in – and looking to the audience for reactions. For example, *King Hedley* had a waltz moment, so I had to teach the actors how to waltz, and they stand as a couple, when they start, *she* pushes her foot forward first.¹⁹ I'd seen this in the rehearsal room, and I liked it because it felt real to the characters; although they have this knowledge of waltzing, the fact that she makes the choice to move her foot forwards, as opposed to allowing her male partner to do so, added another layer to the movement – a layer about power play and personal dynamics, as well as revealing the history of their relationship. And I kept it in.

You asked me if my world of dance feeds into theatre and how has it shaped and helped; I find that it's actually the reverse – I've become a better contemporary dance choreographer because of working in theatre.

How?
Because theatre has opened up my mind with regards to not setting limitations, not setting boundaries and to being fluid and to allowing beautiful things to become ugly and ugly things to become beautiful in their own way. I find that in theatre we create that baseline, and we keep layering on. Because I've applied that back into contemporary dance now, it's really altered my practice in a great way.

How do you see the field of movement direction developing?
Well, one, I think that thanks to people that went before it's become more dominant in theatre. A lot more directors are using movement directors, and a lot more movement directors are being acknowledged for their work in productions. Now you receive a credit because there is an acknowledgement that the work that you're doing is becoming an important process of the rehearsal room. It is that acknowledgement of voice, of movement and of the acting body and that they work together as a unit.

It can go in many ways; the idea of a movement coach and a movement director are going to become a little bit more separate – not that you can't do both, but those two titles will become energies in their own right. And a movement coach will be someone that's doing one-on-one work with an actor in such a way that embeds into their process of creating a character. And the movement director will again become more of an overseer.

There are going to be more plays where they are co-directed by the director and the movement director, because I can already feel that pull where they will share their vision and create the vision together. It's the open collaborative method of directing, but it's also a shift in our view of it; not that it didn't happen before, but before there wasn't always public acknowledgement of it. Whereas now everything is more open and more visible, and there's more acknowledgement of all of the creative team and what they do.

Does that mean the end of movement directors? Because actually what they will become is directors?
Not at all; I've had a lot of people in the last two years go to me, 'Are you going to become a director, you should be a director,' and I go, 'No thank you.' Because I also see what that requires. I feel very happy within my world doing what I do. I don't think it would require directors to make a shift, and I don't think that they will need to, but it will be informed by the plays that come about. A lot more plays are leading towards physical theatre, and if it is a play that has a lot of physicality in, you will see a director who is a choreographer, like the musical *Book of Mormon* – Casey Nicholaw who has 'Directed and choreographed by' – because one person is doing both.[20] But what if it's someone who only directs, and they come with this play and they recognize that it needs to be 'Directed and choreographed by'? Then it needs to be co-directors. I don't think this is the end of an era, this is just the tip of the iceberg.

I think times are changing, with all the women directors as well. I love to learn from people. You can constantly keep re-evaluating self and learning. I've worked loads in a short amount of time and I'm thankful for that and I don't take anything for granted. I also acknowledge that there are many people out there that have been doing this for decades and they have a wealth of experience and we're all still learning and we're all fighting for the same thing – we're all doing it for the passion and love of artistry and that's what comes first and foremost.

Notes

1   This interview took place on 5 June 2019 at the National Theatre, London.
    Shelley Maxwell's credits include *Hansard* (National Theatre, 2019); *Master Harold and the Boys* (National Theatre, 2019); *Equus* (Theatre Royal Stratford East

and Trafalgar Studios, West End, 2019); *Nine Night* (National Theatre and Trafalgar Studios, West End, 2018); *Antony and Cleopatra* (National Theatre, 2018); *A Streetcar Named Desire* (Nuffield, Clwyd Theatre Cymru and UK tour with English Touring Theatre, 2018); *Tartuffe* (Royal Shakespeare Company, 2018); *Winter* (Young Vic, 2018); *Why It's Kicking Off Everywhere* (Young Vic, 2017); *Cuttin' It* (Royal Court, 2017); *Twelfth Night* (National Theatre, 2016–17); *Rules for Living* (Royal & Derngate, the Rose Kingston and on UK tour for the English Touring Theatre, 2017); *Hamlet* (Royal Shakespeare Company, 2016, as Assistant Movement Director); and dance research and development team for Julian Fellowes' production of *The Wind in the Willows* (Theatre Royal Plymouth, 2016). Selected performance credits include *Fela!* (National Theatre, 2010) and *The Lion King* (Lyceum Theatre, 2012–14).

2 The 2016 Royal Shakespeare Company production of *Hamlet* was directed by Simon Godwin and starred Paapa Essiedu as Hamlet. The movement director was Mbulelo Ndabeni. Originally from South Africa, Ndabeni is a London-based choreographer, dancer, teacher and mentor. He is founder and director of N'da Dance Company.

3 An influential, complex history of dance in Jamaica is comprised of a network of indigenous forms, African diasporic forms, religious practices, political resistance practices, hybrid Latin American forms, modern dance and colonial European influences. The reader can discover more about the multitude of dances and dance cultures to which Maxwell refers in an index created by Tabanka African and Caribbean People's Dance Ensemble. Available online: https://tabankadance.com/caribbean-dance-index/ (accessed 29 June 2019). Specifically, dance hall is a popular form of music and dance that evolved from reggae.

For further investigation into modern dance theatre in Jamaica in the twentieth century, refer to two influential dance pioneers: first, Trinidadian dancer and teacher Beryl McBurnie (1914–2000), remembered as the Caribbean's 'mother of dance' and a major influence on Katherine Dunham; and second, US-born Lavinia Williams, an inheritor of Katherine Dunham methods. The cross-pollination of early modern dance with their unique techniques informed by Caribbean folk dance, percolates through the history of dance in Jamaica and beyond into the twentieth century. McBurnie was celebrated in Alvin Ailey Dance Company's 1978 tribute, which located her as 'one of the three extraordinary Black women who have had a profound influence on American dance', alongside Pearl Primus and Katherine Dunham (Sorgel 2007: 60). For a comprehensive evaluation of dance theatre in Jamaica, see Sorgel 2007 where Sorgel suggests that 'What differentiates Caribbean modern dance theatre thus from its modern progenitors in the US and Europe, is precisely its shared African Creole background in such as religious rituals as Vodou, Shango and Revival/Myal. Dance scholars Robert Farris Thompson, Kariamu Welsh-Asante and Brenda Dixon-Gottschild have argued to regard such continuity of religious practice as the foundational source of a common African aesthetic in the New World diaspora.' Readers can also refer to Robert Farris Thompson's essay, 'An Aesthetic of the Cool: West African Dance' (1966).

4 Barbara McDaniel was the director of Wolmers Dance Troupe.

5 Escuela Nacional de Arte, Cuba.

6 Cuba has a far-reaching history and culture of dance. Very broadly, this includes groupings of dance such as social dances including danzon, salsa and mambo; ritual dances, mainly of African-Cuban origin, and festival dances; religious and political dances; carnival dance, ballet and contemporary. The reader might like to watch

7   the documentary film *A History of Cuban Dance* (2016) by Lucy Walker by way of introduction to the richness of dance within Cuban culture.

7   Cuban ballet dancer Carlos Acosta CBE had just been appointed as Director of Birmingham Royal Ballet during the writing of this book. His is arguably the most globally recognized dancer from Cuba with a sizable influence on the British ballet scene as a dancer and choreographer. The Royal Ballet website provides a first-person account of his route into dance, as well as highlighting some touch points of Cuban dance, including the influence of Alicia Alonso, ballet dancer and choreographer, who established the Ballet Nacional de Cuba. Available online: https://www.roh.org.uk/news/a-cuban-dance-history-part-i (accessed 29 June 2019); https://www.roh.org.uk/news/a-cuban-dance-history-part-ii (accessed 29 June 2019).

8   See Sabine Sorgel's detailed investigation into the origins of National Dance Theatre Company of Jamaica in her book *Dancing Postcolonialism: The National Dance Theatre Dance Company of Jamaica* (Sorgel 2007).

9   MA in Choreography from Trinity Laban Conservatoire of Music and Dance, London.

10 A 'swing' is a dancer or performer who understudies several different roles so that they can step in to cover an absent colleague. It is more usual to have 'swings' in musical theatre productions. They have to be able to retain many individual performance tracks and step in seamlessly to any of those roles at short notice. Also see Glossary.

11 Dancers' Career Development Agency is a charitable organization that helps dancers transition into new careers. Available online: https://thedcd.org.uk.

12 *Tartuffe* (2018), RSC production directed by Iqbal Khan, a British theatre and opera director.

13 Asif Khan is an award-winning British actor and writer who played Tahir Taufiq Arsuf (*Tartuffe*) in the 2018 RSC production.

14 The 2018 production of Peter Shaffer's *Equus* at Theatre Royal, Stratford East, was directed by Ned Bennett. Maxwell's work was critically acclaimed. The *Evening Standard* wrote, 'The sinuous movement – a big shout-out to movement director Shelley Maxwell – is a wonder to behold; when the cast tramples impatiently as horses, it's easy to imagine we can feel their panting breath on us' (Mountford 2019). Michael Billington, in the *Guardian*, wrote: 'Shaffer's published stage directions are modelled on John Dexter's original production: "the actors wear tracksuits of chestnut velvet" and "tough masks of silver wire and leather". But Bennett, designer Georgia Lowe and movement director Shelley Maxwell have totally reimagined this. The opening image is of Ethan Kai's Alan nuzzling a horse in the shape of Ira Mandela Siobhan, who sports grey shorts and reveals a muscular torso. The eroticism of the relationship pays off later when Alan orgasmically bestrides the horse in question, Nugget, and when that memory intrudes on his attempt to have sex with a stable-girl. An idea latent in Shaffer's text, of Alan's equine fixation as a metaphor for same-sex love, is made explicit in Bennett's production' (Billington 2019).

15 National Theatre (2016–17), directed by Simon Godwin and starring Tamsin Greig as Malvolia – a regendered Malvolio.

16 Maxwell is referring to an exploration of Malvolia's relationship to cross-gartering and wearing the colour yellow in the form of yellow stockings.

17 Maxwell is referring to 'tech notes', which is a meeting that involves all the technical departments and the creative team who evaluate how each preview went that night from their specialist perspective. Based on that conversation, the director will allocate time for working the next day – as a movement director you will often input into the scheduling once you and the director have shared movement-specific notes. Also see Glossary.

18 In theatre parlance, what is not 'reading to the audience' is a question of the legibility of an image or the articulation of a stage moment in terms of time and space.

19 *King Hedley II* by August Wilson at Theatre Royal Stratford East (2019), directed by Nadia Fall, British director and artistic director of Theatre Royal Stratford East.

20 *The Book of Mormon* was directed and choreographed by Casey Nicholaw, an award-winning choreographer and director of musicals. It is of note that Maxwell drew on the musical theatre world to tease out the ways of attributing an authorial aspect of movement, dance and staging.

15 FUTURE VOICES

Diane Alison-Mitchell, Polly Bennett, Lucy Cullingford, Ioli Filippakopoulou, Natasha Harrison, Chi-San Howard, Vicki Igbokwe, Jennifer Jackson, Ingrid Mackinnon, Rebecca Meltzer, Coral Messam, Anna Morrissey, Sue Mythen, Sacha Plaige

This chapter emerged from short conversations with movement directors who responded to an open invitation to take the pulse of the profession and to speak about their hopes for their work. What follows is a tapestry of voices. Happenstance means that this group is all women; they are representative of the large numbers of female movement directors currently on the British scene. Some of these practitioners already have substantial experience working on opera, film, television, mass movement, musical theatre and theatre, and might be considered mid-career movement directors. Others are very early in their careers. It is useful to listen to their voices with those differences in mind.

The rehearsal room is a workplace as well as a site of artistic endeavour. Today, it is being questioned and reshaped in very productive ways. What follows is organized thematically:

- reinventing time and space (of rehearsals);
- creativity and potential;
- plurality, equality and place;
- sustainability and development.

Reinventing time and space (of rehearsals): Visions of flexibility and consultation

There is broad agreement amongst these movement directors that time, space and human resources should be organized more creatively, intuitively and productively in production contexts. A consistent theme emerged: theatre systems could be more responsive to how movement might be woven into a production process. Polly Bennett explores the complications associated with a freelance career – specifically, those that arise when several projects overlap and run concurrently.[1] She articulates her craving 'to have rehearsal processes accommodate a movement director's process', since current practices could be restrictive. Bennett speaks of a need to find collaborators who can 'staunchly challenge' the way that institutions manage actors and movement directors alike. A thorough evaluation would cast scrutiny upon multiple aspects of a freelancer's working life – from contract negotiations to rehearsal calls. Bennett has practical suggestions for improving how movement work is structured ahead of rehearsal processes, such as weekly pre-rehearsal meetings of the creative team, and involving the movement directors in auditions (where creative conversation between director and actors is seeded).[2] During rehearsal periods, enhanced cooperation between stage management teams in different theatres would allow movement practitioners to work more coherently in different environments. Bennett notes that 'the more normal and regular it becomes for movement directors to be in the room, the more important it is to bring your working methodology to the forefront'. Lucy Cullingford talks of an increase in requests to attend design meetings and auditions.[3] Whilst she sees this as creatively and logistically productive, she observes that this valuable input is based on goodwill, rather than factored in to the formal scope of work as agreed by the host organization.[4]

Movement is practical. These practitioners understand how movement work can be managed and shaped to produce a particular outcome. Anna Morrissey highlights a common experience – that while 'how much time you need *does* get factored in', this time invariably expands.[5] From the planning period (that is, the settling of contracts) to the actual development of the work, the workload can increase sizeably. This means that the movement director is caught between the creative needs of the work, and the constraints of the time and fee that have been arranged (maybe months or a year ahead). For Sue Mythen, her contribution benefits from a shared language that is built through repeated collaborative relationships.[6] She notes that she was able to be more influential in planning processes as her relationship developed with a director. Her preference is 'ideally being there [in rehearsal] every day'. She argues that movement directors must clearly communicate the 'conditions that work for [them]', artistically and logistically, in a production. Diane Alison-Mitchell suggests that 'movement needs to be more strongly positioned' in rehearsal by being 'there, from the start' in order to be seen as 'critical to the process'.[7] In her view, this would help dismantle unhelpful hierarchies within theatre – for example, the implicit ways the word is valued over the body.[8] She argues that a stronger stance would also lead to clearer credits.[9] She observes that movement has become a recognized part of the rehearsal process and anticipates that TV and film are likely to follow suit.

Alison-Mitchell speaks for many when she highlights that 'each project is different and requires a different response'. If these nuances remain buried in the dialogue between director and movement director, she observes, it is little wonder that the movement can feel intangible and mysterious to those not involved in those conversations. At a producer level, there appears to be a stronger understanding of the work of a choreographer, but less so of a movement director (Alison-Mitchell). Greater dialogue is needed between movement directors and those responsible for organizational infrastructures, so that the latter understand the working processes of the former. Movement directors must articulate what they do and how they do it, and suggest how their work can flourish within theatre structures. Jennifer Jackson speaks of the importance of developing the dialogue about movement with producers and other creatives, like designers.[10] She seeks a working environment that is better informed by current ideas of movement direction. Jackson argues that better communication between producers and movement directors would enhance the delivery and understanding of movement work within a production.

These movement directors, like those in Chapters 3 to 14, are negotiating the shape, parameters and effectiveness of their creative and logistic input. A pattern emerges – that with greater dialogue and transparency, and through repeat working relationships, movement creativity could flourish and grow.

Creativity and potential

The practitioners whose voices inform this chapter share a commitment to creating ambitious and responsive movement processes. Yet, a feeling that their skills can be underused forms an undercurrent to our conversations.

Cullingford sees potential to 'invite a more holistic approach' to the working relationships between director and movement director. Some directors are not fully capitalizing on the input of the movement directors with whom they collaborate. Movement directors frequently articulate a desire to operate on a deeper level within rehearsal, in relation to actor's processes or the shape of a scene. In this regard, Cullingford sees how her movement work can 'unlock a creative, open space and tap into primal instinct'; this potential sometimes remains unharnessed. Successful, repeated working relationships can offer a platform for deeper involvement. It might also be time to include more directors within the movement work in warm-up, for example.[11] If they, too, can feel the benefit of their body moving, then they will also connect to a deeper potential of movement in the wider framework of their process.

For Vicki Igbokwe, her background in choreography and mass movement laid the ground for movement direction.[12] Such experiences helped her to acquire skills in 'managing personalities, reading a room, taking people who are not necessarily movers on a journey of building confidence'. She echoes the words of many movement directors when she talks of seeing 'the challenge and the unknown' of each new project as creative. Igbokwe observes how each project's unique circumstances stimulate the need to 'keep producing something really bespoke to every production; for those actors and uniquely to that production'.

Early-career movement director Sacha Plaige speaks of her experience of Russian and French actor training, each characterized by a strong ensemble ethos.[13] She notes an absence of ensemble culture in British theatre. For her, movement direction is inextricably linked to the creation of 'the feeling of the ensemble and knowing how to create the idea of ensemble' where 'creativity comes from everywhere'. She suggests that movement is a potent method of creating a shared culture and challenging the division between the creative team and the actors. For Plaige, a new genre of theatre is emerging directly out of movement practices. She draws attention to the work of Imogen Knight (see Chapter 13) as director of *Nuclear* at the Royal Court (2017) as an example of a 'new art form' led by movement directors. She feels that movement will be the starting point for further theatrical works, rather than one component of the whole. Whilst this is more common within the field of dance or site/immersive/devised theatre or performance art, it is still uncommon in text-led theatre. There are examples of movement-driven work by companies such as Clod Ensemble, Gecko, Frantic, DV8, Lost Dog or Rash Dash, but they occupy a space that is still thought of as physical theatre, or dance theatre, rather than simply theatre. Is it time that text-based theatre organizations open themselves to alternative origination points?[14]

Several of the movement directors whose voices inform this chapter now work between different performance contexts. Most frequently, they develop their skills in theatre first, and then take these skills into their work on opera, film or TV. Rebecca Meltzer is an early-career movement director working in opera, a form that has been reinventing itself in relation to the accepted wisdom associated with the physical training that opera singers undergo.[15] Meltzer suggests that because 'in opera, directors *are* being more ambitious physically', there is a need to develop new approaches to the movement training that singers receive. In her view, radically different movement capacities would transform the aesthetic and expressive range of choruses and principals in opera productions. Movement director Coral Messam, whose main practice has been within theatre, sees her future work developing in the field of TV and film.[16] She is seeking opportunities for 'shifting her gaze on to the limitlessness of movement through another medium', that is, film.

The growth of creative families that move from one project to the next suggests that opportunities for collaboration and influence in terms of movement are multidirectional within a creative team and not only contained in the triangle of actor, movement director and director. A close relationship with actors unites the movement directors I spoke with for this chapter, too. They all notice that, in the last decade, their dialogue with actors has blossomed – now, it matches the scale and quality of the dialogue that movement directors enjoy with directors. Morrissey notes, 'Actors *are* more open'; Cullingford says, 'Actors expect to work physically towards their character'; and Mythen agrees that 'actors are more open expecting movement to be part of the process'. More than ever, actors are ready to work with a movement director and want and expect to approach work in a physical way.[17] Actors clearly value approaching their craft through their bodies. Movement directors attribute this to the increased prevalence of actor movement training and the growing trust in physical aspects of the acting process. Building confidence and empowering actors through movement is an important part of movement direction. These practitioners constantly emphasize bespoke processes structured around the unique capacities of particular actors.

Visions of plurality, equality and place

The voices in this chapter articulate experiences of female freelance practitioners in a profession that has been slowly changing. Our differences are enriching; equality and inclusion are fundamental; and that parity of opportunity often means changing working systems and approaches. Movement director Ingrid Mackinnon, who participated in Shakespeare's Globe's *250 Black Womxn in Theatre*[18] photo the day before our conversation, recounts how it felt to be standing with three other movement directors – Diane Alison-Mitchell, Shelley Maxwell and Coral Messam. The power and uniqueness of this moment was echoed by Messam.

Mackinnon grew up in Canada, trained in the United States and lives and works in the UK. She says, 'In these places, a woman of colour is always in the minority.' She recalls the power of critical mass and the dissolving of otherness in a dance class with Black Dance Theatre, Dallas, Texas. Here, she was within the majority of a class of diverse ethnicities, where 'I didn't know I was missing it until I was in it'. If that is true of movement directors, it must also be true of the bodies that constitute a company of actors and creatives.

Mackinnon describes the nature of her connection to movement within plays that deal with real issues in a socially conscious way. She is part of works that 'tell stories that don't get told, by people who don't get an opportunity to tell stories'. She identifies opportunities to draw her industry persona and her personal identity closer together whilst creating movement material; these instances nourished her work. She describes how her 'presence, experience and voice as a black woman within the work' could shift cultures and create new movement responses. Working on *Typical* (Ryan Calais Cameron's play about the experience of a black ex-serviceman) ignited a desire in Mackinnon 'to find a deeper movement response to *this* story'; this is testament to the way that movement directors change and are changed by the work they encounter.[19]

The revisionist stance of this book echoes the perspective of this group of movement directors, particularly in terms of gender; many of them observe that 'being left out is gendered'. Anna Morrissey's reading of the predominance of female movement directors is linked, in her mind, to a larger picture of histories of invisible female labour. This is a complex area to consider fully here (see Chapter 16), but recalibrating pay and ensuring visibility will start to address the imbalances of fees and enhance recognition (for example, in reviews and omissions in the artistic memory of work).[20]

Sue Mythen problematizes perceptions that emphasize the *craft* of the movement director. She makes an interesting distinction: 'Movement is practical, more akin to artisanal craft rather than seen as high art – it's an "artistry versus artisan debate", and as movement directors we must be given the resources in a rehearsal space to elevate the work to its full potential artistically.' The proximity to the body serves to emphasize practical aspects of movement skill and technique that might, for some, eclipse artistry. Most movement directors recognize the symbiotic relationship between craft and art in their practice, as one cannot exist without the other.

The cultures of rehearsal rooms have been undergoing significant shifts in the last decade. These were accelerated by the #MeToo movement which exposed malpractice in the creative industries and elsewhere. This has led to greater professional scrutiny of the ethics in artistic working relationships, treatment of actors and languages deployed around the body (for example, judgement-laden language in reviews about weight, skin colour and age). For years, movement directors have been stepping into the space of intimacy and creating techniques to help maintain the private self of the actor in relation to their performing body. This remains a fundamental part of their creative and ethical practice. As actors navigate their career, it is important that they possess the tools to articulate *their needs* around *their bodies*.[21] The focus of movement practitioners must remain on empowering actors to understand their own working methodologies in relation to intimacy, violence and sex acts. Movement practitioners can be instrumental in establishing working methods and contexts for intimate scenes ahead of rehearsal and through the production process. The emergence of 'intimacy coordination' is playing a part in communicating the extant practices of actor movement and movement directors in the form of protocols for the film and TV industry.

Sexism in theatre workplaces still exists, as it does in wider culture. As movement directors, we have witnessed the discomfort that change requires and recognize that equality is still some way off. However, more mechanisms for addressing this problem are being implemented by theatre organizations. Change will accelerate as groups of practitioners are able to challenge outdated language; model simple, direct working methodologies; and address sexist behaviour in artistic practices within rehearsal rooms (see also Chapter 16). Movement practice can be an agent for change.

Many movement directors acknowledge that working habitually with actors of various ages, physical capacities and body types develops multimodal, inclusive movement practice that then can be redeployed to create work with non-professional performers. Early-career movement director Chi-San Howard is interested in how the transformative process that she has seen with actors can be translated to other people, possibly into environments for social benefit rather than artistic creation.[22] Howard's idea of 'movement as a force for social good' is built on 'the ability to express oneself, to feel visible and entitled to occupy space, and to make space for others'. Alison-Mitchell, Morrissey and Bennett are three of the ten movement assistants who worked with Sedgwick on the 2012 Olympic opening ceremony, an event that synthesized their transferable movement skills and presented mass movement to a global audience. Vicki Igbokwe has also learnt from her work with mixed groups of performers from both professional and non-professional backgrounds on mass movement choreography in London and at the Sochi Winter Olympics. These experiences have fed back into her movement direction practice.

These movement directors are united by the endeavour to reveal the movement capacities of all the actors they work with. This, in turn, enhances the lived experience of the rehearsal process and supports the ambitions of the production.

Sustainability and development – visions of connectivity

Whilst movement is occupying a significant place in the rehearsal room, these movement directors felt their work became peripheral in the wider setting of the profession. In a working life characterized by jumping from production to production, where might movement practitioners find creative continuity and a supportive environment where they can develop their practice? Morrissey points out the need for companies to 'recognize you as an artist, and that you want to explore and play and want to *grow* through the job'. Movement directors should enjoy a sense of growth through accumulating a body of work, like other creatives such as lighting designers and designers. How might a movement director deepen their creative practice? As Jennifer Jackson expresses it, without progression there is a danger that accumulated knowledges and practices might 'dissolve' away. Might movement directors join other creatives to run theatres in the form of artist-led directorship? Alison-Mitchell articulates a widely held desire for greater responsibility and impact upon decision making when she envisages being in 'a theatre as part of a leadership team as a movement director'. She posits the idea that every theatre in the UK might have a 'movement director in residence', to enable a core contribution to the artistic process and to have a say in programming. Cullingford's vision extends into Europe where she can see herself evolving within art forms like festivals, opera and gig theatre and being part of collectives who work internationally. This is echoed by Ioli Filippakopoulou, whose long-term aspiration is to create a movement director's collective that might work between Greece, Germany and the UK.[23] Might we envisage a consultative process in the future where movement directors select projects to develop their work in specifically new directions? This might be made possible if movement directors were embedded into theatre organizations. Does the working model need to shift from the peripatetic to the 'home' model, that is, opportunities for freelance movement directors and in-house practitioners? Could a horizontal creative space, as Morrissey suggests, act as 'an antidote to freelancing' by 'making some space for a movement director as a contributor with original ideas'?

Some of these movement directors feel that opportunities lie outside the theatre. They believe they could enrich their careers and the discipline by applying their movement skills to a broader range of forms in the wider creative industries. In the words of Bennett, 'The most interesting development in movement is in its broad application. The range of applications is huge, from "public speaking" to working with "Hollywood film actors"'. Chi-San Howard notices that actor-centred processes are driving the movement languages of new musicals; she sees this in contrast to the US heritage of dance-led movement in musicals. In her words, she 'was involved in actor-led processes that fed into choreography that fed into the narrative', and her process was not to bring 'steps' into the room but to start by really looking at *who* is in the room, and in her process, 'choreography is a spoke in the wheel of movement direction'. Howard's wide frame of reference includes circus, fashion, music videos, motion capture, video games, film and TV. She sees a future where she would be able to 'experience movement in every possible medium' – crucially, 'beyond the boundaries of theatre'. There are potentially other disciplines where the skills of movement direction could be valued and applied.

For these working movement directors, the instability of freelance work combined with strictly limited fees (even when you have a full year of work) is a problem. Bennett echoes many when she asks, 'How can making a living and making theatre *talk* to each other?' This question underpins various discussions of finances, parenting and well-being. Chapter 16 explores how inequalities associated with the working conditions of movement direction may be ameliorated.

The growth of the population of movement directors working today has certainly been noticed by this group of practitioners. Although this is generally seen positively, it also raises some concerns about the practice not being viewed as a discrete vocation or being seen as a secondary career for those who did not work their way through a training or apprenticeship. As with any discipline there is the desire that those following behind you undertake a type of apprenticeship – a process of authentic investment to merit the title of the practice. Jackson cautions that 'being good at movement is not the whole thing: it's a really skilful job, and by doing it over years lets you understand the really subtle navigation of the rehearsal room'. She speaks of her desire to be able to share her knowledge with others; to enrich her own practice by shadowing other movement directors. For her, processes of growth and learning parallel movement direction, which she describes as 'marking out landmarks on an imaginary landscape' with 'craft and rigour'. Increased definition and visibility of the role are viewed positively, and with that comes responsibility. Messam says that 'the practice needs to be respected and invested in' and advises newcomers to '[be] patient, watch, take time, invest in the art and the skill'.

Theatre has some formal and informal routes to apprenticeship.[24] Morrissey, Bennett and Natasha Harrison have been active in mentoring other movement directors by nurturing early career practitioners on placements or assistantships.[25] Teamwork amongst movement directors can build confidence, create cultures of resilience and model creative cooperation. The practical aspect of job sharing might also enable new practitioners to enter the creative industries and support those with caring duties.[26] The subtext here is that rehearsal rooms require a level of confidence that takes time to build, and they may appear overwhelming or hostile to less experienced practitioners.

The movement directors who inform this chapter are unified by the value they place on cooperation, lifelong learning and development. As the body changes, so does the way you experience and use your body. Ongoing development is seen as necessary to keep nourishing movement knowledge with new physical skills and creative expansion. Morrissey, with over fifteen years of movement direction experience on national and international platforms, points out the value that mentorship would have for the artistic development that is central to her career progression.

Recent initiatives have focused on building community amongst movement directors. One such initiative, MoveSpace, originated from regular but informal professional discussions between two movement directors.[27] These meetings acted as an inspiration and a resource as they moved through the vagaries of freelance work. MoveSpace opens up a closed, informal relationship into a wider domain. It is the first network of its kind. Other initiatives have capitalized on the open access nature of the web and have included rehearsal room insights in the form of blogs, programme notes, videos, interviews and panels. The network aspect of social media allows for informal exchange, conversation, connection and dialogue around movement work.

Natasha Harrison, speaking as an early-career practitioner, was awarded a place in the Old Vic 12 scheme for emerging artists as a movement director; with this scheme, the Old Vic is the only British theatre to formally develop movement directors. Alongside her developing practice Harrison initiated the Movement Podcast, which capitalizes on free access to technology and the emergence of this spoken form to offer insights from the profession.

In the UK, there are currently no professional awards specifically for movement direction. However, in 2018 the *Irish Times* created a new category, 'Best Movement Director', and as an Irish artist working in Ireland, Mythen was the second movement director to be rewarded specifically for her work as a movement director in a category that names her work as such. As an award winner, she notes that 'the future of the role of Movement Director is expanding in Irish theatre not least because it is now recognized in the *Irish Times* Theatre Awards since 2018. However, most of the nominees have a dance/choreography background. My feeling is that the judges need to be further educated about embodied acting/character and see this as well as the stylized/choreographed movement sequences in shows ... there is still a way to go before the delicate, interwoven, invisible work is recognized as a specific discipline.'

The open conversations that inform this chapter have a messy richness, because each interviewee is at different point in her career. Looking at the future through their eyes, I am able to see a profession that is characterized by intersectionality, connection and a type of vitality that bodes well for the development of the field. This group talked to me with indefatigable energy and expressed their commitment to the importance of movement with seriousness. Wider developments in the industry will benefit them, and they will also lead on those developments. Some of the questions raised by their observations inform the final chapter, in which the future development of the field is discussed.

Notes

1   Polly Bennett, in conversation 29 July 2019, London. Polly Bennett is a movement director, choreographer and practitioner working across the broadest applications of movement. From professional theatre to amateur performance, Polly creates physical worlds for theatre, dance, live performance and film, as well as doing extensive work as a performance coach, workshop facilitator and mentor. She holds a Movement MA from the Royal Central School of Speech and Drama (RCSSD), is an Associate Artist of the Bush Theatre and the National Youth Theatre, and is co-director of The Mono Box, a company founded to help emerging theatre artists connect to the industry and continue training.

2   Movement directors are often included at the early stages of project planning, that is, design meetings and auditions, but these can be hard to difficult attend when productions are overlapping or if the fee does not include preparatory meetings.

3   In conversation, 29 July 2019, London. Lucy Cullingford collaborates regularly with the Royal Shakespeare Company (RSC). Recent productions include *Measure for Measure*

(2019); *The Taming of the Shrew* (2019); *Coriolanus* (2017), *Snow in Midsummer* (2017); *The Tempest* (2016); *Don Quixote* (RSC and West End, 2016) and *The Jew of Malta* (2015). Other credits include *King Lear* (Chichester Festival Theatre and West End, 2017); *Constellations* (Royal Court, West End, Broadway and National tour, 2012). Further credits include *East is East* (Northern Stage, 2017); *Jenufa* (Revival, Grange Park Opera, 2017); *101 Dalmatians* and *Of Mice and Men* (Birmingham Repertory Theatre, 2016); *The Night Before Christmas* (West Yorkshire Playhouse, 2015); *The Spanish Golden Age Season* (Ustinov, Arcola and Belgrade Theatres, 2014). Recent choreography includes *The Last Mermaid* (Wales Millennium Centre, 2016); *Alice In Wonderland* (CBBC, 2013); *The Secret Adversary* (Watermill Theatre, 2015); *Rusalka*, Revival (Royal Danish Opera, 2012). Lucy worked as Children's Dance Repetiteur on *Matilda* in Stratford upon Avon and the West End (see Ellen Kane, Chapter 9).

4   Making requests to attend meetings has become a common practice in my experience at the RSC in the past decade, where there is an opportunity to meet with the director, designer and composer six to twelve months before the production process proper begins. These meetings are always of value, both creatively and practically. This experience, and this sentiment, are echoed by several of the practitioners in Chapters 3 to 14. Such invitations may indicate that it is the more established practitioners who tend to be contracted much earlier than less experienced practitioners. This enables longer lead-in time for a project.

5   In conversation, 29 July 2019. Anna Morrissey works as movement director, choreographer and director in theatre, opera and dance. Her theatre work as choreographer and movement director includes *Emilia* (West End, Shakespeare's Globe, 2018); *ANNA* (2019), *Translations,* (2018) and *World of Extreme Happiness* (2013), The National Theatre; *Queen Anne* (West End, 2017); *Imperium* (2017), *Pericles* (2012), *Antony and Cleopatra* (2010), *Dunsinane* (2011), *The Grain Store* (2009), *The Drunks* (2009) and *Marat/Sade* (2011), the RSC; *King Charles III* (West End, Almeida, 2014); *Wings* (2017), *My Dad's a Birdman* (2010) Young Vic; *Rise* (2016) *and Ages* (2015) Old Vic; the London 2012 Olympic Games opening ceremony (as Movement Assistant). Opera credits include *Macbeth* (2016) and *Sweeney Todd* (2015) Welsh National Opera; *Swan Hunter* (2015) and *Hansel and Gretel* (2017) Opera North; *Salome* (2015), *Macbeth* (2014), *The Flying Dutchman,* (2013) and *Noye's Fludde* (2012), Northern Ireland Opera; *The Barber of Seville* (2014) and *Manon Lescaut* (2019), Opera Holland Park; *Orpheus in the Underworld* (Scottish Opera, 2011). Morrissey was Artist in Residence at Historic Royal Palaces in (2014).

6   In conversation, 29 July 2019, between Dublin and London. Sue Mythen is based in Ireland. She was Movement Director on over twenty plays at the Abbey, National Theatre of Ireland. With ANU Productions since 2012, she directed movement for many productions, including *The Lost O'Casey,* (2018), for which she won an Irish Theatre Award for Best Movement Direction 2019. Mythen works with other companies include: Druid, Shakespeare's Globe, Everyman, Verdant, Opera Ireland, Northern Ireland Opera, Landmark, Project Theatre, Soho Theatre, Dublin Theatre Festival, Canadian Opera Company and Lyric Belfast. Movement for film and television includes *Northanger Abbey* (2007), *Capital Letters* (2004), *Normal People* (2020) and *History's Future* (2016). Mythen is Head of Movement at the Lir Academy, Trinity College, Dublin.

7   In conversation, 29 July 2019. Diane Alison-Mitchell is a movement director, choreographer and movement tutor who recently co-directed *Bones* by Tanika Gupta at the Courtyard Theatre, RCSSD (2019). Credits include *Wife* (Kiln Theatre, 2019);

Our Lady of Kibeho (Royal and Derngate, 2019); *The Hoes* (Hampstead Theatre, 2018); *Holy Sh!t* (Kiln Theatre, 2018); *Never Vera Blue*, *Offside* (Futures Theatre, 2018); *The Island* (Theatre Chipping Norton/Dukes Lancaster 2017); *Roundelay* (2017), *Klippies* (Southwark Playhouse, 2015); *They Drink It in The Congo* (Almeida Theatre, 2016); *SOUL* (Royal & Derngate/Hackney Empire, 2016); *Othello* (2015); *Julius Caesar* (RSC, 2012); *How Nigeria Became: A Story, and a Spear that Didn't Work* (Unicorn Theatre, 2014); *Porgy and Bess* (Regent's Park Open Air Theatre, 2014); *We Are Proud to Present* (Bush Theatre, 2014); *The Island* (Young Vic, 2013); London 2012 Olympic Games opening ceremony; *Lola* (Trestle Theatre Company, 2008).

8 Being part of the core creative team might constitute 'being there from the start', and that is more and more common for movement directors with experience. There might be another issue expressed here; the need for theatre organizations to appreciate the value of engaging a movement director for the whole production process, rather than a portion of it. Only once in the last ten years have I been asked to step in very late in a process to rapidly enhance an aspect of the movement – it is potentially very disruptive for actors to work in this way.

9 Alison-Mitchell noted that Shakespeare's Globe Theatre was adopting an alphabetical listing of creatives and cast rather than a billing of implied importance.

10 Jennifer Jackson is a movement director, theatre maker and actor who trained at East 15. She is a Leverhulme Arts Scholar. Movement credits include *I Wanna Be Yours* (Paines Plough, Tamasha, the Bush, 2019), *Amsterdam* (ATC, Orange Tree, TRP, 2019); *Death of a Salesman* (2018), *Queens of the Coal Age* (2018), *Our Town* (Royal Exchange Theatre, 2017); *Parliament Square* (Bush Theatre, Royal Exchange Theatre, 2017); *Be My Baby*, *Around The World in 80 Days* (Leeds Playhouse); *The Trick*, *Philoxenia* (Bush Theatre); *The Mountaintop* (Young Vic and tour, 2016); *Mayfly* (2018), *Out of Water* (Orange Tree, 2019); Paines Plough Roundabout seasons 2014, 2017 and 2018; *Macbeth* (Sam Wanamaker Playhouse, 2014).

11 As a movement director, I work with several directors who frequently participate in the warm-up and recently had the participation of a composer, a musical director, a lighting designer/costume designer – and I believe this is enriching for all involved. When I can, I join the company for voice warm-up or for singing with the hope that also working out of my comfort zone is helpful to the culture of the room and experiencing other's expertise through my body.

12 Vicki Igbokwe is the founder, Creative Director and Choreographer of Uchenna Dance, a London-based dance company on a mission to 'Empower, Entertain and Educate' through the medium of dance. Independently, she works as a choreographer, movement director and facilitator. She is the facilitator for The Fi.ELD (Future Innovators East London Dance), a trustee for One Dance UK, and a Work Place artist (associate artist) at The Place.

13 Sacha Plaige is a graduate of L'École Internationale de Théâtre Jacques Lecoq and a founding member of award-winning Clout Theatre. As a young person she was an ice-dancer for ten years. Prior to her training at Lecoq, she attend the four-year acting course at the University of Cinematography in Moscow. Sacha also holds a MA in Movement: Directing and Teaching from RCSSD. Her teaching experience is with the International Film School of Paris, Bedfordshire University and Northampton University. Movement direction credits include Garsington Opera and National Trust Runnymede. She has performed with Clout Theatre, Royal Opera House and ZOU Theatre.

14 The Old Vic has had several recent projects led by choreographers such as Kate Prince and Drew McOnie. Jane Gibson and Sue Lefton also have led movement-driven works and adaptations in the past as co-directors.

15 Rebecca Meltzer is a movement director and teacher, and director primarily working in opera. Rebecca trained at Durham University and RCSSD, and her work focuses on interdisciplinary techniques of performance practice, uniting her backgrounds in music, dance and fine art. She has worked with companies and institutions including Royal Opera House, Wexford Festival Opera, Opera Holland Park, British Youth Opera, Blackheath Halls Opera, Shadwell Opera, National Opera Studio, Iford Arts, Bury Court Opera, Dorset Opera Festival, Royal Conservatoire of Scotland, Trinity Laban, Royal Academy of Music and Tête à Tête. Rebecca is also a founding director of Waterperry Opera Festival.

16 Coral Messam is a performer, choreographer and movement director with over twenty years of experience working in the arts. As movement director productions include *Small Island* (2019), *Ma Rainey* (2015), *The Amen Corner* (2013) National Theatre; *Fantastic Follies of Mrs Rich* (RSC, 2018); *The Convert* (Young Vic, 2018). TV includes *Small Axe* (2020), with Steve McQueen, and *January 22nd* with Michaela Coel; *Cursed* (Netflix, 2019); *Game of Thrones* (choreographer and performer, 2010); *Britannia* (as movement director, 2019). Her film experience includes *London Road* (2014), and her directorial debut was *Run It Back* (2018) at Hackney Showrooms, which returns in spring 2020 to Talawa's new theatre space. Messam also works as a visiting movement lecturer at RCSSD and practitioner at the National Theatre Learning Department.

17 This is echoed in the relationship in the 1960s between Litz Pisk and Vanessa Redgrave or, more recently, between Eddie Redmayne and Alexandra Reynolds; Polly Bennett and Rami Malek; or Toby Sedgwick and Steve Coogan. Actors frequently talk with eloquence about the impact of movement work on their work and themselves.

18 Skype conversation, 27 July 2019. Ingrid Mackinnon is a London-based movement director, choreographer, teacher and dancer. Movement direction credits include *Typical* (Nouveau Riche, Soho Theatre), *#WeAreArrested* (RSC, 2019), *#DR@CULA!* (RCSSD, 2017), *Kingdom Come* (RSC, 2017), *Fantastic Mr Fox* (associate at Nuffield Southampton and National/International tour, 2016). Choreography and rehearsal direction credits include *The Headwrap Diaries* (assistant choreographer and rehearsal director, 2017) for Uchenna Dance; *Our Mighty Groove* (rehearsal director) for Uchenna Dance (2015); *Boy Breaking Glass* (rehearsal director, 2018) for Vocab Dance and Alesandra Seutin; *Hansel and Gretel* (assistant choreographer and rehearsal director, 2018); *Imoinda* (choreographer, 2019). Mackinnon holds a MA in Movement: Directing and Teaching from RCSSD.

19 *Typical*, written by Ryan Calais Cameron and directed by Anastasia Osei-Kuffour at Soho Theatre (2019).

20 In 2017, the UK government legislated that organizations with over 250 employees would have to publish statistics of gender pay differences in their work force. *The Stage* reported that 'statistics from the latest round of data (2018–19) show the gender pay gap remains broadly similar to the previous year, with a median hourly gap of 6.5%', and where women remain disadvantaged financially. See Snow (2019).

21 Thanks to Vanessa Ewan's workshop as part of the International Community for Movement for this clarity and centring of the actor. See also Ewan and Green 2015: Chapter 9.

22 Chi-San Howard is a movement director who trained at RCSSD. Movement work for theatre includes *World's End* (Kings Head Theatre, 2019); *Catching Comets* (Pleasance Edinburgh, Royal Exchange, 2019); *A Midsummer Night's Dream* (Oxford Playhouse, 2018); *Variations* (NT Connections, Dorfman Theatre, 2019); *The Curious Case of Benjamin Button* (Southwark Playhouse, 2019); *Let Kilburn Shake* (Kiln Theatre, 2019); *Skellig* (Nottingham Playhouse, 2019); *Under the Umbrella* (Belgrade Theatre, Tamasha, Yellow Earth, 2019); *American Idiot* (Mountview, 2018); *Carmen the Gypsy* (Arcola Theatre and tour, 2018); *Describe the Night (*Hampstead Theatre, 2018); *Bury the Dead* (2018), *Homos or Everyone in America* (2018), *Adding Machine: A Musical* (Finborough Theatre, 2016); *Parade* (Mountview, 2018).

23 Ioli Filippakopoulou is a movement teacher and movement director originally from Greece, based in London. She holds an MA in Movement Directing and Teaching from RCSSD, where she is currently a visiting lecturer. Ioli is a movement teacher at East 15 Drama School – specializing in Laban for actors – and also works as a movement coach for animation (Royal College of Art) and motion capture performance. Her most recent credits in the UK include *Metamorphosis* (New Diorama & HOME, 2019); *Timon of Athens* (RSC; co-movement director with Jon Goddard, 2018); *Troy* (Voila Europe Festival, 2018); *Tejas Verdes* (Ugly Duck, 2017).

24 The MA/MFA Movement: Directing and Teaching has mentoring schemes and actively seeks placements. International Community for Movement is a series of rolling professional development workshops for movement practitioners. Theatre mentoring schemes include Old Vic 12, informal networks, Frantic Assembly Associates and workshops at Paines Plough, run by Bennett.

25 In conversation, 29 July 2019. Natasha Harrison is a movement director, choreographer and teacher based in London. After studying at the Northern School of Contemporary Dance, Natasha went on to complete her Masters in Movement: Directing and Teaching, graduating from RCSSD. Aside from movement directing productions, Natasha is an associate artist for Red Ladder Theatre Company and is the Old Vic 12 Movement Director for 2018/19, an education associate practitioner for the RSC and creator and host of the Movement Podcast.

26 Job sharing has been particularly successful in enabling those with caring duties to manage the classic theatre schedules and maternity career breaks.

27 Ingrid Mackinnon and Laura Dredger, founders of MoveSpace, sought to inject inspiration into the community of emergent movement practitioners. Their meetings and workshops have become a place for sharing, nurturing and problem solving with peers. Available online: http://movespace.org.uk (accessed 4 August 2019).

16 BEYOND THE ROOM: CONTEXTS AND STRUCTURES

The movement practitioners who feature in this book are unified by their roles as creators, facilitators, enablers, collaborators, translators and problem solvers. Their descriptions of their careers demonstrate how the influence of movement on production is growing and proliferating, and the artistic input from movement directors and theatre choreographers is widely felt to be dynamic and fruitful. Significantly, all of the interviewees work as freelancers. As such, they create workplaces which are temporary, with many discontinuities from one project to another. Where are the spaces and structures for continuity and reflection? How might movement practitioners create – and articulate – impact which endures beyond the immediate effects of their work within individual rehearsal environments? This book constitutes one possible solution to this quandary. This is the first book to give a platform to contemporary, working moving directors. Here, through their own voices, practitioners have revealed and analysed their unique ways of working in the rehearsal room and how their own individual work relates to the broader profession. This will enable future movement directors to locate themselves on a continuum of practice. I hope that this book will also clarify the nature of movement direction and theatre choreography for whom the practices are enigmatic or obscure.

When I set out on this project, I was expecting much divergence amongst practitioners. In the event, I discovered a considerable degree of congruence in perspectives on movement. A critical unifying theme also emerged: the need for change in a growing field. In this concluding chapter, it will become apparent that movement as a profession is shaped by the unstable nature of its position within theatre organizations and the wider industry.[1] I will argue that movement directors need to be recognized and afforded a greater sense of belonging within theatrical contexts for the field to flourish.

Movement directors and theatre choreographers collectively could ask, 'What might *we* do to celebrate growth and cultivate the field?' I would like to suggest, first, that future growth will have to mean 'deeper and different' rather than simply 'more'. And secondly, I suggest opportunities for theatre organizations to play a more active role in the future and to benefit from movement practice in a wider sense. Here are some provocations and observations for the future of our field, organized into two themes: belonging and recognition.

Belonging

Consultation, collaboration and continuity are aspects of belonging that will be explored in the following section. My aim is to highlight how the inclusion of movement voices in the wider remit of theatre organizations could nourish and develop the field of movement and the theatre organizations themselves, simultaneously.

These movement directors and theatre choreographers belong to teams of theatre artists and to companies creating work in rehearsal rooms. As freelancers, there is an itinerant aspect to their work, as they move from production to production. On the whole, they are part of creating temporary rehearsal cultures in which actor's movement can take place and theatre choreography can be created. This gives rise to a physical practice that remains embedded within one production. As they progress from show to show, they endeavour to ameliorate the way movement occurs in any given rehearsal room. This feeds into the development and sustainability of the work for actors. It also shapes the interviewees' sense of artistry in movement and their place within creative collaboration. With each project, they start the whole movement process anew. However, progressing from show to show rarely allows movement directors opportunities to offer regular movement practice or witness deep development in the embodied practices that are offered to actors.

All interviewees express how unique each project is and highlight the differences amongst the directors they work with. Artistically, that is stimulating. But other differences suggest instability and precariousness in timescales and working structures. There are big variations within the planning and rehearsal periods discussed. This might suggest diversity amongst the needs and practices of these practitioners; or equally, it might be a consequence of lack of consultation by host organizations on how movement could best unfurl across a production. I noticed that even the most experienced movement practitioners were buffeted by organizational structures such as obtaining dedicated warm-up space or time during a tech or pre-show. Or they had to strongly assert their way of working; instances where movement directors managed to secure thirty minutes ahead of rehearsal, or an hour of morning practice throughout a whole production, are of note because they are still very much the exception.[2]

Organizations do not, as yet, appear to fully appreciate the conditions needed to work with movement optimally. A step towards improving conditions would be to have work contracts for movement practitioners that enable continuity with an acting company. The next step would be to have suitable spaces and allocated time for movement to happen, during all phases of a production, from rehearsal through to the run. All theatre departments could centralize the actors' physical (and vocal) preparation ahead of a performance and after a performance – with paid, allocated time/space for actors to warm up and cool down as a form of personal practice.

As a creative, your contract formally ends on press night. There is often sporadic provision for movement practitioners to return to see and sustain their work beyond this point. 'Dance captains' can play an invaluable part in the maintenance of movement work.[3] However, movement directors need to be able to 'maintain' their contribution, especially on a long run. It is becoming more and more common for contracts to have provision for a movement practitioner to maintain their work, and this is a positive development that could be more consistently anticipated, and adopted by theatre organizations.

Being freelance means that offering constructive feedback to a host organization can happen in an ad hoc manner. Your professional persona as a willing and productive collaborator can override any critical feedback, and this can leave change unsought, unexpressed and internalized.[4] If the rapport between producing houses and freelancers were more open and discursive, opportunities for innovation, which so often is seeded in critical feedback, would increase. Host theatres could invite suggestions and input from movement practitioners or set up holistic planning meetings. Both actions would start to dissolve any real or perceived 'risk' in offering frank or critical feedback. The potential exists, therefore, to create a platform for innovation.

Inclusivity and movement practices

The wider creative industries are in the process of addressing barriers that prevent and inhibit the participation of a wider range of artists and audiences. In Britain, the Equality Act 2010, disability laws and activism have instigated theatres to take action around protected characteristics in the broader setting of the theatre as a workplace.[5] Theatres are in the process of adapting spaces and systems for greater inclusivity of otherly-abled theatre artists. There are also initiatives underway to enrich creative teams through race equality. Systems for addressing unethical and disempowering behaviours in the workplace are being implemented. Those who run buildings in which rehearsal rooms exist – theatre administrators, artistic directors, stage managers, producers – are changing cultures.[6]

Movement for actors frequently models innovative, inclusive practice. Movement practitioners could be at the forefront of modelling this inclusivity, as it is frequently already embedded in their artistic practice and languages. With the ensemble approach they are creating space for all actors within movement. Their work aims to empower all bodies to move and to take up space during the production's movement work. Enhancing capacity and connection is part of the fabric of creating bespoke movement material. Movement practice is playing its part in building confidence and freedom to move, but this remains contained in the production process and rarely communicates outwards to the host organization.

Rather than discussing notions of belonging directly, many of these interviewees articulate the ongoing nature of awareness. Trying to work with awareness within the room is sometimes in tension with the organizational and directorial infrastructure offered to them. A movement director can hold, manage and shape the energy of a rehearsal room in unique and enormously valuable ways, yet their ability to utilize this awareness is framed by the structures within which they work. The rehearsal room is a shared space, and their access to it is determined (and, at times, limited) by organizational structures and directorial priorities.

These movement practitioners highlight the necessity to remain current and attentive to shifts in language and approaches to the performer's body. Their focus is directed into the rehearsal room. Part of future growth is to also redirect that practice outwards and to ask how movement directors might collectively share their actor-centred approach, and disseminate strategies that are clearly enabling, beyond one project. Likewise, how could a movement director, needful of development, resource themselves ethically and artistically for a career that is in tune with contemporary practices and has longevity?[7]

Heads of Movement and resident movement directors

At present, there are no resident movement directors or Heads of Movement in any national theatre in the UK. Two national companies, the Royal National Theatre and the Royal Shakespeare Company (RSC), are amongst the biggest employers of freelance movement directors. They are well positioned to create models of continuity for the practitioners who movement direct for their companies. Both institutions have had Head of Movement posts in the past, but with changes to artistic leadership, or through financial restructuring, these were dissolved. For over seven decades, informal groups of de facto movement directors have also been weaving their way through both institutions. Freelance practitioners who work for consecutive seasons for these theatres inevitably have an impact on the productions. But they rarely have agency, and they certainly have few opportunities for wider involvement in the institution. The National Theatre of Scotland has felt the full force of leading movement directors on the success of its productions – as freelancers. The more recently established National Theatre of Wales has no visible place for movement directors in its infrastructure, although its programming is often movement based. This constitutes a noticeable gap in potential for actors, education departments and productions of our national institutions.

Continuity is instrumental for developing artists. With some continuity, movement directors could contribute to the vision and leadership of the creative culture of a building. Their practices could extend outwards from a rehearsal room to inform research and development of new work, and participate in audience development, education and outreach work. The connectivity and accessibility of movement practice is demonstrated in the ensemble approaches articulated by these interviewees. This can be readily extended to other groups such as young artists, school children and third-age groups. The creative strategies and languages embedded in their artistic involvement could be shared with audiences and other theatre practitioners alike. Some workshop initiatives are in evidence, but they are disjointed and lacking in any cumulative effect. Movement directors and theatre choreographers could play a bigger part in the future of theatre organizations, and it is time that they were invited to the table in decision making at an institutional level. This would harness creative thinking that is physically led. It is also time that movement practitioners express their wish to be involved.

One may argue that there is continued dominance of word over body at the very centre of some theatre institutions. This may explain the current absence of Heads of Movement or movement directors in residence in any national theatre institution in the UK. Theatre organizations that have the potential to lead change by acknowledging the physical dimension of theatre works are choosing to focus resources elsewhere. Another reading may be that artistic demands of multiple productions in one organization will always outstrip one movement director's reach, style and time, and that incoming creative teams will always want to work with their chosen practitioner. If the model of a 'Head' was deemed unworkable, then our national institutions might consider other rhizomatic models: for example, rolling groups of movement directors working in concert over several seasons; or artist residencies with mentoring schemes; or embedding movement directors in artistic leadership. There are many ways to imagine and design continuity.

Shakespeare's Globe Theatre has a Master of Movement (who is female) and whose role is a valuable backdrop to the work of the company and may be thought of as movement support rather than movement direction.[8] Smaller companies do have a more coherent track record of continuity with movement directors, such as Shared Experience and Cheek by Jowl, where one or two practitioners work consistently over many shows and over time. As a consequence, movement plays a large part in the overall picture of these company's language and style. An increase in the number of movement directors being honoured as Associate Artists may herald the future.[9] Now those institutions could consider facilitating their Associates to influence the wider work of the company, whilst simultaneously enabling creative growth for those movement directors. This could be achieved with modest resources – movement often only needs space and bodies, for example, to run open, weekly actor's movement classes. Institutions could convene meetings of regional movement directors for creative exchange or host residencies reminiscent of writer's residencies. For an early-career movement director there currently exists only one formal British theatre scheme designed to develop their practice. Hosted by the Old Vic as part of the Old Vic 12 scheme, this develops one practitioner per year. Imagine how potent it would be if every British theatre developed an early-career movement director for a year? Apprenticeship schemes could include watching rehearsals across several productions, shadowing a variety movement directors and soaking up the craft of actors and directors.

Theatre organizations are taking action around 'protected characteristics' amongst their creative workforce. They do so partly in response to external forces (often associated with funding).[10] The response of cultural institutions to questions of diversity and inclusion is also shaped by the artistic directors – their tone and their cultural priorities. Who they are, what they do and what they say are of relevance. Recent developments have prompted a long overdue recalibration process.[11] The privileges afforded white male artistic directors have been challenged, and in their stead a new wave of artistic directors is emerging.[12] This new wave is more diverse in terms of gender, orientation and ethnicity. Attention to the lived experiences of artists from minority backgrounds and female workers has prompted organizations to wrestle with the politics of exclusion and omission. On the whole, these new artistic directors have successfully integrated movement directors into the heart of their creative teams, and their intersectional and/or feminist gaze has started to celebrate, rather than tolerate, the power of movement.[13] This bodes well for belonging – a type of belonging that is uncomplicated, respectful and genuinely empowering. New artistic directors with innovative programming, reshaped working practices and sensitivity to the power dynamics within collaboration are changing the context of artistic production. Belonging to artistic homes might be a potent, reciprocal way to feed and nurture movement directors to develop the field.

British theatre has historically underrepresented artists of colour and otherly-abled artists. And whilst there is some growth in the numbers of movement directors from a range of backgrounds and orientations, this author has yet to meet an otherly-abled movement practitioner and notices a dearth of British East Asian or South Asian movement directors. Awareness of intersectionality and actions for inclusion must be built into the future growth of the field.[14] Development and inclusion of all sorts of artists can only progress if it is a shared responsibility of every branch of our creative industry. This will require a shift from passive to active and from fragmented to joined up. When we, as a profession, ask, 'Who is missing from this picture?', we are prompted to take positive action. This may include questioning how we decide who assists us or what forms of movement actors are embodying through our work.[15] Enabling a wider range of trainee movement directors into the profession will need industry infrastructure – one approach might include schemes and apprenticeship models. The aim has to be opening the doors to movers from a mix of heritages and socioeconomic backgrounds, and with a range of bodies and orientations.[16] Then, once those practitioners are on board and developing, how can they be embedded in creative teams? Without increased opportunities for continuity and development within the field of movement direction, we will only address diversity in a fragmented manner.

Movement direction is shaped by a combination of professional skills and personal, lived experience. These interviews clearly show that it is characterized by hybridity of movement trainings. What constitutes this hybridity is significant. There is a close relationship between a movement director's skills and their own embodied history with movement. 'Who' they are and 'what' they bring to the creative process are intimately interwoven. Diversity amongst practitioners can bring unique embodied knowledge through first-hand experience of forms and cultures.[17]

The interviewees highlight many models of positive working relationships between directors and movement directors. As a witness to artistic growth, I have seen a flourishing of theatre works driven by a female gaze. In female teams of director and movement director, feminist discourses have questioned the framing of bodies on stage. Those discourses are also having a positive influence on working cultures in rehearsal rooms. Practitioners are more able to take up space. They are being consulted about rehearsal. Revivified cultures of artistic respect, deep-rooted mutual support, shared ambitions and a fearless approach to the body are permeating certain rehearsal rooms. As a movement director, my movement practice has benefited from the creative and political enquiry of the feminist directors I have worked with, and I have many positive experiences of open creative cultures of rehearsal. Collaborative models of consultation and practice are increasingly prevalent, and these bode well for the future of belonging and flourishing.

Recognition

In the first two decades of the twenty-first century, the presence of movement directors and theatre choreographers has increased on the British theatre scene. The interviewees in this book have witnessed their profession grow, and they feel that they have contributed to that growth. Their experience chimes with the Arts Council's evaluation that freelance employment has grown on productions with larger casts and larger creative teams in theatre in England.[18] In 2004, the MA in Movement at Royal Central School of Speech and Drama was established as the first formal training in Europe with a remit to develop movement teachers and movement directors, and in the last fifteen years it has influenced the field through cultivating new, specialist practitioners and academics.

In the following section, I will examine how movement directors, despite all this growth and increased institutionalization, have not yet achieved professional parity with other roles in the creative team in relation to crediting, critical recognition, associations and awards. The conversations featured in this book point to a subtle but significant disjunction between the greater inclusion of movement directors in creative production and their continued absence (or *omission*) in a wider forum.

Beyond credits

Early movement directors suffered from invisibility in several ways: their work was ignored or misattributed in reviews; their input was undocumented and unrecognized in the traces of productions; and they were, at times, either uncredited or miscredited on programmes. Progress has been made: today, critics *do* sometimes write about movement and practitioners *are* credited in programmes and are sporadically involved in the allied events of a production.

Apt crediting is certainly more prevalent; movement directors do now appear in programmes consistently. Yet the scale and/or nature of their contribution is not always accurately represented.[19] This is professionally undermining and artistically dispiriting. The requirement for crediting to be truthfully located is a matter not of inflating the work but of simple professionalism. It is useful to note that practitioners working in musical theatre did not raise credits as a problem. A theatre *choreographer* tends to be more easy to identify, name and locate. Movement directors might look to musical theatre for guidance. We could collaborate more clearly with marketing departments to communicate what is preferable in relation to the *actual* contribution to the production. It is worth noting that it is as uncomfortable being undercredited as it is being overcredited.[20] Host institutions could generate credits as part of an inclusive consultative process, rather than passively adhering to existing and unrepresentative 'house' style. If producers and publicity departments ask the question, 'What is important for you?' rather than assert, 'This is how we do it,' then this problem will immediately evaporate. The shifting, ephemeral nature of movement work and the vastly differing amounts of input from show to show mean that movement directors must be responsible for articulating their presence and contribution in as many ways as possible to external parties. Producing houses and agents could consult more with movement directors about the naming and positioning of their work. Then the 'house style' of programme or credits would no longer be a place to reduce or inflate the scale of a movement director's input and inadvertently contribute to the obfuscation of their work.[21]

Critics are slowly starting to include movement in their reviews and articulate the contribution of movement directors in writing. Production programmes that reveal the role of movement in rehearsal processes and clearly credit movement directors are helpful, allowing critics to track individuals from production to production.[22] Increasingly, critics are writing about theatre creation as collaborative, which is more representative and helps make a wider range of practitioners visible to audiences. This is supported and enhanced by some institutions that have started to highlight the collaborative nature of productions by crediting movement practitioners on production photos and including them in audience talks, allied video material, production interviews and blogs.[23]

Association

I identify a continual tension around the way that logistics can support artists. In the theatre profession, employment conditions are seen to be lagging in relation to freelance creatives, including movement directors.[24] Many movement directors would benefit from the structures provided by the main theatre union in the UK, Equity. But currently, the organization does not have a division that includes movement directors. Thus, the majority of practitioners do not recognize themselves within the organization, and they operate outside its resources, protections and advocacy. This will need to change in the future, with Equity creating specific provision for movement directors. Negotiating productive work time is inextricably linked to contracts. These rarely or sporadically include adequate provision for pre-meetings, preparation or maintenance over long runs.

Movement direction is a creative role that has suffered from modest fees. The majority of British movement directors are women, and their pay reflects the larger history of lower pay for women workers. Historically, this role has been an invisible part of the workforce. There are instances of movement directors being omitted for transfer fees and royalties or, more commonly, overworking to deliver the movement on a show. Furthermore, the presence of female practitioners has been largely rendered invisible in the way work and processes are documented. These are areas that are almost impossible to address as a solo freelance practitioner.

As yet, there is no association for movement directors.[25] The idea of a unifying professional body is notable by its absence from the interviews. Movement directors need a forum to articulate their ideas about the shape of their work: the moment that a guild of practitioners is formed, a discipline can advocate and instigate change. This is clearly demonstrated by recently formed associations for sound designers and casting directors. Both are already operating effectively to define and celebrate their field. Guilds function to motivate their members with professional development opportunities, build community and achieve recognition, all of which would contribute to future growth.

As a mid-career movement director looking forwards and backwards between these interviewees, I was led to ask how movement directors and theatre choreographers might keep developing their practice. How can practitioners develop their methods ever more deeply and creatively? Members of this group are unified by their thirst for development and lifelong learning. Where might they find that space for development and impact? My worry is that they would have to switch to an allied theatre profession to feel that they had agency and progression.

If movement direction is seen as a stepping stone to some other theatre career, then the field of movement direction will stultify into a constantly 'emergent' field.

Currently, there are no categories for movement direction in any theatre awards in Scotland, Wales, Northern Ireland or England. Awards are a simple way for theatre professionals to be recognized for their work.[26] My research into movement director's absence from awards illuminates the disparities at work amongst members of the creative teams (often on the same shows).[27] In the context of awards, naming your artistic role becomes critical.[28] The picture is muddled and out of date for movement directors – the awards that *have* been presented to movement directors have sat in the 'choreography' categories. This is perplexing when the work they created was not recognizably dance material but the broader creation of physical language. This acts to eclipse movement work and confuse audiences and theatre professionals alike. It also means that plays and opera are frequently omitted in favour of musical theatre.

Ireland is leading the way. In 2018, the *Irish Times* Theatre Awards created two new categories: 'Movement Direction' and 'Ensemble'. These both go a long way towards recognizing movement creation and collective artistry in production processes. It is noticeable that even newer, small-scale awards – which otherwise have excellent inclusive agendas – have failed to recognize movement directors.[29] Awarding bodies and panels need to be clearer about what kind of work they recognize as movement direction. Once movement directors form an association, they can campaign for change amongst awarding bodies.

By sharing my observations about missed opportunities, I hope not only to articulate a range of future possibilities, but also to mobilize all invested parties. Theatre is a collaborative art, and movement is playing an ever larger part within the matrix. Growth in the creative dimension of the work has outrun change at an institutional level. By addressing the resulting omissions and confusions, movement directors and theatre choreographers will be able to flourish and build on a sense of belonging and apt recognition. This will create the conditions to tend to growth more clearly within the artistic realm.

In its purest form, there is something hugely simple and life-giving about being a human within the flow of your body in movement. The future for the actual practice of movement in production is full of creative thinking, dreaming, tangible physical skills and connectivity through movement. This is evident in the voices of the practitioners in this book. As movement directors and theatre choreographers, we will continue to step into all of our rehearsal rooms with our whole selves, full of wonder at the discoveries of human movement and the unending wisdoms that the body gives rise to - imagination and emotion. My hope for the future of the field is that movement creativity finds a more lasting place in the memory of work and more space to flourish within the wider setting of the theatre profession.

Notes

1. This final chapter was written over the course of spring 2019, when I sat on three industry panels dedicated to the voices of movement directors and a discussion group on 8 June in collaboration with Diane Alison-Mitchell. All of this serves as a backdrop for this look at the future.
2. Jane Gibson's career has been underpinned by strong continuity – both during her time as Head of Movement and during her long-term engagement with Cheek by Jowl; Steven Hoggett's Frantic Assembly days will have given him opportunity to build a model of practice that continues to inform his current movement direction.
3. A 'dance captain' is a member of the acting company who is chosen, inducted and trained by the movement director to maintain the movement work throughout the run. In musical theatre, the dance captain is probably in place from the start of the rehearsal, and in theatre they normally are appointed towards the end of the rehearsal. Their role is to maintain the movement work as set by the movement director and to facilitate any small changes that arise from a change of theatre venue or actor injury. See Glossary, p. 213.
4. A full production debrief between the creative team and the in-house team is a model used in some theatres, for example at the RSC, and offers a setting for the exchange of ideas and suggestions. If these were also attended by other departments, such as marketing and education, then a holistic approach would permeate and potentially activate change. This is not common practice, however, across other theatre companies.
5. According to the Equality Act 2010, it is against the law to discriminate against someone because of age, disability, sex, sexual orientation, gender reassignment, pregnancy and maternity, marriage and civil partnership, race, beliefs and religion.
6. Theatres are increasingly offering training for crew, cast and creatives to work knowledgeably with particular disabilities and conditions so that rehearsal rooms can meet the needs of all the actors. Some rehearsal rooms also have principles of respect articulated in visible formats, and some inductions include information on safeguarding, etc. All these methods of working have been embedded in higher education (HE) settings for many years but have started to infiltrate professional rehearsal spaces, too. Vicky Featherstone and the team at the Royal Court modelled a variety of reporting methods for sexist and sexually predatory behaviours within the theatre as workplace.
7. Few professional development opportunities are available for movement practitioners, and their ongoing training is very much in their own hands. As a beneficiary of HE training, in the last decade I have undertaken training in trans awareness, risk assessment, learning differences, safeguarding and sexual violence, British Sign Language, unconscious bias and many more. As a practitioner I have also attended Tonic Theatre and Parents and Carers in Performing Arts (PIPA) events to develop best practice for child carers and to hear of hurdles that women encounter in the workplace. This training has led me to question my language in productive ways and has invaluably informed my movement practice.

8   Glynne MacDonald is the Master of Movement and draws on her background in Alexander technique to support actors in the productions.

9   These include, but are not limited to, the Bush (one), the RSC (three), Watford Palace (three), the Globe (two), King's Head (one), Dundee Rep Theatre (one), Cheek by Jowl (one), Complicité (one), Volcano (one), Old Vic (two choreographers), Shared Experience (one).

10 See note 5.

11 Feminist and/or intersectional organizations have proliferated in the last decade, with ERA 50:50, Blacktress, Tonic Theatre and PIPA all campaigning to address the inequalities of opportunity and recognition in the creative industries. Available online: http://equalrepresentationforactresses.co.uk; http://www.blacktress.co.uk; https://www.tonictheatre.co.uk; http://www.pipacampaign.com.

12 These include, but are not limited to, the following: Ellen McDougall at the Gate; Rachel O'Riordan at the Lyric Hammersmith; Roxana Silbert, at the Hampstead Theatre; Lynette Linton at the Bush; Kwame Kwei-Armah at the Young Vic; Alexander Wise and Bryony Shanahan at Manchester Royal Exchange; Michael Longhurst at the Donmar; Sean Foley and Amit Sharma at the Birmingham Rep; Tarek Iskander at Battersea; Justin Audibert at the Unicorn; Suba Das at HighTide; Nadia Fall at Theatre Royal, Stratford East; Chris Sonnex at the Bunker; Charlotte Bennett and Katie Posner at Paines Plough; Michelle Terry at Shakespeare's Globe; and Vicky Featherstone at the Royal Court. See Clapp 2019.

13 I have noted this while working with a number of directors in the last decade. Of note are artistic directors Ellen McDougall (the Gate), Roxana Silbert (Hampstead Theatre), Erica Whyman (Deputy Artistic Director, RSC), and freelance directors Maria Aberg, Kimberley Sykes and Phillip Breen.

14 The movement course that I co-lead with Vanessa Ewan at Royal Central School of Speech and Drama has been playing its part in increasing the range of movement practitioners entering the profession, but we must acknowledge the potential obstacles created by the financial commitment that HE study requires.

15 For example, what non-Western forms of movement practices might be used in the training of actors? Yoga is already occupying a sizeable place in actor training – but what about capoeira or South Asian dance, for example?

16 See Arts Council report 2017/18 and 'Panic!' report funded by the Arts and Humanities Research Council Both suggest people from black and minority ethnic backgrounds are more likely to see a pathway in the arts as high risk.

17 For one detailed examination of how a movement director unites trainings and influences, see Alison-Mitchell (2017: 46–53).

18 A report looking at theatre by the Arts Council of England, entitled 'Theatre Assessment 2009', evaluated the growth of the arts in the first decade of the twenty-first century. It begins, 'The first years of the 21st century was a boom time for the arts' (7). The authors go on to flesh out the statistics for that growth during the period of review (2001–9): 'The theatre industry grew considerably with the number of people employed by the theatre organisations in our constant sample increased by more than half [sic]. Permanent artistic staff numbers increased by 81 per cent. The number of freelance staff increased by even more, indicating that there has been more work created by larger casts and creative teams. This is a useful indicator of the

ambition of theatre organisations and we hope theatre organisations will be able to maintain or increase current levels, providing valuable employment to actors, stage managers, etc., as well as large scale productions for audiences' (16).

19 A billing of implied importance where movement directors may feel their work to be diminished by a low position on the list, such as
Director
Designer
Composer
Lighting Designer
Sound Designer
Movement Director
Some theatres have started using an alphabetical listing of creatives and cast.

20 It is rare that a movement director has been under-deployed on a project. It is notable that many directors and movement directors have successful repeat working relationships: Hoggett and Tiffany, Yee and Cracknell, Knight and Longhurst, to name a few. This shows us that collaboration is felt and celebrated but still under-recognized beyond the rehearsal room.

21 In the last year, the author has noticed that marketing departments and producers are including the full creative team's credit on social media, printed matter and photos.

22 In *The Stage*, Matthew Trueman writes, 'If it takes one great performance to notice an actor and one great play to spot a playwright, other creatives can be harder to clock. Their stamp isn't so obvious; their style bends to fit. When work catches your eye – a design or some direction – you delve into your programme only to find the name staring back is the same as last time' (Trueman 2015). Also in *The Stage*, Fergus Morgan asks, 'What exactly does a movement director do?' and observed that 'It's an increasingly common question as the job title has started appearing more frequently in programmes' (Morgan 2018).

23 One effective model is offered by Dr Sita Thomas, who produced a series of short films for the National Theatre:

What is a Movement Director? (2014), https://www.youtube.com/watch?v=KY-gWqj-FIk&index=9&list=PLJgBmjHpqgs4s6c0MrG-pniFOTtvKncpG;

History of Movement Direction at the National Theatre by Ayse Tashkiran (2015), https://www.youtube.com/watch?v=8NjU8gttsZo&list=PLJgBmjHpqgs4s6c0MrG-pniFOTtvKncpG&index=4;

Creating an Ensemble by Imogen Knight – warm-up (2015) https://www.youtube.com/watch?v=2FWAUncAvv4&index=8&list=PLJgBmjHpqgs4s6c0MrG-pniFOTtvKncpG;

Movement Direction: Creating Character, by Vanessa Ewan (2014); https://www.youtube.com/watch?v=1RRc4tq2kpE&list=PLJgBmjHpqgs4s6c0MrG-pniFOTtvKncpG&index=3.

Another model is in the form of the podcast curated by movement director Natasha Harrison. Available online: https://podcasts.apple.com/gb/podcast/the-movement-podcast-hosted-by-natasha-harrison/id1464005842.

24 Allied professions (such as musicians or teachers) have had pension funds, holiday pay, maternity and paternity leave and childcare structures in place for many years.

25 A movement directors' association is currently under construction.

26 The Olivier Awards have a Choreographer category and a Dance Work category which means that there is a bias towards the genre of dance or musical theatre. The transatlantic nature of large-scale, commercially successful work has theatre choreographers and movement directors at the centre of that success. There is a pattern of exchange between Broadway or London, with productions moving between the two, then undertaking national and international touring. This type of work enters the framework of awards such as the Olivier Awards and Tony Awards. It is here that a job title seems to make a sizeable difference. Theatre choreographers sit more easily within award structures and are nominated and win or lose; movement directors are nominated in ill-fitting Choreography categories and, unsurprisingly, normally lose. That is either because judging panels are not comparing like for like – a play with a musical – or because judges are not including movement directors in the awarding panels. No one in the industry works for awards, but once nominated it is noticeable that the rest of the creative team of a show are rewarded, and the movement director is not. That is demotivating and suggests a problem that all awards givers could usefully address. It might be clearer to have two categories, or at least separate movement on musical theatre from movement on opera and plays.

The following summary indicates the sheer number of movement directors whose work was in Olivier-nominated shows for the 2019 awards:

Misty at the Bush and Trafalgar Studios, Movement by Rachael Nanyonjo
A Monster Calls at the Old Vic, Movement by Dan Canham
King Lear at Duke of York's Theatre, Movement by Lucy Cullingford
Nine Night at NT Dorfman and Trafalgar Studios, Movement Director Shelley Maxwell
Quiz at Noël Coward Theatre, Movement by Naomi Said
The Phlebotomist at Hampstead Theatre Downstairs, Movement by Michela Meazza
Katya Kabanova at Royal Opera House, Movement Director Sarah Fahie
Lessons in Love and Violence at Royal Opera House, Movement Director Joseph Alford
The Turn of The Screw at Regent's Park Open Air Theatre, Movement Director Jenny Ogilvie
The Inheritance at Young Vic and Noël Coward Theatre, Movement Director Polly Bennett
The Lehman Trilogy at National Theatre Lyttelton, Movement Director Polly Bennett
Sweat at Donmar Warehouse, Movement Director Polly Bennett

27 As I was writing this book, britishtheatre.com published an article entitled 'Time to step up recognition of movement direction' (Ludman 2019), and movement directors Polly Bennett and Shelley Maxwell appeared on *Front Row* arts programme on BBC Radio 4; each highlighted the need for change.

28 An analysis of the input of movement on National Theatre productions from 1963 to February 2020 (436 shows with movement input were considered) indicates that 'Movement Director' is the most common role title in use at the National Theatre,

followed by 'Choreographer', followed by 'Movement'. The author was surprised at how few composite titles were in fact used, for example 'Choreographer and Movement Director' (six instances). 'Director of Movement' credit was only used thirty-three times and 'choreography' in twenty six instances. In the early years of the National Theatre, variations of 'Dance by' or 'Dances arranged by' (including Dance set by/Advisor/Consultant/ Coach) were the norm and account for fifty credits.

29   Such as *The Stage* Debut Awards.

GLOSSARY

Room refers to the rehearsal room.

Creative team constitutes any combination of the following roles: director, designer, composer, movement director or theatre choreographer, lighting designer, video designer, sound designer, and stage combat person. Professional shorthand includes **creative team** or **the creatives**.

Tech is an abbreviation for technical rehearsal, a phase of the production process where the performers move from the rehearsal room into the theatre space. This is the time when the technical aspects of the creative process are realised. Design elements, costumes, lighting, music and sound, are all practically and creatively integrated into the overall arc of the production during the technical rehearsal. This is followed by a phase of work called 'previews' where the audience is present and sees the show. The creative and technical departments are still able to make improvements and changes in the daytime before the next preview. Most creatives' contracts finish with the press night, by which time the design and material of a production are deemed to be completed.

A **run** is the phase when the production performs at a particular venue.

A **job** is a professional engagement that lasts for one full production process from pre-planning to press night.

First night and **press night** are two different stages in the process. 'First night' means the first audience, that is, first 'preview'; then, after several previews, is 'press night', which is when critics are also invited to see the production. A creative team's work is completed by press night.

A **dance captain** is a member of the acting company who is chosen, inducted and trained by the movement director to maintain the movement work throughout the run. In musical theatre, the dance captain is likely to be in place from the start of the rehearsal, and in theatre they are normally appointed towards the end of the rehearsal. Their role is to maintain the movement work as set by the movement director and to facilitate any small adjustments that might arise from a change of theatre venue or actor injury.

A **swing** is a dancer or performer who understudies several different roles so that they can step in to cover an absent performer. It is more usual to have swings in musical theatre productions. They have to be able to retain many individual performance tracks and step in seamlessly to any of those roles at short notice.

REFERENCES

Books

Au, S. (1988), *Ballet and Modern Dance*, London and New York: Thames and Hudson.
Carter, A. and R. Fensham, eds (2011), *Dancing Naturally: Nature, Neo-Classicism and Modernity in Early Twentieth-Century Dance*, London: Palgrave Macmillan.
Dexter, J. (1993), *The Honourable Beast: A Posthumous Autobiography*, New York: Nick Hern Books.
Damasio, A. (2002), *The Feeling of What Happens: Body, Emotion and the Making of Consciousness*, London: Vintage.
Ewan, V. and D. Green (2015), *Actor Movement: Expression of the Physical Being*, London and New York: Bloomsbury Methuen Drama.
Ewan, V. with K. Sagovsky (2019), *Laban's Efforts in Action: A Movement Handbook for Actors*, London and New York: Methuen Drama.
Gallagher, S. and D. Zahavi (2008), *The Phenomenological Mind: An Introduction to Philosophy of Mind and Cognitive Science*, New York: Routledge.
Ginner, R. (1933), *The Revived Greek Dance: Its Art and Technique*, London: Methuen and Co.
Graham, S. and S. Hoggett (2014), *The Frantic Assembly Book of Devising Theatre*, 2nd edn, Abingdon, Oxon: Routledge.
Hodgson, J. (2001), *Mastering Movement: The Life and Work of Rudolf Laban*, New York and Abingdon, Oxon: Routledge.
Hodgson, J. and V. Preston-Dunlop (1990), *Rudolf Laban: An Introduction to His Work and Influence*, Plymouth: Northcote House.
Lecoq, J., ed. (1987), *Le Théâtre du Geste: Mimes et acteurs*, Paris, France: Bordas.
Lecoq, J. with J.-G. Carasso and J.-C. Lallias (2000), *The Moving Body (Le Corps Poétique)*, trans. David Bradby, London: Methuen Drama.
Konstan, D. and K. Rutter (2003), *Envy, Spite and Jealousy: The Rivalrous Emotions in Ancient Greece*, Edinburgh: Edinburgh University Press.
Mawer, I. (1932), *The Art of Mime: Its History and Technique in Education and the Theatre*, London: Methuen and Co.
Newlove, J. (1993), *Laban for Actors and Dancers: Putting Laban's Movement Theory into Practice: A Step-by-Step Guide*, London: Nick Hern Books.
Nicholas, L. (2007), *Dancing in Utopia: Dartington Hall and its Dancers*, Binsted, Hampshire: Dance Books.

Novack, J. C. (1990), *Sharing the Dance: Contact Improvisation and American Culture*, Madison, WI: University of Wisconsin Press.

Quirey, B. (1987), *May I Have the Pleasure: The Story of Popular Dancing*, London: Dance Books.

Sorgel, S. (2007), *Dancing Postcolonialism: The National Dance Theatre Company of Jamaica*, Bielefeld, Germany: Transcript Verlag.

Trewhitt, B. and J. Hastie, eds (1997), *Margaret Morris: Modern Dance Pioneer: A Resource Pack for Teachers and Students of Dance History*, Biggin Hill: International Association of Margaret Morris Movement.

Chapters in edited collections

Barker, C. (2000), 'Joan Littlewood', in A. Hodge (ed.), *Twentieth Century Actor Training*, 113–28, London: Routledge.

Elliott, M. ([1975] 2018), 'Foreword', in L. Pisk (ed.), *The Actor and His Body*, 4th edn, London: Bloomsbury Methuen Drama.

Garner, S. B. Jr. (2019), 'Watching Movement: Phenomenology, Cognition, Performance', in Rick Kemp and Bruce McConachie (eds), *The Routledge Companion to Theatre, Performance and Cognitive Science*, 203–15, Abingdon, Oxon and New York: Routledge.

Humphrey, D. (2002), 'The Art of Making Dances', in Michael Huxley and Noel Witts (eds), *The Twentieth Century Performance Reader*, 229–37, Abingdon, Oxon and New York: Routledge.

Perret, J. (1987), 'Entretien avec Ariane Mnouchkine', in J. Lecoq (ed.), *Le Théâtre du Geste: Mimes et acteurs*, 127–30, Paris, France: Bordas.

Tashkiran, A. (2016), 'British Movement Directors', in M. Evans and R. Kemp (eds), *The Routledge Companion to Jacques Lecoq*, 227–35, Abingdon: Routledge.

Journal articles

Blair, R. (2009), 'Cognitive Neuroscience and Acting: Imagination, Conceptual Blending and Empathy', *TDR: The Drama Review*, 53 (4): 93–103.

Flatt, K. and S. Melrose (2006), 'Finding – and Owning – a Voice: Choreographic Signature and Intellectual Property in Collaborative Theatre Practice', *Dance Theatre Journal*, 22 (2): 41–6.

McGaw, D. (2001), 'Lifelong Listening: An Appreciation of the Fifty-Year Career of the Teacher and Choreographer Geraldine Stephenson', *Dance Theatre Journal*, 17 (1): 20–4.

Ostermeier, T. and P. M. Boenisch (2014), '"The More Political We Are, the Better We Sell": A Conversation about the Political Potential of Directing Classical Drama and the Nasty Traps of Today's Cultural Industry', *Performance Paradigm*, 10: 17–27. Available online: https://www.performanceparadigm.net/index.php/journal/article/viewFile/142/141 (accessed 31 August 2019).

Paxton, S. with N. S. Stark (2018), 'The Politics of Mutuality: A Conversation with Steve Paxton at the Table', *Contact Quarterly*, 43 (1): 36–8.

Thompson, R. F. (1966), 'An Aesthetic of the Cool: West African Dance', *African Forum*, 2 (2): 85–102.

Walker, K. S. (1984), 'The Festival and the Abbey: Ninette de Valois' Early Choreography 1925–1934, Part One', *Dance Chronicle*, 7 (4): 379–412.

Magazine and newspaper articles

Bryden, R. (1966), 'John Osborne's Perfect Hero', *The Observer*, 12 June: 24.
Goodrich, J. (2003), 'Five Decades Dedicated to Dance', *Dancing Times*, September: 29–31.
Grace, N., V. Redgrave and B. Rawson (1997), 'Prime Mover and Shaker in the Arts', Litz Pisk Obituary, *The Guardian*, 14.
Macauley, A. (2008), 'Celebrating a Leader of Britain's Modern-Dance Vanguard', *New York Times*, 5 October. Available online: https://www.nytimes.com/2008/10/06/arts/dance/06alst.html?_r=2&scp=3&sq=%22Richard%20alston%22&st=cse (accessed 19 February 2020).
Shulman, M. (1966), 'Lope de Osborne', *Evening Standard*, 7 June: 9.
Young, B. A. (1966), 'A Bond Honoured', *Financial Times*, 7 June: 24.

Online resources

Billington, M. (2019), '*Equus* Review: Peter Shaffer's Homoerotic Classic Is Exhilarating', *The Guardian*, 25 February. Available online: https://www.theguardian.com/stage/2019/feb/25/equus-review-peter-shaffer-horse-blinding-theatre-royal-stratford-east-london-ned-bennett (accessed 29 June 2019).
Clayton, B. (2007), 'Barry Clayton – Interview Transcript', Interviewed by Kate Harris, *Theatre Archive Project British Library*, 8 October. Available online: https://sounds.bl.uk/related-content/TRANSCRIPTS/024T-C1142X000185-0100A0.pdf (accessed 30 November 2019).
Hageli, U. (2014), 'Ballet Evolved - Enrico Cecchetti 1850-1928', *Royal Opera House Insights*. Available online: https://www.youtube.com/watch?v=mG1WuZViibU (accessed 28 March 2020).
Hemming, S. (2016), 'Interview: Director and Choreographer Struan Leslie', *Financial Times*, 27 May. Available online: https://www.ft.com/content/1f6aee1c-21bc-11e6-9d4d-c11776a5124d (accessed 28 May 2016).
Hench, J. D. (2017), 'How to Make the Most of Stillness Onstage', *Dance Spirit*, 31 October. Available online: https://www.dancespirit.com/how-to-make-the-most-of-stillness-onstage-2502557437.html (accessed 2 May 2018).
Horwell, V. (2014), 'The Jig Is Up – Shakespeare's Globe Sends Them Out Dancing', *The Guardian*, 1 October. Available online: https://www.theguardian.com/stage/2014/oct/01/shakespeare-jig-music-choreography-globe-theatre (accessed 28 August 2019).
Jando, D. (n.d.), 'Johnny Hutch', *Circopedia*. Available online: http://www.circopedia.org/Johnny_Hutch (accessed 28 August 2019).
Jays, D. (2016), 'How Choreographer Ann Yee Got Andrew Scott and Ralph Fiennes into the Groove', *The Guardian*, 22 June. Available online: https://www.theguardian.com/stage/2016/jun/22/ann-yee-andrew-scott-ralph-fiennes-interview?CMP=share_btn_link (accessed 28 May 2018).
Macel, E. (2008), 'Brits on Broadway', *Dance Magazine*, 27 October. Available online: https://www.dancemagazine.com/brits-on-broadway-2306880918.html (accessed 1 July 2018).
Massom, G. (2019), 'Movement Director Shelley Maxwell: "Being Open Is Good – There's a Wide Rainbow of Things We Can Do"', *The Stage*, 12 February. Available online: https://www.thestage.co.uk/features/interviews/2019/movement-director-shelley-maxwell-open-good-theres-wide-rainbow-things-can/ (accessed 28 May 2019).

Morgan, F. (2018), 'Sian Williams: Theatres Are Waking Up to the Value of Movement Directors', *The Stage*, 1 October. Available online: https://www.thestage.co.uk/features/interviews/2018/sian-williams-theatre-movement-director-wolf-hall-rsc-kate-bush/# (accessed 2 October 2018).

Mountford, F. (2019), '*Equus* Review: Mesmerising Intensity and Intimacy in Disturbing Modern Classic', *Evening Standard*, 27 February. Available online: https://www.standard.co.uk/go/london/theatre/equus-review-theatre-royal-stratford-east-a4077671.html (accessed 29 June 2019).

Newlove, J. (2007), 'Jean Newlove – Interview Transcript', Interviewed by Kate Harris, *Theatre Archive Project British Library*, 6 November. Available online: https://sounds.bl.uk/related-content/TRANSCRIPTS/024T-C1142X000193-0100A0.pdf (accessed 1 September 2019).

Petherbridge, E. (2018), 'Geraldine Stephenson', *Peth's Staging Post*, 7 January. Available online: http://edwardpetherbridge.com/geraldine-stephenson/ (accessed 27 May 2019).

Pozzoli, S. and G. Siciliani (2013), 'Poetics of Touch: Nancy Stark-Smith, a Pathway into Contact Improvisation'. Available online: https://www.youtube.com/watch?v=v6Pt0OXK7es (accessed 6 December 2019).

'Shelley Maxwell: A "likkle Jamaican Girl" Doing Big Things Abroad' (2018), *Jamaica Observer*, 12 August. Available online: http://www.jamaicaobserver.com/career-education/shelley-maxwell-a-likkle-jamaican-girl-doing-big-things-abroad_141138?profile=1443 (accessed 27 June 2019).

Snow, G. (2019), 'Theatre Employers Blame Gender Pay Gap on Imbalance in Technical Departments', *The Stage*, 12 April. Available online: https://www.thestage.co.uk/news/2019/theatre-employers-blame-gender-pay-gap-on-imbalance-in-technical-departments/.

'Struan Leslie' (2015), Digital Theatre Plus: Creative Learning Panel. Available online: https://www.digitaltheatreplus.com/about-us/creative-learning-panel/struan-leslie (accessed 13 July 2019).

Trueman, M. (2015), 'Imogen Knight: "I Never Set Out to Be a Choreographer"', *The Stage*, 8 August. Available online: https://www.thestage.co.uk/features/interviews/2015/imogen-knight-never-set-choreographer/ (accessed 7 July 2016).

Film

Making War Horse (2009), [DVD], Dir. Phil Grabsky and David Bickerstaff, UK: National Theatre/Seventh Art Productions.

Unpublished interviews

Tashkiran, A. (2016), Cicely Berry CBE, unpublished interview, Stratford upon Avon, 16 May.

Tashkiran, A. (2014), Sarah Chagrin Cohen, unpublished interview, London, 5 September.

FURTHER READING

Books

Baldwin, J. (2003), *Michel St Denis and the Shaping of the Modern Actor*, Westport, CT and London: Praeger Publisher.
Brinson, C. and R. Dove, eds (2013), *German Speaking Exiles in the Performing Arts in Britain after 1933*, Amsterdam, Netherlands and New York: Editions Rodopi B.V.
Carter, A., ed. (2004), *Rethinking Dance History: A Reader*, Abingdon, Oxon and New York: Routledge.
Chambers, C. (2004), *Inside the Royal Shakespeare Company*, Oxon: Routledge.
Corbin, A., J.-J. Courtine and G. Vigarello (2006), *Histoire du Corps: 3. Les Mutations du Regards. Le XXe siecle*, Paris, France: Editions du Seuil.
Craine, D. and J. Mackrell (2010), *The Oxford Dictionary of Dance*, 2nd edn, Oxford: Oxford University Press.
Cross, R. (2004), *Steven Berkoff and the Theatre of Self-Performance*, Manchester: Manchester University Press.
Damasio, A. (2000), *The Feeling of What Happens: Body, Emotion and the Making of Consciousness*, London: Vintage.
Doat, J. (1944), *L' expression corporelle du comedien*, Grenoble, France: Les Éditions Françaises Nouvelles BORDAS Frères.
Degaine, A. (1992), *Histoire de Théâtre Dessinée*, Saint Genouph, France: Librairie AG Nizet.
Evans, M. (2009), *Movement Training for the Modern Actor*, New York and Oxon: Routledge.
Evans, M. and R. Kemp, eds (2016), *The Routledge Companion to Jacques Lecoq*, London and New York: Routledge.
Findlater, R., ed. (1981), *At the Royal Court: 25 Years of the English Stage Company*, Ambergate, Derbyshire: Amber Lane Press.
Flatt, K. (2019), *Choreography: Creating and Developing Dance for Performance*, Ramsbury, Marlborough: Crowood Press.
Frank-Manuel, P., ed. (2000), *Elizabeth Duncan Biography 'Isadora and Elizabeth Duncan in Germany'*, Koln, Germany: Deutsches Tanzarchiv.
Garner, S. (1994), *Bodied Spaces: Phenomenology and Performance in Contemporary Drama*, New York: Cornell University Press.
Ginot, I., and M. Michel (2002), *La Danse au XXe siècle*, Paris, France: Larousse/ Veuf. Hirschbach.
Gottschild, B. D. (2003) *The Black Dancing Body, a Geography from Coon to Cool*, New York: Palgrave Macmillan.

Hartnoll, P., ed. (1983), *The Oxford Companion to the Theatre*, 4th edn, Oxford; New York; Toronto, Canada; and Melbourne, Australia: Oxford University Press.
Jacques-Dalcroze, É. (1912), *The Eurythmics of Jacques-Dalcroze*, London: Constable and Co.
Kershaw, B., ed. (2004), *The Cambridge History of British Theatre Vol. 3*, Cambridge: Cambridge University Press.
Laban, R. (1971), *The Mastery of Movement*, 3rd edn, London: MacDonald & Evans.
Lakoff, G., and M. Johnson (1999), *Philosophy in the Flesh: The Embodied Mind and Its Challenge to Western Thought*, New York: Basic Books.
Lakoff, G., and M. Johnson (2003), *Metaphors We Live By*, Chicago, IL: University of Chicago Press.
Lecoq, J. (1987), *Theatre of Movement and Gesture*, ed. David Bradby, Oxon: Routledge.
Lecoq, P. (2016), *Jacques Lecoq: Un point fixe en movement*, Arles, France: Actes Sud.
Littlewood, J. (2003), *Joan's Book: The Autobiography of Joan Littlewood*, London: Methuen.
Madden, D. (1996), *You Call Me Louis, Not Mr Horst*, Amsterdam, Netherlands: Harwood Academic Publishers.
McCall, M., ed. (1978), *My Drama School*, London: Robson Books.
Morris, M. (1969), *My Life in Movement*, London: Peter Owen Publishers.
Morris, M., and F. Daniels (1926), *Margaret Morris Dancing: A Book of Pictures*, London: K. Paul, Trench, Trubner & Co.
Mitchell, K. (2009), *The Director's Craft. A Handbook for Theatre*, Oxon and New York: Routledge.
Newlove, J. (2013), *Yum Di Dee Dah* [e-book]. Available online: www.amazon.co.uk/Yum-Dee-Dah-Jean-Newlove-ebook/dp/B00EIRDDSC (accessed 29 August 2014).
Rebellato, D. (1999), *1956 and All That: The Making of Modern British Drama*, Oxon and New York: Routledge.
Robertson, A. and D. Hutera (1988), *The Dance Handbook*, London: Longman UK.
Robbins Dudeck, T. (2013), *Keith Johnstone: A Critical Biography*, London and New York: Bloomsbury Methuen Drama.
Rosenthal, D. (2013), *The National Theatre Story*, London: Oberon Books.
Rudlin, J. (1986), *Directors in Perspective: Jacques Copeau*, Cambridge: Cambridge University Press.
Saint-Denis, M., and J. Baldwin, ed. (2009), *Theatre: The Rediscovery of Style and Other Writings*, Abingdon, Oxon and New York: Routledge.
Shawn, T. (1963), *Every Little Movement: A Book about Francois Delsarte*, 2nd edn, New York: Dance Horizons.
Shepherd, S. (2009), *The Cambridge Introduction to Modern British Theatre*, Cambridge: Cambridge University Press.
Simpson, B. (1936), *Notes on the Theory of Teaching Margaret Morris Movement*, Whitfield, Francis.
States, B. O. (1987), *Great Reckonings in Little Rooms: On the Phenomenology of Theatre*, Oakland: University of California.
Stebbins, G. (1885), *Delsarte System of Dramatic Expression*, New York: Werner.
Stodelle, E. (1984), *Deep Song: The Dance Story of Martha Graham*, London: Macmillan.
Susi, L. (2006), *The Central Book: A 100 Year History of the Central School of Speech and Drama*, London: Oberon Books.
Susi, L. (2010), *An Untidy Career: Conversations with George Hall*, London: Oberon Books.

Toepfer, K. (1997), *Empire of Ecstasy: Nudity and Movement in German Body Culture, 1910–1935*, Berkeley, CA: University of California Press.
Wilms, A. (1987), *Lindsay Kemp & Company*, London: GMP Publishers.
Winearls, J. (1958), *Modern Dance: The Jooss-Leeder Method*, London: Adam and Charles Black.

Chapters in edited collections

Alison-Mitchell, D. (2017), 'Dancing Since Strapped to Their Mother's Backs: Movement Directing on the RSC's African Julius Caesar', in D. Jarrett-Macauley (ed.), *Shakespeare, Race and Performance: The Diverse Bard*, 46–53, Abingdon, Oxon and New York: Routledge.
Amort, A. (2009), 'Free Dance in Interwar Vienna', in D. Holmes and L. Silverman (eds), *Interwar Vienna: Culture between Tradition and Modernity*, 117–42, Rochester and New York: Boydell and Brewer, Camden House.
Duncan, I. (2002), 'The Dancer of the Future', in Michael Huxley and Noel Witts (eds), *The Twentieth Century Performance Reader*, 171–6, Abingdon, Oxon and New York: Routledge.
Gaines, D. (2016), 'Full-face Masks, Pantomime Blanche and Cartoon Mime', in M. Evans and R. Kemp (eds), *The Routledge Companion to Jacques Lecoq*, 135–41, London and New York: Routledge.
Kampe, T. (2013), 'The Choreographer Hilde Holger: Between Three Worlds', in C. Brinson and R. Dove (eds), *German-speaking Exiles in the Performing Arts in Britain after 1933 in The Year Book of the Research Centre for German and Austrian Exile Studies*, Vol. 14, 187–206, Amsterdam, Netherlands and New York: Rodopi.
Leach, R. (2000), 'Meyerhold and Biomechanics', in Alison Hodge (ed.), *Twentieth Century Actor Training*, 39–54, London: Routledge.
Malet, M. (2013), 'Litz Pisk Dance and Theatre', in C. Brinson and R. Dove (eds), *German-speaking Exiles in the Performing Arts in Britain after 1933 in The Yearbook of the Research Centre for German and Austrian Exile Studies*, Vol. 14, 89–103, Amsterdam, Netherlands and New York: Rodopi.
Rudlin, J. (2000), 'Jacques Copeau: The Quest for Sincerity', in Alison Hodge (ed.), *Twentieth Century Actor Training*, 39–54, London: Routledge.
Tashkiran, A. (2016), 'British Movement Directors', in Mark Evans and Rick Kemp (eds), *The Routledge Companion to Jacques Lecoq*, 227–35, Abingdon: Routledge.

Journal articles

Carter, A. (2010), 'Archives of the Dance (22): Pioneer Women: Early British Modern Dancers, The National Resource Centre for Dance, University of Surrey', *Dance Research: The Journal of the Society for Dance Research*, 28 (1): 90–103.
Cox, F. (1964), '1964: Actor in the Studio', *Plays and Players* (December): 8–11, 50.
Evans, M. (2012), 'The Influence of Sports on Jacques Lecoq's Actor Training', *Theatre, Dance and Performance Training Online Journal*. Available online: http://www.tandfonline.com/doi/full/10.1080/19443927.2012.686451?needAccess=true.

Hulton, D. (2015), 'Review of *The Actor and His Body*, *Theatre, Dance and Performance Training*, 6 (3): 368–71.
Paxton, S. (1996), 'Still Moving: … To Touch', *Contact Quarterly* 9 and 21 (2, Summer/Fall): 50–1.
Robaton, J. (1969), 'Isadora's Teacher', *Times Educational Supplement* (7 March): 724–5.
Rodosthenous, G. (2007), 'Billy Elliot the Musical: Visual Representations of Working-Class Masculinity and the All-Singing, All-Dancing Bo[d]y', *Studies in Musical Theatre*, 1 (3): 275–92.
Scrivener, D. (1998), 'Belinda Quirey', *Historical Dance*, 3 (5): 17–18.
Zhang, I. R. (2018), 'The Figure: Adornment & Identity', *British Journal of Photography*, 7870: 84–7.

Magazine and newspaper articles

Anderson, J. (1984), 'Dance: Tribute Paid to Louis Horst', *New York Times*, 19 April: Section C 15.
Clarke, M. (2003), 'Nina Fonaroff: Obituary', *The Guardian*, 29 August.
Hall, G. (1997), 'Litz Pisk Obituary', the *Independent Newspaper*, 29 March.
Hope-Wallace, P. (1964), 'Review of Royal Hunt of the Sun', *The Guardian*, 9 December.
Kellaway, K. (2005), 'Power Play', *The Observer*, 10 April.
Les Archives Internationales de la Danse (1933), 1 (15 January): 26–33, Paris.
Maclain, J., and K. Syliva (1968), 'Isadora: A Remarkable Film Reincarnation', *Dance Magazine*, 43–8 (February).
Watts, J. (1975), 'Moving Figure', *Arts Guardian* (22 July): 10.

DVD

Margaret Morris Movement (1973) [DVD] Educational Films of Scotland, Scottish Film Council.
Tea with Trish: The Movement Work of Trish Arnold, Parts 1 and 2 (2008) [DVD] Merry Conway, New York.

Online resources

Arts Council England (2009), 'Theatre Assessment 2009'. Available online: https://www.artscouncil.org.uk/sites/default/files/download-file/Theatre_Assessement_2009.pdf (accessed 18 August 2019).
Arts Council England (2019), 'Equality, Diversity and the Creative Case: A Data Report 2017–2018', January. Available online: https://www.artscouncil.org.uk/sites/default/files/download-file/Diversity_report_1718.pdf (accessed 18 August 2019).
Blacktress: A Grassroots Network and Support Group for Self-Defined Black Womxn Actors of the African Diaspora (n.d.). Available online: http://www.blacktress.co.uk/ (accessed 7 August 2019).

British Pathé (n.d.), 'Margaret Morris Movement 1938'. Available online: https://www.britishpathe.com/video/margaret-morris-movement and https://www.britishpathe.com/video/margaret-morris-movement-1/query/Margaret+Morris+Movement (accessed 4 April 2018).

Brook, O., D. O'Brien and M. Taylor (2018), 'Panic! Social Class, Taste and Inequalities within the Creative Industries', *Arts and Humanities Research Council*. Available online: http://createlondon.org/wp-content/uploads/2018/04/Panic-Social-Class-Taste-and-Inequalities-in-the-Creative-Industries1.pdf (accessed 3 May 2019).

Burns, S., and S. Harrison (2016), 'Dance Mapping: A Window on Dance 2004–2008', *Arts Council England*, 7 April. Available online: https://www.artscouncil.org.uk/publication/dance-mapping (accessed 7 July 2019).

Burrows, J. (2007), 'Parallel Voices 2007: The Narrative Body' with Nicholas Hytner, Katie Mitchell and Lloyd Newson, [YouTube Video], 22 March. Available online: https://www.youtube.com/watch?time_continue=7&v=f2VjGlT7HSk&feature=emb_title (accessed 8 June 2009).

Burt, R. (1995), 'Rudolf Laban and the Yorkshire Connection: 50 Years of Dance 1947–1997: A History of Yorkshire Movement and Dance'. Available online: https://dora.dmu.ac.uk/handle/2086/6166 (accessed 29 December 2018).

'Caribbean Dance Index' (n.d.), *Tabanka: African & Caribbean Peoples Dance Ensemble*. Available online: https://tabankadance.com/caribbean-dance-%20index/ (accessed 29 June 2019).

Christiansen, R. (2001), 'Invisible Heroes of the Theatre', *Telegraph*, 12 July. Available online: https://www.telegraph.co.uk/culture/4724523/Invisible-heroes-of-the-theatre.html (accessed 12 July 2011).

Clapp, S., with K. Fox and L. O'Kelly (2019), 'All Change: Meet the New Artistic Directors Shaking Up British Theatre', *The Guardian*, 23 June. Available online: https://www.theguardian.com/stage/2019/jun/23/artistic-directors-shaking-up-british-theatre-lynette-linton-suba-das-tarek-iskander (accessed 31 August 2019).

'Creating an Ensemble' (2015) [YouTube Video], National Theatre, curated by Dr Sita Thomas, 6 January. Available online: https://youtu.be/2FWAUncAvv4 (accessed 2 August 2019).

'Cruel Garden by Christopher Bruce and Lindsey Kemp' (1982) [YouTube Video]. Available online: https://www.youtube.com/watch?v=duxtr1KFOfc (accessed 4 August 2019).

Dramatic Need (n.d.), 'Dramatic Need Frankenstein Miller and Cumberbatch Q&A Transcript'. Available online: https://dramaticneed.tumblr.com/post/4833906913/qanda-transcript (Accessed 15 February 2020).

Early Dance Circle (n.d.), 'Belinda Quirey MBE (1912–1996)'. Available online: http://www.earlydancecircle.co.uk/belinda-quirey-mbe-1912-1996/ (accessed 10 July 2016).

Eddleston, P. (2017), 'Remembering Matt Mattox', Imperial Society of Teachers of Dancing, 26 October. Available online: https://www.istd.org/news/news-archive/remembering-matt-mattox/ (accessed 4 June 2018).

Equal Representation for Actresses, ERA 50:50 Campaigning for 5050 Gender Balance on British Stage and Screen by 2020 (n.d.). Available online: http://equalrepresentationforactresses.co.uk/ (accessed 18 July 2019).

English National Orchestra (n.d.), 'ENO Chorus'. Available online: https://www.eno.org/about/whos-who/chorus/ (accessed 16 August 2019).

Estate of Léonide Massine (n.d.), 'Léonide Massine: Biography'. Available online: http://massine-ballet.com/html/about_massine.php (accessed 16 August 2019).

'Front Row: Cary Grant and Notorious, Festival Cancellations, Movement Directors, Anna Symon' (2019) [Radio] presenter John Wilson, BBC Radio 4, 9 August. Available online: https://www.bbc.co.uk/sounds/play/m0007dkh?fbclid=IwAR0--X5qXoUHHjJDx1HBZ0XgHO6Cvw4BtHaiM4sSEKHBUlbL_byXnxZgSiQ (accessed 19 August 2019).

Gilbert, J. (1996), 'A Bad Blow for the Kosh', the *Independent*, 24 November. Available online: https://www.independent.co.uk/life-style/a-bad-blow-for-the-kosh-1353986.html (accessed 31 December 2018).

Harrison, N. (2019), 'The Movement Podcast'. Available online: https://podcasts.apple.com/gb/podcast/the-movement-podcast-hosted-by-natasha-harrison/id1464005842 (accessed 30 July 2019).

Hemley, M. (2019), 'Photo Captures More Than 250 Black Women, Trans Women and Non-Binary People Working in Theatre', *The Stage*, photo by Sharon Wallace, 26 July. Available online: https://www.thestage.co.uk/news/2019/photo-250-black-women-trans-women-non-binary-working-theatre/ (accessed 1 August 2019).

Hench, J. D. (2017), 'How to Make the Most of Stillness Onstage', *Dance Spirit*, 31 October. Available online: https://www.dancespirit.com/how-to-make-the-most-of-stillness-onstage-2502557437.html (accessed 1 March 2018).

'History of Movement Direction' (2015) [YouTube Video], National Theatre, curated by Dr Sita Thomas, 22 January. Available online: https://youtu.be/8NjU8gttsZo (accessed 2 August 2019).

Houston, W. (2012), 'Nigel Charnock: Choreographer and Dancer Celebrated for His Raw Energy and Punk Attitude', *Independent*, 15 September, Available online: https://www.independent.co.uk/news/obituaries/nigel-charnock-choreographer-and-dancer-celebrated-for-his-raw-energy-and-punk-attitude-8139989.html (accessed 9 August 2019).

Jack, I. (2008), 'It's in the Blood: Ian Jack Looks at What Makes Black Watch so Affecting', *The Guardian*, 14 June. Available online: https://www.theguardian.com/books/2008/jun/14/saturdayreviewsfeatres.guardianreview18 (accessed 9 August 2019).

'Jean Newlove Public Lecture: Jean Newlove at The Teesside University, October 9 2014' (2014) [YouTube Video], Teesside University, 13 October. Available online: https://www.youtube.com/watch?v=DMyqa-TI7I4 (accessed 24 June 2015).

Kirkup, J. (2007), 'A Life in Focus: Marcel Marceau, Sculptor of Silence Whose Name Became Synonymous with Mime', *Independent*, 24 September. Available online: https://www.independent.co.uk/news/obituaries/marcel-marceau-remembered-obituary-mine-dancer-blip-lindsay-kemp-a8517291.html (accessed 15 November 2019).

London Contemporary Dance School (n.d.), 'History of London Contemporary Dance School'. Available online: https://www.lcds.ac.uk/history-london-contemporary-dance-school (accessed 30 December 2018).

Ludman, M. (2019), 'Time to Step Up Recognition of Movement Direction', *British Theatre.Com*, 5 August. Available online: https://britishtheatre.com/time-to-step-up-recognition-of-movement-direction/ (accessed 18 August 2019).

McGaw, D. (2018), 'A Celebration of the Life of Geraldine Stephenson 1925–2017: Funeral Elegy', *Laban Guild*, 16 January. Available online: http://www.labanguild.org.uk/wp-content/uploads/2018/03/Geraldine-Stephenson-Celebration.pdf (accessed 19 July 2018).

Middleton, C. (2009), 'Secrets of the War Horse Puppeteer', *Telegraph*, 26 March. Available online: https://www.telegraph.co.uk/lifestyle/wellbeing/outdoors/5050116/Secrets-of-the-War-Horse-puppeteer.html (accessed 15 September 2014).

Monsegur, T. (1999), 'Laban, Leeder ... Memory of Movement', *International Council of Kinetography Laban/Labanotation*. Available online: http://html.ickl.org/conf99_proceedings/monsegur.pdf (accessed 29 December 2018).

'Movement Direction: Creating Character' (2014) [YouTube Video], National Theatre, curated by Dr Sita Thomas, 19 November. Available online: https://youtu.be/1RRc4tq2kpE (accessed 29 October 2014).

'MoveSpace', http://movespace.org.uk (accessed 4 August 2019).

Orts, N. E. (2010), 'Louis Horst', *Dance Teacher*, 9 February. Available online: https://www.dance-teacher.com/louis-horst-2392289666.html (accessed 29 December 2018).

Patton, A. (2010), Rosalind Knight: interview transcript, British Library Theatre Archive Project, 11 June. Available online: https://sounds.bl.uk/Arts-literature-and-performance/Theatre-Archive-Project/024 M-C1142X000192-0001V0; transcript at: https://sounds.bl.uk/related-content/TRANSCRIPTS/024T-C1142X000192-0001A0.pdf.

Sher, A. (2006), 'Johnny Hutch Obituary', *The Guardian*, 21 December. Available online: https://www.theguardian.com/news/2006/dec/21/guardianobituaries.artsobituaries (accessed 31 December 2018).

Snape Maltings (2016), 'Struan Leslie Researching Les Illuminations at the Red House's Britten Archive', 17 May. Available online: https://www.youtube.com/watch?v=SjSvHfcltGc (accessed 28 May 2016).

Sulcas, R. (2018), 'Harry Potter Doesn't Dance: But He Sure Can Move', *New York Times*, 10 July. Available online: https://www.nytimes.com/2018/07/10/arts/dance/harry-potter-and-the-cursed-child-choreography.html (accessed 12 July 2018).

Thomas, R. (2014), 'Cuban Dance History: Part 1', *Royal Opera House*, 14 July. Available online: https://www.roh.org.uk/news/a-cuban-dance-history-part-i (accessed 29 June 2019).

Thomas, R. (2014), 'Cuban Dance History: Part 2', *Royal Opera House*, 16 July. Available online: https://www.roh.org.uk/news/a-cuban-dance-history-part-ii (accessed 29 June 2019).

Tonic Theatre (n.d.), Supporting Theatre and the Arts to Achieve Greater Gender Equality, Diversity & Inclusion. Available online: https://www.tonictheatre.co.uk/ (accessed 7 August 2019).

Train, L. (2019), 'BWW Interview: Movement Director Shelley Maxwell Talks EQUUS', *Broadway World UK*, 12 February. Available online: https://www.broadwayworld.com/westend/article/BWW-Interview-Movement-Director-Shelley-Maxwell-Talks-EQUUS-20190212 (accessed 28 May 2019).

Trueman, M. (2017), 'Let's Get Physical: The Growing Role of Movement Directors in Theatre', *Financial Times*, 13 April. Available online: https://www.ft.com/content/d7ba0ea0-1def-11e7-b7d3-163f5a7f229c (accessed 13 May 2017).

Victoria and Albert Museum (n.d.), 'London Contemporary Dance Theatre'. Available online: http://www.vam.ac.uk/content/articles/l/london-contemporary-dance-theatre/ (accessed 15 August 2019).

Volcano Theatre (n.d.), 'About Us', http://www.volcanotheatre.co.uk/about-us (accessed 9 August 2019).

'What Is a Movement Director?' (2014) [YouTube Video], National Theatre, curated by Dr Sita Thomas, 28 October. Available online: https://youtu.be/KY-gWqj-FIk (accessed 29 October 2016).

Wrigley, A. (2011), 'Greek Plays: Viewing *Women of Troy* (BBC, 1958)'. Screen Plays: Theatre Plays on British Television. Available online: https://screenplaystv.wordpress.com/2011/11/30/viewing-women-of-troy-bbc-1958/ (accessed 17 August 2016).

Video

A History of Cuban Dance (2016), [Video] Lucy Walker, Broad Green Pictures.
Dartington (2012), 'Joos-Leeder School of Dance "Danse Macabre" 1935' [YouTube Video] Dartington TV, 6 June. Available online: https://www.youtube.com/watch?v=tHR5eL1OCtU&amp=&list=PL6D2B8591FA27BD25 (accessed 18 July 2018).
Dartington (2012), 'Joos-Leeder School of Dance "Danse Macabre"' (*c.* 1935) and Dartington's Mime Theatre School 'Women of Voe' (*c.* 1938)' [YouTube Video] Dartington TV, 25 June. Available online: https://www.youtube.com/watch?v=pWqSqNdDlnc (accessed 18 July 2018).
Les Deux Voyages de Jacques Lecoq (2006) [Video] Jacques Lecoq, Jean-Gabriel Carasso, Jean-Claude Laillas and Jean-Noël Roy, Paris: La Sept ARTE and SCÉRÉN CNDP, Online Productions – ANRAT.
William Forsythe Improvisation Technologies: A Tool for the Analytical Dance Eye (2003), [Video] William Forsythe, Digital Arts edn.

Presentations

Carter, A. (2009), 'Constructing the Natural: A Critical Appraisal of Selected Forms of British Theatre Dance in the Early 20th Century', presented at International Academic Symposium – Moving Naturally: Re-thinking Dance 1900s–1930s, University of Surrey, 31 October.

ABOUT THE AUTHOR

Ayse Tashkiran is a movement director, teacher and researcher in the field of movement direction and actor movement. She obtained her undergraduate degree in Drama from Bristol University and then trained with Lecoq at L'École Internationale de Théâtre Jacques Lecoq, Paris. After a career as a physical theatre performer, she started to movement direct and teach. She joined the Royal Central School of Speech and Drama, University of London, in 2003, where she co-leads the MA/MFA Movement: Directing and Teaching. She is also an Associate Artist at the Royal Shakespeare Company.

Movement direction productions include: *Europeana* (Royal Shakespeare Company (RSC), the Swan, 2020); *BLANK* (Donmar Warehouse, 2019); *As You Like It* (RSC, Royal Shakespeare Theatre (RST), the Barbican and national tour, 2019–20); *The Provoked Wife* (RSC, the Swan, 2019); *The Wolves* (Theatre Royal, Stratford East, 2018); *Shakespeare in Love* (national tour, 2018); *The Duchess of Malfi* (RSC, the Swan, 2018); *Romeo and Juliet* (RSC, the RST, Barbican and National Tour, 2018); *Dido, Queen of Carthage* (RSC, the Swan, 2017); *Othello* (Sam Wanamaker at Shakespeare's Globe, 2017); *Fantastic Mr Fox* (Nuffield Theatre, national and international tour, 2016–17), UK Theatre Awards 2017, Renee Stepham Award for Best Presentation of Touring Theatre; *Tidy Up* Peut-Être Theatre, international and national tour, 2017–20); *Lady Chatterley's Lover* (English Touring Theatre, Crucible Theatre, national tour, 2016); *Doctor Faustus* (RSC, the Swan and Barbican, 2016–17); *York Mystery Plays* (York Minster, 2016), winner of Best Production, York Culture Awards, 2016; *The Government Inspector* (Birmingham Repertory Theatre, national tour, 2016), production nominated for Olivier Awards 2017; *Barbarians* (Young Vic, 2015), production nominated for Olivier Awards 2016; *Shh … Bang!* (Peut-Etre Theatre, national tour, 2015–20); *Hecuba* (RSC, the Swan, 2015), *The Shoemaker's Holiday* (RSC, the Swan, 2014), *The White Devil* (RSC, the Swan, 2014), *As You Like It* (RSC, RST and national tour, 2013–14), *The Merry Wives of Windsor* (RSC, RST, 2012), *Richard III* (RSC, the Swan, 2012), *King John* (RSC, the Swan, 2012), *Measure for Measure* (RSC, the Swan, 2011), *Little Eagles* (RSC, Hampstead Theatre, 2010), *The Gods Weep* (RSC, Hampstead Theatre, 2010), *Days of Significance* (RSC, national tour, 2009); *Belongings* (Hampstead Theatre, 2011); *The Chairs* (Theatre Royal Bath, 2010); *The Tempest* (Gdansk Shakespeare Festival, 2009); *Sarajevo Story* (Lyric Hammersmith, 2008); *Feast on the Bridge* (Thames Festival, 2008); *Silent Tide* (Institute of Contemporary Arts, 2008); *Stacy* (Trafalgar Studios, 2007); *Ma Vie en Rose* (Young Vic, 2007); *Macbeth* (Regent's Park Open Air Theatre, 2007); *La Songe du 21 Juin* (national tour of France, 2007); *Brixton Stories* (Lyric Hammersmith, 2006); *Here's What I Did With My Body One Day* (national tour and Pleasance, Theatre, 2006).

Opera includes *The Sleeper* (Welsh National Opera Max, Coal Exchange, Cardiff, 2011); *Sweeney Todd* (Welsh National Opera Max, Millennium Centre, Cardiff, 2009); *The Beggar's Opera* (Blackheath Concert Halls, 2006); *L'Orfeo* (Greenwich Theatre, 2005).

Publications include: 'Introduction', in Litz Pisk, *The Actor and His Body* (London: Bloomsbury Methuen Drama, 2018) and 'British Movement Directors', in Rick Kemp and Mark Evans (eds), *The Routledge Companion to Jacques Lecoq* (Abingdon: Routledge, 2016).

www.ingramcontent.com/pod-product-compliance
Ingram Content Group UK Ltd.
Pitfield, Milton Keynes, MK11 3LW, UK
UKHW021907220326
469204UK00008B/230